Working with Couples for Marriage Enrichment

A Guide to
Developing, Conducting,
and Evaluating Programs

Diana S. Richmond Garland

Working with Couples
for Marriage Enrichment

Jossey-Bass Publishers

San Francisco • Washington • London • 1983

WORKING WITH COUPLES FOR MARRIAGE ENRICHMENT
A Guide to Developing, Conducting, and Evaluating Programs
by Diana S. Richmond Garland

Copyright © 1983 by: Jossey-Bass Inc., Publishers
433 California Street
San Francisco, California 94104
&
Jossey-Bass Limited
28 Banner Street
London EC1Y 8QE

Library of Congress Cataloging in Publication Data

Garland, Diana S. Richmond, date
Working with couples for marriage enrichment.

Bibliography: p. 307
Includes indexes.
1. Marriage. 2. Marriage counseling. 3. Groups
relations training. 4. Interpersonal relations.
I. Title.
HQ734.G254   1983   362.8'286   83-48158
ISBN 0-87589-573-5

The paper in this book meets the guidelines for
permanence and durability of the Committee on
Production Guidelines for Book Longevity of the
Council on Library Resources.

JACKET DESIGN BY WILLI BAUM

FIRST EDITION

Code 8320

The Jossey-Bass
Social and Behavioral Science Series

Preface

Over the past fifteen years there has been considerable growth in the number and types of preventive mental health services in the United States. A category of services that has undergone particularly notable growth and development has been family life education, which includes marriage enrichment services. Marriage enrichment classes are now available on most college campuses, in mental health centers, and through other human service systems and churches.

The leadership of marriage enrichment groups is varied and includes clergy, specifically trained lay couples, and professionals—social workers, psychologists, and psychiatrists. Although several resources are available for marriage enrichment leaders, these have primarily been written by and for pastoral counselors. Moreover, each of the works currently available tends to be limited to one theoretical framework. Lacking up to now have been an overview of the various approaches to marriage enrichment, guidelines for adapting any one model to the needs of a particular population or context, and guidance concerning program evaluation, a step that is essential to increasing the effectiveness of marriage enrichment services. *Working with Couples for Marriage Enrichment* addresses all these needs. Written mainly for helping professionals, this book provides a brief introduction to the history and current status of enrichment services along with guidelines for developing, providing, and evaluating these services.

My basic assumption in writing this book has been that services must be adapted to the context and needs of a particular group rather than group needs being adapted to a particular program model. Thus my focus is on providing the marriage enrichment leader with the tools for developing models of marriage enrichment that fit the unique needs of each group of couples. In addition, it is my hope that this book will be a catalyst for increased interaction between practitioners and researchers. My discussion of evaluation and review of evaluation instruments is designed to address the needs of an academic audience involved in developing research methodologies in this field. Sections of this book, particularly those on group development, group leadership, and the structured activities, may also be used by the practitioner training lay couples to provide marriage enrichment services under professional supervision.

Contents and Organization

Chapter One traces the development of enrichment services, describing their relationship to the more traditional professional services such as marriage counseling, and outlining some of the advantages of educational approaches such as marriage enrichment in the helping process. The professional helper's roles in providing direct leadership for marriage enrichment groups, consulting with lay leaders and marriage enrichment associations, developing theoretical bases for marriage enrichment services, and defining the goals and objectives of marriage enrichment programs are discussed. Qualifications of group leaders, criteria for evaluating leadership capability, and some common problems leaders of marriage enrichment programs face are detailed.

Chapter Two presents the theoretical bases of marriage

enrichment programs that have been developed from these theoretical bases and reviews the research conducted on each of these approaches. The theoretical bases presented include General Systems theory, Rogerian theory, behavioral theory, the ground swell marriage enrichment movement in churches, and other theoretical approaches that have had a lesser impact on these services, such as Gestalt theory, transactional analysis, Maslow's self-actualization theory, Rankian philosophy, and others. Suggestions are given for choosing an approach from the variety of models available on the basis of group needs and goals.

Chapter Three is a pragmatic description of how to design and implement a successful marriage enrichment program. Among the issues it addresses are selection of participants to achieve homogeneity or heterogeneity of a group with regard to specific characteristics of participants, family life-cycle stages, degree of marital adjustment, and group size; the frequency and length of group meetings; building a program from a specific theoretical base, which has been selected on the basis of group goals; establishing an appropriate leadership configuration; and ensuring that learning in the group transfers to and lasts in the home life of participating couples.

Chapter Four provides practical suggestions for implementing the program developed for a particular group. The stages of group development and the leader's task in integrating group development and couple learning are described. Strategies for leading a group through the process of forming relationships and building group norms are discussed.

Chapter Five presents two marriage enrichment programs, emphasizing the use of structured activities, the processes of leadership, and the dynamics of group development. The two programs include a group focusing on communication skills for couples who have successfully engaged in marriage counseling, and a weekend retreat for a Sunday school class of young married couples. Detailed are the rationale for choosing activities, and illustrations of group discussion and leader activities are given in examples of group and leader dialogue.

Chapter Six describes in detail a variety of problems that

may arise when a personal or marital crisis erupts in a marriage enrichment group or when group issues surface that impede progress (such as lack of participation, domineering behavior on the part of participants, and disagreement with the leader's approach). It suggests strategies leaders can use to keep the group focused on group goals rather than on individual couples' needs. This chapter emphasizes the importance of distinguishing between issues that can be dealt with in marriage enrichment groups and ones that are too complex and demanding to be managed in this setting. It provides insights helpful to leaders who must decide when to suggest that a couple leave the group and enter another more in-depth counseling situation, whether to counsel such a couple or refer them to another source, and how to help participants cope with feelings of doubt and loss so that productive work can continue after a couple leaves the group.

Chapter Seven suggests approaches to evaluating marriage enrichment services, taking into consideration the usually limited resources of the community agencies and churches that provide them. The advantages and methods of making evaluation an integral part of marriage enrichment are explored. The objectives and criteria of evaluation are discussed; for example, improving spouses' understanding of one another and increasing marital satisfaction are significantly different goals and require different approaches in planning as well as in evaluation.

Chapter Eight suggests that marriage enrichment services are one aspect of a much larger movement toward enhancing the growth and development of individuals, families, and communities through education. This movement has as its aim serving people throughout the life cycle rather than focusing on crises and remediation. Marriage enrichment services, as an example, simultaneously fulfill the functions of prevention, therapy, and enrichment. The future of marriage enrichment lies in developing theoretical approaches, leadership styles, and models of group development and evaluation, and integrating professional enrichment services with family support and education networks.

Resource A includes twenty-five program activities with step-by-step instructions for use in marriage enrichment groups. Examples of handouts and questionnaires are also provided. There are five activities in each of the following categories: group formation, communication, problem solving and conflict management, values and priorities, and intimacy and sexuality.

Resource B is a comprehensive listing of instruments for evaluating marriage enrichment programs. Twenty-six of these methods are described in detail and suggestions are given for their use. Bibliographical sources are provided for all instruments named or annotated in this section. To my knowledge this is a unique review of evaluation methodologies that can be used as they are or adapted to fit the evaluation needs of a given group.

This book provides a comprehensive overview of the field of marriage enrichment. The variety of theoretical frameworks is defined and explored, and there is a discussion of how leaders can choose among and integrate these frameworks. Designed as a basic sourcebook for conducting marriage enrichment services, it incorporates group leadership models, a discussion of group development issues, a guide to structured activities and evaluation methods, and a comprehensive bibliography of the marriage enrichment field.

Acknowledgments

No book is written alone; this book has been enriched by the contributions of many. I am very grateful to my colleagues, Anne Davis, Robin Rogers, and Judy Lester, who have been generous with their encouragement and their helpful criticism as they have read several drafts of this work. Penny Marler has assisted me throughout with the research and in the manuscript preparation. I am also very grateful to Pattie McCollum and others at The Southern Baptist Theological Seminary who have been so patient and so helpful in typing the manuscript drafts. David Garland has been chief encourager throughout the development of methods and ideas and the committing of them to paper. Our relationship has been my constant source of inspiration. My children, Sarah and John, have lengthened the time involved in the writing but have enriched it immeasurably.

My chief source of learning and growing excitement about marriage enrichment has been the many couples who have allowed me to share in their lives through marriage enrichment groups. To them I am indeed grateful.

Louisville, Kentucky   Diana S. Richmond Garland
July 1983

Contents

Preface ix

The Author xvii

1. Marriage Enrichment: Development, Goals, and Leadership 1

2. Foundations of Marriage Enrichment Services 17

3. Designing and Implementing Group Programs 48

4. Leading the Group and Achieving Goals 76

5. Examples of Group Programs and Activities 109

6. Common Problems in Marriage Enrichment Groups 151

7. Evaluating Marriage Enrichment Services 183

8. Marriage Enrichment: Current Status
    and Future Prospects   217

    Resource A: Structured Activities   231

    Resource B: Evaluation Tools   281

    References   307

    Name Index   337

    Subject Index   345

The Author

Diana S. Richmond Garland is an assistant professor of social work at The Southern Baptist Theological Seminary in Louisville, Kentucky, and a staff member of Personal Counseling Services in Jeffersonville, Indiana. She received her M.S.S.W. from the Kent School of Social Work at the University of Louisville in 1975 and her Ph.D. in interdisciplinary studies in social work and clinical psychology from the University of Louisville in 1979. Garland's professional experience includes social work with River Region Community Mental Health Services and the Kentucky Baptist Board of Child Care. She has also served as administrative director of Personal Counseling Services and as an adjunct professor at the Kent School of Social Work and Indiana University Southeast.

Garland is a member of the Academy of Certified Social Workers, a clinical member of the American Association of Marriage and Family Therapists, and a member of the National Council on Family Relations. She has previously authored *Workshop Models for Family Life Education: Couples Communication and Negotiation Skills* (1978).

To my husband, David E. Garland

Working with Couples for Marriage Enrichment

❧❧❧❧❧❧❧❧❧❧❧❧❧❧❧❧❧

*A Guide to
Developing, Conducting,
and Evaluating Programs*

1

Marriage Enrichment: Development, Goals, and Leadership

Marriage enrichment is a term which refers to a philosophy of marriage and its functions for persons and for societies, to an educational model of couple and group services offered by the helping professions, and to a number of specific programs for providing these services. The major focus of all three—the philosophy, the model for services, and the resulting programs—is the improvement of married life. There are at times differences in how *improvement* is defined and in the processes by which it is thought to be achieved. Most commonly, however, this improvement is described as enabling partners "to create a climate between them which will enable them to increase self- and other-awareness of the growth potential of the marriage; to explore and express their thoughts and feelings with honesty and empathy; and to develop and use the skills needed to relate together effectively, solve their problems and resolve their conflicts. In such a climate, it is believed that the individual and the couple are best able to maximize their potential for relationship satisfaction and personal and couple growth" (Hof and Miller, 1980, p. 5).

Although marriage enrichment is often conceptualized as a preventive service by the helping professions, it really moves beyond the dichotomy between prevention and treatment to the overarching belief that teaching persons the knowledge, attitudes, and skills they can use to develop relationships unique to their needs serves not only the functions of treatment and prevention but also enhances and enriches the lives of many who are not at risk or in need of preventive or therapeutic services. Marriage enrichment is an approach to the use of professional knowledge about marriage and the family which potentially is applicable to all marriages. It gives couples the opportunity to define the nature of their commitment to one another, to determine the purposes of their relationship, and to develop the skills, knowledge, and attitudes they need to accomplish those purposes. When spouses are equipped in this manner, they can develop a strong, flexible relationship that changes over time as their needs change and that enhances the personal growth of each partner within the marriage.

Marriage enrichment has emerged from two quite different sources—the human service professions and religious groups. In the human service professions, marriage enrichment has its roots in interpersonal relationship groups and related research of the late forties and fifties. That work gave rise to the human potential movement, which emerged in the sixties and was also a significant precursor to marriage enrichment. The human potential movement encouraged criticism of the medical model of "illness" in human relations and stressed strengths and assets rather than limitations. It conceptualized the family as the matrix for a lifelong growth process involving all family members (Otto, 1979). Paralleling the human potential movement were increases in the use of self-help groups and paraprofessionals (L'Abate, 1981), which created widespread acceptance of group experiences among educated people (Otto, 1976). Affective education and humanistic psychology, accompanied by a major emphasis on preventive services, also had an impact during the sixties.

Other trends that enhanced the development of marriage enrichment services were the growth of consumerism and a push toward brief, demonstrably effective treatments (L'Abate, 1981). The enormous growth of behavior therapy and behavioral technology, with their emphases on self-control strategies and step-by-step approaches to teaching interpersonal skills, were also influential (L'Abate, 1981). Developments in the fields of human sexuality, family sociology, and family life education have provided additional understanding of marital relationships and the variables that influence interpersonal satisfaction (Ball, 1979).

Finally, the need for marriage enrichment services has been heightened by sociological changes in our culture. The move from traditional to companionship marriage, with its basis in intimacy, equity, and flexible interpersonal interaction, has changed the requirements for effective performance in marriage. "What we have been calling 'the failure of marriage' has rather been the failure of large numbers of individual marriages as they tried to undertake a transition for which the partners concerned simply lacked the necessary equipment" (Mace and Mace, 1975, p. 133).

The impact of these movements on the helping professions can be seen in the array of services now offered by most agencies—parent and family life education; marriage enrichment; and life transition groups for young adults, single parents, the newly divorced or widowed, the homemaker entering the job market, the retiree, and women and men questioning traditional sex roles. Almost all these services emphasize educational-experiential approaches to overcoming difficulties or producing intrapersonal and interpersonal growth, rather than the more traditional one-to-one verbal method (Drum and Knott, 1977).

Educational services for marital couples are such a useful alternative to traditional services that they have become a movement in the helping professions practically independent of other kinds of educational services. Organizations exist that train and certify marriage enrichment leaders; university undergraduate and graduate courses offer marriage enrichment services and train professionals to provide these services; practitioners specialize in leading marriage enrichment groups.

Thus a wide variety of marriage enrichment services is

available. Although there are a number of theoretical and philosophical bases for these services, they share a common goal—to teach spouses interpersonal skills that will enable them to initiate as well as adjust to changes in their relationship. Through this kind of continuing change, the personal growth and development of both spouses is enhanced throughout the marriage. Practically all models emphasize an educational, not therapeutic, approach that is designed to "make good marriages better" (Otto, 1976). However, increasing acceptance of family therapy has developed concurrently with marital enrichment services. This shift in the therapeutic arena, from focusing on the individual to considering the whole family system, has strengthened the rationale for family and marriage enrichment (L'Abate, 1978).

Marriage enrichment as offered by the secular helping professions differs in some respects from marriage enrichment as it has developed in church settings. The church-related marriage enrichment movement is more a philosophy than a methodology for human services. Historically, the church has supported the family as an institution. Marriage enrichment as it comes from the church represents the concerned response of religious groups and their leaders to changes in modern family life and, especially, to the rising divorce rate. It is important to distinguish between church-related and secular approaches to marriage enrichment, not only because they have different institutional origins, but also because their goals differ in several respects.

The helping professions offer marriage enrichment services that are designed to enhance people's ability to communicate within and derive satisfaction from their marriages. These services strive for effects that can be described in terms of the skills couples learn and the happiness they report in their marriages. The church's approach to marriage enrichment is also concerned with these objectives but places much greater emphasis on influencing people's attitudes by, for example, instilling hope in couples that they can attain their relationship goals, strengthening their belief in the validity of the institution of marriage, and eventually influencing societal institutions and values through these couples.

Church-related marriage enrichment programs have developed methodologies of their own and have also incorporated aspects of the secular approaches that are compatible with their philosophies. Likewise, secular professionals have recently begun to incorporate some of the methdologies of church-related marriage enrichment into their services. In fact, exchanges, which have enhanced the growth of both areas, have taken place largely because of helping professionals practicing in church-related settings.* Therefore, despite marked differences in their historical development and purposes, there has been a significant shading of the distinctions between the church-related and secular approaches to marriage enrichment.

Given the church's emphasis on changing societal values and the secular services' emphasis on observable change in individual couples, interdisciplinary sharing will no doubt continue to be greatly beneficial to practitioners in both areas. The focus of this book on the development, implementation, and evaluation of marriage enrichment services is based on the assumption that these two emphases can be addressed from a common base of theory and intervention strategies.

Marriage Enrichment Services and Marriage Counseling

Human service professionals have had to develop criteria for determining whether marriage enrichment or marital therapy is the treatment of choice. In making this decision, it is important first to define the differences between the two kinds of intervention. Two aspects of marriage enrichment—its time-limited nature and its structured approach—generally distinguish it from marital therapy, although this is not always the case.

---

*Throughout this book "church" and "church-related" are terms used to refer to marriage enrichment as a movement within religious groups. The main thrust of the movement has come from Catholics, Methodists, Quakers, Baptists, and the Christian Church. Among these groups, marriage enrichment is seen as a significant means of accomplishing the goals of the church, goals which extend beyond the more specific goals of marriage enrichment in the lives of participating couples. These goals include the demonstration of Christian love in action, evangelism, and the development and growth of Christian communities.

L'Abate (1981, p. 634) offers some helpful considerations: (1) in therapy, client factors that may prevent client families from learning directly structured skills are emphasized; (2) in therapy, it is *not* assumed that a person's lack of skills is primarily due to lack of opportunity to learn them, but this is a common assumption in skills programs; (3) therapy may be to skills programs as teaching learning disabled children is to normal classroom education; (4) therapy models generally seem to place more importance than skills programs do on recipients' ambivalence about change; and (5) skills programs operate according to therapist- or leader-generated agendas, while therapy sessions usually center on what the client thinks is important.

Generally, marriage enrichment services are considered most appropriate for couples who are committed to their marriages and who are not in the midst of marital crisis; marriage enrichment is designed to "make good marriages better," not to patch up shaky ones. This is not to say that couples who have "good marriages" are automatically eliminated from marriage counseling. Indeed, counseling tends to be viewed as the basic service for couples. However, marriage enrichment services are frequently reserved for couples who have successfully completed therapy or do not need counseling. By way of analogy, counseling services are like a required university course, and marriage enrichment services are like a course with a prerequisite—one must have a good marriage or "instructor permission" to participate.

Ordinarily it is considered inappropriate to offer marriage enrichment services to couples who are considering separation or divorce; it is assumed that these couples need help in deciding whether to continue their marital relationship, not help in enhancing it. Some practitioners would argue, however, that couples can make such a decision with greater certainty if they first get a glimpse of what the relationship might become with work and commitment. Thus, for couples who are interested, marriage enrichment may provide an opportunity to develop the relationship's potential before they decide to end it. Furthermore, couples in the midst of crisis benefit by receiving input and support from other couples and by learning the skills that are presented in marriage enrichment groups.

It is commonly assumed that if troubled couples are to be included in a marriage enrichment group, the leader needs to have special counseling skills. Therefore, the use of lay leadership in the marriage enrichment movement may be partly responsible for the exclusion of couples in crisis: lay leaders may not consider themselves competent to deal with these couples.

A second and probably more significant reason for designing marriage enrichment for healthy marriages is the desire to avoid a connection with therapy and the stereotypes of weakness and illness associated with remedial services. The emphasis on education and prevention identifies enrichment services as acceptable for healthy couples. This approach to avoiding the labels of dysfunction and illness in some ways, however, reinforces those very labels. An assumption that some couples are categorically to be excluded from educational services suggests that such divisions between the healthy and the dysfunctional have validity.

The educational approach has a number of advantages over counseling services, even for troubled marriages. First, in marriage enrichment programs, couples learn interpersonal skills that are applicable not only to various aspects of their current relationship, including areas of crisis, but also to changes that take place over months or even years of marriage. Such skills include empathizing, defining and resolving problems, managing conflict, and establishing trust, intimacy, and respect. Those who train helping professionals believe that teaching clients the interpersonal skills that are ordinarily taught to professional helpers can be a useful alternative to traditional counseling services (see, for example, Egan, 1975; Ivey, 1971; Ivey and others, 1968; Middleman, 1977). Carkhuff and Berenson (1977) have suggested that teaching such skills is the preferred mode of treatment: "The helping process is in the end a skills-acquisition model; a learning process by which the helpee with a limited repertoire of responses is transformed into a person with an extensive repertoire of responses. . . . In our work in social action, we have found that we are only as good as the skills we have to offer the community we service. Indeed, we are only as good as the skills in which we train others to service themselves" (pp. 249, 274).

A second advantage of an educational model of services to couples is that the helper can time the intervention to correspond to developmental needs. Traditional methods frequently are unable to provide intervention until a developmental issue has deteriorated into a problem or crisis (Drum and Knott, 1977). For instance, studies of the family life cycle (Rollins and Feldman, 1970; Burr, 1970) have shown that during the period when there are elementary school age children in the home marital satisfaction is relatively low; childbearing and rearing have a profound negative effect on the happiness of couples. Enrichment services can be designed to correspond to these stages and address the issues of maintaining couple intimacy and mutual growth in the midst of assuming and performing parental roles. Services could similarly be designed for couples in the midst of the "launching" and "empty nest" stages of the family life cycle. Enrichment services could also address the virtually ignored needs of the couple facing retirement and the crises of aging.

A third advantage of marriage enrichment services over counseling services is greater access to the population in general. Educational services are deemed more acceptable by consumers than counseling services. Couples are more likely to participate in a program, class, or retreat offered by their church, school, or club than they are to call a community mental health agency and ask for marital counseling.

Fourth, such enrichment services place responsibility for problem resolution on the couple, not on a therapist, as sometimes happens in counseling. Couples are encouraged to discover and build on the strengths of their relationships rather than to focus on areas of weakness.

Fifth, marriage and family counselors have suggested that change occurs at a faster rate with multiple than with individual family units (Bowen, 1975). In a multiple-family group, couples support each other in breaking the strong taboo against seriously discussing one's marriage with other couples, a taboo that isolates couples, stigmatizes conflict, and stifles growth (Mace and Mace, 1976b). The group engenders a sense of normalcy about conflict and developmental crises. Also, the group provides a means of gaining new perspectives on old problems and of giving members opportunities to model various interactional skills for one another. The group format, which is the norm for marriage enrichment/educational services, is thus a significant advantage. Counseling services are less often provided for groups; most couples who seek counseling believe their unique problems cannot be dealt with sufficiently in a group environment.

Sixth, because trained leaders rather than helping professionals provide educational services, enrichment programs are less costly than marital therapy. It is considerably less expensive, for example, for trained nonprofessionals to use training films, tapes, and practice materials than it is for professionals to generate and present such programs.

Finally, the educational approach is more suitable than the counseling approach for conducting research. First, enrichment programs usually have content and procedures that can be easily replicated for study. Second, groups of participants are widely attracted to the programs, thus enabling leaders to compose several groups simultaneously whose program processes and outcomes can be compared. Finally, it is easier in educational programs to specify relevant evaluation criteria than in most counseling approaches in which treatment goals must be defined in individualistic terms (Guerney, 1977). Since marriage enrichment services can be studied more easily, there is a greater likelihood that relevant research will provide suggestions for meeting client needs more effectively.

The major limitation of educational programs is that they are not designed to provide remediation for problems that do not lie within the programs' intervention structure. However, educational services at pre- and postcrisis points can be quite useful in dealing with these problems (Guerney, 1977). L'Abate (1978) reports the use of successful combinations of therapy and enrichment: therapy followed by enrichment and vice versa, therapy and enrichment offered concurrently, enrichment preceding and following therapy and vice versa. He even suggests eliminating the distinction between the two: "It would be more accurate to speak only of family enrichment and eliminate the medical term 'therapy' when we refer to family intervention.

The terms 'structured' and 'unstructured' may differentiate between the different modes of intervention, especially when they are placed as polar opposites on a continuum, with an equal mixture . . . in the middle" (L'Abate, 1978, p. 61).

In support of the advantages of enrichment approaches, Wildman (1976), using self-evaluation of marital happiness measures, reports significant improvement for 92 percent of clinical couples (those defining their relationships as troubled) in unstructured therapy and for 88 percent of such couples in enrichment programs. In this same study it was found that clinical couples participating in enrichment services provided by first-year graduate students derived as much benefit as similar couples in therapy with professionals with an average of twelve years of experience. It should be noted that the model of enrichment used in these studies is a leader working with one couple in a structured program. Nonetheless, the implications are that enrichment services are a viable alternative to therapy for some couples.

In an extensive review of the research in both marriage enrichment and marriage therapy, Birchler (1979) has similarly concluded that despite little overt recognition of the similarities between the two approaches, there has been an impressive convergence in the actual intervention strategies used.

Couples can be offered counseling as an adjunct to marriage enrichment, just as students in classrooms can be provided with remedial services for reading, speech and other learning problems. Thus it seems practical to consider marital enrichment services as the basic course in the curriculum of services available to married couples and counseling, crisis intervention, and family therapy as the remedial measures for those with special needs.

The Role of the Professional Helper
in Marriage Enrichment

Because of the advantages of educational services, helping professionals are using marriage enrichment programs as an alternative to traditional counseling. Professionals have referred clients to programs sponsored by the marriage enrichment movement and have also offered marriage enrichment services themselves.

These practices raise some interesting issues. It could be argued that it is nonproductive for professionals to offer clients services that might be obtained at less cost from nonprofessional couples who have been trained to lead groups and support groups. Furthermore, it seems a misuse of the professionals' time to duplicate services available from other sources. If professionals offer marriage enrichment services, do they have a responsibility to provide services beyond those already being provided by trained lay leaders?

There are, in fact, a number of roles available to professional helpers that are vital both to the increased effectiveness of marriage enrichment services and to the achievement of the goals of the marriage enrichment movement. First, professionals can guide lay leaders and can serve as group leaders themselves for couples whose marriages are more at risk than those usually treated in enrichment programs. Second, professionals can make a significant contribution by becoming involved in the training of lay and paraprofessional leaders. Third, professionals can work in consultative roles with the support groups and organizations of the marriage enrichment movement.

A fourth critical area of involvement for professionals is the development of theoretical bases for marriage enrichment services and translation of these bases into program models. Much of what is currently being offered by lay leaders in marriage enrichment has been borrowed from various schools of thought. Frequently, more emphasis has been put on intuitively selecting and constructing activities than on developing programs from theories of human behavior, social systems, and the family. Thus leaders have at times chosen to adapt prepackaged programs to meet the needs of specific groups. This process may have resulted in a hodgepodge of skills training, values clarification, and self- and other-awareness activities. Leaders have often lacked guidance in how to conceptualize theoretically the structuring of a specific group to meet its unique goals.

Defining these goals is a fifth role for helping professionals. Is marriage enrichment aimed at making couples happier with their marriages? teaching them more finely developed skills for relating to one another? or enhancing individual adjustment, which may or may not be possible within the existing marriage? These three goals may or may not be mutually exclusive. Attempting to achieve all three without specifying relevant evaluative criteria can result in ineffectual enrichment programs.

Specifying the purpose(s) of a program is a prerequisite both to developing an appropriate methodology and to assessing its effectiveness. Different services may be designed to achieve different goals, but all the goals must be clarified. Only then can the effective approach be determined for each goal.

For example, research has indicated that learning the skills to better understand one's spouse does not necessarily result in greater marital happiness and adjustment (Garland, 1981). In a review of marriage enrichment evaluation studies, Gurman and Kniskern (1977) found that although marriage enrichment services are consistently effective, they are much more effective in changing the actual behaviors of spouses than they are in changing spouses' evaluations of and feelings about the marriage. It becomes essential, then, to decide whether a service is designed to increase marital happiness, to develop the skills people use to communicate with and understand one another, or to enhance individual adjustment.

A better understanding of one's spouse does not necessarily result in a happier relationship. What does make partners happier with their marriages—participation in a group where spouses can get some sense of context from sharing experiences with and observing the interaction of other couples? resolving specific conflicts? going out one night a week alone together, away from the kids, to talk about "us"? It is the role of the professional helper to research how and why marriage enrichment works to create marital attitude changes, teach interpersonal skills, and enhance the individual adjustment of spouses, and then to translate these research results into appropriate program strategies.

Qualifications of the Marriage Enrichment Leader

The most pervasive role of the professional helper in marriage enrichment is leading groups for couples who are experiencing problems in their marital relationships. Yet the professional is also called on to lead groups, and to consult with trained paraprofessionals who lead groups, in which relatively well-adjusted couples are seeking opportunities for growth. While educational preparation for clinical certification by a professional association such as the American Association of Marriage and Family Therapists is important to the professional status as a marriage enrichment leader, it may not be sufficient. I will return to the matter of professional qualifications later in this chapter. First I propose to look closely at another group of people who work in marriage enrichment programs: paraprofessionals who have had special training.

The Association of Couples for Marriage Enrichment has established the most widely accepted standards for the training of paraprofessional couples who lead marriage enrichment groups. Couples who are members in the Association must meet the following criteria for selection as leaders:

1. The couple must be committed to marital growth and be currently working effectively on their own marriage.
2. The couple must be able to function well as a team, cooperating smoothly and not competing or getting in each other's way.
3. The couple needs to be able to communicate in a warm and caring attitude to other couples in the group.
4. The couple needs to be ready to share their own experiences, to be open and make themselves vulnerable if necessary, in order to help other couples.
5. The couple must be sensitive to the others in the group and aware of what is going on.
6. All prospective leader couples need to have some basic knowledge about human development, marital interaction, and group process. In the case of couples who have no formal training in any of the helping professions, evidence of some acquaintance with these areas (through attendance at workshops, training sessions and the like) may be required (Hopkins and others, 1978, p. 75).

Couples must participate in two marriage enrichment experiences and be recommended by two qualified leader couples in order to participate in a basic training workshop. Such a workshop extends over at least four and one half days and involves, for each couple, participation in a marriage enrichment event; reflection on marriage enrichment experiences; learning a variety of styles, resources, and support systems for marriage enrichment; practice in planning and leading groups; exploring their marital relationship; and developing a continuing education plan for themselves. If a couple completes these requirements, they are provisionally certified. After leading five marriage enrichment events under supervision, they participate in an advanced training workshop and are then eligible for full certification, which must be renewed at three year intervals. (Hopkins and others, 1978).

For the professionally trained leader, with whom this book is primarily concerned, there are some additional criteria by which preparedness for leading marriage enrichment groups can be judged. The educational background of the professional should include mastering the concepts and skills of small group leadership, marriage counseling, and crisis intervention.

In addition, the marriage enrichment leader needs to be a skilled teacher. In a sense, marriage enrichment can be conceptualized as a teaching function: teaching couples interpersonal skills they can use to augment their relationships and teaching groups skills that will enable skill learning and relationship building to occur in them. For example, the leader needs to be able to teach problem-solving skills; in doing this, the leader is not primarily solving problems but, rather, is providing tools for group participants to use in solving their own problems, inside or outside the group setting. Leaders, therefore, need to avoid being pulled into the role of problem-solver and therapist for couples, roles in which the focus is often on negative aspects of the relationship that need to be changed through outside intervention. Instead, the marriage enrichment leader focuses on translating problems into opportunities to develop each couple's skills. Even dealing with problems, then, becomes translated into a growth and learning activity, for which the group provides the context.

The marriage enrichment leader needs to be skilled in presenting concepts and information didactically as well as through structured group experiences and structured and unstructured group discussion. Beyond teaching, the leader needs to be able to model the values and skills the group is learning. Thus the leader's role includes enacting the values and skills as well as presenting them in such a way that participants can learn them. The process involves helping participants conceptualize the bits of behavior that compose skills and enacted values, encouraging participants to enact these in a progressive way until the skills are learned, and reinforcing the participants' learning. The complexity of skill learning will be explored further in Chapter Three.

The marriage enrichment leader's focus needs to be on growth goals, rather than problem resolution goals, and on the relationships of participants with each other—spouse to spouse and couple to couple—rather than on their relationships with the leader. For example, they are encouraged to talk to one another rather than to channel communication through the leader. This is particularly difficult to do if participants see the leader as an expert whose function is primarily problem solving. Participant-leader relationships will be further explored in the examination of group development in Chapter Four.

Although marriage enrichment groups are not designed to solve specific problems or provide therapy, it is not uncommon for individual or relationship crises to be discovered or to erupt in the course of a program. The marriage enrichment leader needs to be a skilled counselor in order to provide crisis intervention in such an instance. The leader may then need to decide either to provide counseling to a couple experiencing crisis or to refer them to another professional. A major consideration in such a decision is whether the roles of group leader (focusing on relationship strengths) and therapist (focusing on resolving problems) might become confused if the couple continues in the group. Because it is sometimes necessary to refer couples to another professional for counseling services, leaders need to maintain consultative relationships with other professionals. Consultation is also useful for obtaining feedback on leadership style, group development, and participant and program "fit." Such a consultative relationship can enhance a leader's ability to develop skills, to explore and utilize thoughts and feelings about the work and the people involved in it, and to evaluate the effectiveness of the services being provided. Consultation may take the form of coleadership, live supervision, responses to video and audio recordings of the group, or any combination of these.

Finally, marriage enrichment leaders need to model the attitudes and values that exemplify the goals of marriage enrichment group—hopefulness about the future of the participants' marriages, belief in the value of marriage, warmth, empathy, and genuineness. Some models of marriage enrichment require that the group be led by a married couple who participate equally in the process, along with other couples—disclosing their thoughts and feelings and exploring their own relationship with the group. Other models conceptualize the leader's role as that of facilitating the group's process without participating in it. In both models, however, the leader's role is to model the kind of interpersonal relating that enhances marital communication and intimacy, to listen, express empathy, and convey concern. In the next chapter I will examine the theoretical bases underlying various approaches to marriage enrichment.

2

Foundations
of Marriage Enrichment
Services

Marriage enrichment programs currently being provided to couples are a mixture of attitudinal and skills training experiences, designed to achieve particular goals. These include increasing spouses' satisfaction with their relationship, improving partners' communication with one another, and resolving particular conflictual issues or crises in the relationship. The rationales for these programs have been developed from a number of psychological and sociological theories and approaches to counseling/therapy. The major approaches to marriage enrichment have been based on General Systems theory, Rogerian theory, behavioral and learning theories, and the philosophy of church-related marriage enrichment programs. In this chapter the general principles of each approach are summarized briefly; the marriage enrichment programs that have been developed from each approach are described; any research on the programs is cited.

General Systems Theory

Unquestionably, General Systems theory has become the dominant theoretical framework in the treatment of marital and family relationships (Olson and Sprenkle, 1976) and thus the basis for the development of a variety of marriage enrichment programs. One of the appeals of General Systems theory to those working with marital couples is its basic concern with the processes and structures of relationships rather than specific problems that couples want to resolve; in other words it deals with relationship variables rather than personality variables. Quick and Jacobs's (1973) research indicates that process variables are more important than attribute variables (personality variables) in discriminating between disturbed and healthy couples. They found that empathy, genuineness, openness of communication, and unconditional positive regard were the process variables associated with marital satisfaction. These variables can be translated into skills and taught to couples who can then use them to modify their relationships.

The marital relationship is defined in General Systems theory as a social system, or "a consistent network of interacting relationships between persons, with the persons considered as units of the system, above and beyond their individual characteristics" (Murrell, 1973, p. 9). It includes both the nature of the relationship and the patterns by which the partners relate to one another. A central concept in this theory is that the system functions to develop patterns of coping with and relating to changing input from within the system (developmental, affective, and other changes in each partner) and from the environment (changes in employment, relationships to extended family, and so on). The system uses information from both sources to understand how it is functioning for its members and in its environment. If these data indicate some disparity between the actual effects and the intended effects, the marital system/relationship must change in some way.

For example, spouses experience progressive developmental changes through the life cycle such as the role strain frequently accompanying the addition of a child to the family. The spouses may recognize a resulting decrease in the amount of intimate time spent with one another as an unacceptable change in their relationship, and may therefore attempt to structure more time alone together (negative feedback). *Nega-*

tive feedback is defined as processes used to restore the individual's or relationship's behavior so that it complies with the system's original intentions.

Spouses may also find departures from established routines: fewer gourmet meals, beds left unmade more often, and floors vacuumed fewer times a week. If these changes provide time and energy for other necessary and enjoyable activities such as playing with the baby, the couple may look for additional household tasks that can be eliminated or curtailed to allow more time for family or individual activities (positive feedback). *Positive feedback* is defined as processes used to increase the divergence between what is and what the system originally intended.

Of course, positive and negative feedback are dependent on the ability of the couple system to acknowledge discrepancies between what is expected and what is not expected in their relationship. To acknowledge these discrepancies means to expect a change, one that may or may not be accomplished. Watzlawick, Weakland, and Fisch (1974) and Hill (1974) theorize that the most significant distinction between adequate functioning and dysfunctioning is the degree to which a system is able to generate change by itself or is caught in a process of maintaining the status quo.

Corroborating evidence comes from a number of studies of "pathological" families. In one study, Mishler and Waxler (1968) unexpectedly found that communication in the families of schizophrenics was orderly, with fewer interruptions and longer statements and explanations by family members; their speech was more patterned and predictable than interaction in healthy families. After examination of variability in interaction, they conclude: "There may be an optimum level of such variability that serves an adaptive function for the family and its members. Variability provides new opportunities for change, for the introduction of new information, and for movement and development within the group" (p. 286). Similarly, Haley (1964) found disturbed families to be more rigid in their interactional patterns than healthy families. It appears that interaction in healthy families is less predictable than in pathological families.

By definition, the less predictable communication is, the more new information it carries. Therefore, these healthy families have more information about one another and their environment, which they can use to adjust their relationships to individual needs and to adapt to the environment.

In conceptualizing the marital relationship as a system, spouses' roles are defined as processes requiring adaptation and change in both the individual and the system: "A role is more than simple 'social position,' a position in some social space which is 'occupied.' It involves interaction, adjustments between the components and the system. It is a multiple concept, referring to the demands upon the component by the system, to the internal adjustment processes of the component, and to how the component functions in meeting the system's requirements. The adjustments it makes are frequently compromises between the requirements of the component and the requirements of the system" (Miller, 1978, p. 30). In order for couples to make adjustments, they must go through three processes of communication. First, new information about the components (spouses) and the system (the marital relationship) must be transmitted. Second, spouses must receive this information. Finally, the partners must react to and act upon the information.

If the goal of marriage enrichment is to increase marital adjustment, the enrichment processes should be designed to increase the information available to the spouses about themselves and their environment. This increase in information may or may not "restore order" (Hoffman, 1971) as the couple has experienced it in the past. Lewis (1979) and Lewis and others (1976) have studied healthy families from a General Systems theory framework and relate a variety of healthy relationship characteristics. Three which apply specifically to communication are: I-ness: the ability of individual family members to express themselves clearly as feeling, thinking, acting, valuable, and separate individuals, and to take responsibility for thoughts, feelings, and actions; respect for the unique experience of another: the recognition and acceptance that others may perceive differently; and permeability to others: the ability to hear and respond to others within a system (Lewis and others, 1976).

Marriage Enrichment Programs. One of the most highly structured and well-researched marriage enrichment programs is the Minnesota Couples Communication Program (MCCP) (Miller, Corrales, and Wackman, 1975; Miller, Nunnally, and Wackman, 1975, 1976). It is based on family development theories, symbolic interactionism, and modern systems theory (Nunnally, Miller, and Wackman, 1976). In this program couples are taught two sets of skills: awareness skills, enabling them to understand their interaction patterns and communication skills, enabling them to make changes in those patterns. The program consists of 4 three-hour sessions given once a week by trained, certified instructors. Each session focuses on one of four conceptual frameworks. The first, the awareness wheel, helps participants identify information about themselves and is made up of five components: sensing, thinking, feeling, wanting, and doing. The participants learn skills to express this information. The second framework is the shared meaning process, designed to increase information about the spouse. Spouses learn listening/interaction skills (active listening skills) so that they receive messages as their partners intended them to be received. The third framework, communication styles, is designed to help spouses identify the kinds of communication styles they use and the effects these styles have on their partner. The final framework, I count/I count you, resembles Harris's (1967) *I'm OK—You're OK* but emphasizes spouses' responsibility for their own and their partner's self-esteem. The frameworks are presented in detail in a text designed for participants (Miller, Nunnally, and Wackman, 1975).

A second program developed from the General Systems theory is the Workshop in Couples Communication and Negotiation Skills (Garland, 1978). This program is based on the findings of Lewis and others (1976) in their study of healthy families. The goal of the workshop is that participants understand and analyze their own communication patterns and gain skill in communicating and negotiating effectively. In four weekly three-hour sessions the following communication and negotiation skills are taught through didactic presentations, structured activities, and role plays:

- Paraphrasing: repeating in one's own words what another has said to indicate that one hears and understand what the speaker is saying and to verify any inference one has drawn from what was said.
- Attending: orienting one's body toward another and maintaining eye contact during a verbal communicative sequence.
- Observing nonverbal behavior: calling attention to nonverbal behavior when verbal and nonverbal behaviors are incongruent or when feelings are not being expressed verbally.
- Reaching for information: asking open-ended questions (for example, requesting elaboration of what a speaker has said) when one does not understand what is being communicated, when one would like to explore an issue further or asking a closed question (for example, requesting a specific fact) when one is trying to pinpoint an issue.
- Pinpointing the question: asking the questions "What is it that we do not agree on?" and "If we agree on a solution to this question, will the same argument occur again?" when the issue of disagreement has not been clarified or when the issue of disagreement involves a future behavior.
- Staying with the pinpointed issue: restating the pinpointed question after digressing into past or other issues.
- Deferring the question: agreeing on a mutually convenient time to discuss the issue when an issue has been pinpointed but there is not enough time to discuss it, or when one or both discussants want time to think about the issue.
- Labeling behavior: pointing out a specific behavior of another person, describing its effects, and explaining how it should be changed when a change in another's behavior is desired.
- Determining whether the question is one of fact or of opinion: asking "Is there one answer to this question and all others are wrong, or could there still be disagreement after all the available facts have been researched?" when an issue has been pinpointed and there is still disagreement.
- Negotiating questions of opinion: asking open-ended questions (for example, Why do we have to agree on this, or do we? If so, what *must* we agree on?) in order to specify what

has to be agreed on, and discussing compromises until a satisfactory resolution is reached.

There are three other programs with similar goals. Boyd and others (1974) and Schauble and Hill (1976) have developed programs for use with couples in a therapeutic setting. Carnes and Laube's (1975) program based on General Systems theory was designed for family enrichment in the local church and uses families who have received special training as instructional teams. However, the skills taught are the same as those taught in the MCCP and the Workshop in Couples Communication and Negotiation skills: listening to others, speaking for oneself, sharing of values, problem solving, and contracting.

Elliott and Saunders (1982) have developed a program based on General Systems theory that has a somewhat different approach although a similar focus to the programs already discussed in this chapter. They presume, in fact, that their Systems Marriage Enrichment Program is the only one really based on a systems framework. Their program stems from three core concepts: (1) circular causality, or that a person's behavior both affects and is affected by the partner's behavior; (2) communication patterns which a couple presents that have been organized into predictable patterns; and (3) morphogenesis and morphostastis, or that marital systems have the ability both to adapt to change and to resist change. The program's activities are designed sequentially to develop group cohesiveness, then to raise the intensity of the couples' relationship and to solve problems. The major emphasis of this program is on providing couples the opportunity to first explore the patterns of their relationship and then resolve a conflict while being the focus of the group. Two leaders, one who works with the "couple of focus" and another who works with the observing group, direct the sessions.

In summary, programs developed from General Systems theory emphasize teaching skills that couples can use as tools to develop awareness of their interactional patterns and to modify those patterns to cope with changes in one another and in their environment. These skills may include self-awareness, communication and other-awareness, negotiation, and problem solving.

Evaluation Research. The MCCP, one of the most widely researched marriage enrichment programs, has shown positive results consistently. In comparing couples participating in the Minnesota program with those assigned randomly to a waiting list group, Miller, Nunnally, and Wackman (1976) report that participants in the program significantly increased their interactional awareness and communication skills. Gurman and Kniskern (1977), in a review of unpublished studies, similarly report the positive effects of the Minnesota program. However, because of inadequate follow-up study of participating couples and because of problems in defining the criteria for evaluation, they qualify their conclusions.

In a study designed to deal with these problems, Wampler and Sprenkle (1980) found that married and nonmarried couples participating in the Minnesota program showed more significant improvement on a behavioral measure of communication openness and the perceived quality of the relationship than couples in an attention-placebo control group and those in a no treatment control group. However, follow-up testing indicated that only the positive changes in the perceived quality of the relationship persisted. The researchers conclude that the MCCP has short-term positive effects, but more skills practice, both in training and in the natural environment, and booster sessions may be necessary to create long-term changes in communication behaviors.

Similarly, Joanning (1982) reported that marital adjustment and communication skills ratings increased significantly for couples in the program. However, at a five month follow-up, even though couples maintained their improved ratings in communication skills, marital adjustment had returned to pretest levels. Joanning interviewed couples to determine some of the explanations for the findings and reported that couples complained that skill practice during the sessions was not sufficient to integrate the skills into their lifestyles—although they could demonstrate the skills, they were not actually using them as much as they would like. They also reported that during the program they had felt much closer to one another because they were spending a large amount of time together focusing on their relationship, observing other relationships, and forming friendships with other couples. Joanning concludes that the group training sessions were socially significant, encouraging intimacy that could not be effectively replaced by "real life" routines (Joanning, 1982, p. 467).

In applying the program to engaged couples, Nunnally (1971) found no significant improvement in couples' ability to predict one another's responses to questions about the relationship. Also, participants' degree of adjustment to one another did not increase. These findings suggest that programs found to be effective with marital couples may not be effective with premarital couples and that results cannot always be generalized across these populations.

In summarizing nineteen research studies, many unpublished, Wampler (1982) concluded that there is strong evidence based on behavioral measures that the MCCP increases the use of the desired skills in marital couples' interaction. There also appears to be a positive impact on relationship quality, but evidence of duration of this impact has been less consistent.

Rogerian Theory

The client-centered therapy developed by Carl Rogers (1961) has been the basis for another major group of marriage enrichment programs. Rogers's central hypothesis is that "the growthful potential of any individual will tend to be released in a relationship in which the helping person is experiencing and communicating realness, caring, and a deeply sensitive nonjudgmental understanding" (Meador and Rogers, 1973). Therefore, the theory can be applied to a relationship, such as the marital relationship, in which understanding and individual growth are desired. In a helping relationship, the attitudes considered necessary and sufficient for one partner to effect change in the other are genuineness, congruence, empathy, and unpossessive caring and confirmation of the other. Genuineness and congruence incorporate reliance on one's "moment-to-moment felt experiencing" (Meador and Rogers, 1973, p. 138) in the relationship with the other. One partner is able to imagine, and in this way experience, what the other reports. Empathy involves understanding the world of the other as the other sees it. Unpossessive caring and confirmation of the other, or positive regard, requires a caring that avoids any overtly or covertly judgmental behavior, whether it be approving or disapproving. Rogers (Meador and Rogers, 1973, p. 160) states that if one is successful in communicating these attitudes, the therapist can expect certain things of the client: "He expects that [the other] will move from a remoteness of [his or her] inner experiencing to a more immediate awareness and expression of it; from disapproving of parts of [his or her] self to a greater self-acceptance; from a fear of relating, to relating to him or her more directly; from holding rigid black and white constructs of reality, to holding more tentative constructs; and from seeing the locus of evaluation outside [his or her] self to finding the locus of evaluation in [his or her] own inner experiencing." These expectations are equally applicable to a relationship in which the partners want to understand each other and themselves and are willing to reveal themselves to one another.

Clearly, the Rogerian approach holds an uncompromising belief in the self-actualizing growth motivation of the individual. This theory is as much a value system as it is a guide for therapy and marital enrichment. The Rogerian approach sees individuals as conditionally accepting themselves as worthy or unworthy based on how others seem to see them or on cultural definitions of success and worthiness. Ideally, through the kind of relationships Rogers describes, persons begin to recognize that they are developing organisms with their own desires, feelings, and perceptions, and they can rely on themselves and trust their own judgments.

Rogers (1961, p. 330) points out that individuals' primary reactions to one another are at cross-purposes with his postulated ideal attitude of how people relate: "The major barrier to mutual interpersonal communication is our very natural tendency to judge, to evaluate, to approve, or disapprove, the statement of the other person. . . . In other words, your primary reaction is to evaluate what has been said to you, to evaluate it from *your* point of view, your own frame of reference." This tendency to evaluate rather than to respond empathically and unconditionally to one another is greater in those situations involving conflict or strong emotions: "It is just when emotions are strongest that it is most difficult to achieve the frame of reference of the other person or group. Yet this is the time the attitude is most needed, if communication is to be established" (Rogers, 1961, p. 334).

Thus, to communicate effectively with one another, spouses must avoid being judgmental; the expressed thoughts and feelings of one partner must be understood and felt from the other's point of view so that the other's frame of reference can be achieved. Of course, the task becomes more difficult in a conflictual relationship: "If you really understand another person in this way, if you are willing to enter his private world and see the way life appears to him, without any attempt to make evaluative judgments, you run the risk of being changed yourself. You might see it his way, you might find yourself influenced in your attitudes or your personality" (Rogers, 1961, p. 333).

To improve communication, it is useful for the listener, before making a statement in conversation, to first restate the thoughts and feelings communicated by the speaker. The speaker can then either indicate that the listener has correctly understood the message or clarify any misinterpretation. Thus, before presenting one's own point of view, an understanding of the other's frame of reference is achieved.

Marriage Enrichment Programs. Building on the work of Rogers, Carkhuff (Carkhuff and Berenson, 1977) has developed a method of interpersonal skills training which integrates the skills of client-centered therapy with the systematic action methodology of the behaviorists. These skills are taught systematically to trainees. Using Carkhuff's method as the basis of his approach to marriage enrichment, Pierce (1973) reports a training program that teaches marital couples empathy skills—attending, observing, and listening.

The skills of Rogerian client-centered therapy have also been used as the basis for a comprehensive skills training program known as Conjugal Relationship Enhancement (Guerney,

1977). The Rogerian principles of acceptance, respect, and empathy are blended with an instructional program based on behavioral theory—that is, group leaders use didactic and modeling learning principles to teach the desired skills to participants. The skills are designed to develop greater sharing and psychological intimacy between spouses.

In the Conjugal Relationship Enhancement Program, spouses learn four sets of skills—speaker, listener, mode switching, and facilitator skills. Speaker skills are designed to help speakers' communicate their own feelings to their spouses as openly and honestly as they can without generating unnecessary hostility and defensiveness. As listeners, the spouses are taught to convey acceptance of the other's communication and to understand and empathize with the other's perceptions, thoughts, and feelings. The third set, mode switching, helps to identify the appropriate time and technique to switch from speaker skills to listener skills. Finally, the facilitator skills enable couples in the group to help one another learn the other three sets of skills. (For a comprehensive presentation of these skills and the Conjugal Relationship Enhancement Program, see Guerney, 1977.)

Evaluation Research. The results of programs based on Rogerian client-centered therapy have been consistently positive. Pierce (1973) found that the couples in his training program significantly improved their interpersonal communication skills. The program was more effective than either therapy with insight as its goal or a waiting list group. He also found that the depth of self-exploration, as rated by a trained observer, increased significantly among the couples in the program.

The Conjugal Relationship Enhancement Program has produced significantly positive results in a number of studies summarized by Gurman and Kniskern (1977). In additional studies Ely (1970) has found that couples who went through training showed significantly more improvement than a waiting list control group in skill usage, and reported significantly increased satisfaction with their communication and marital adjustment. Rappaport (1971, 1976), also using the Conjugal Relationship Enhancement model, has found significantly higher levels of self-reported marital adjustment and improvement in measures of skill usage after treatment and not after a baseline waiting period.

Finally, a program developed from a General Systems theory perspective but which uses the training in the Rogerian skills to accomplish its goals, is outlined in Chapter Five. The content and structure of this program are similar to others that have been discussed in this chapter. Research on this program (Garland, 1981) indicates that skills training results in significant increases in spouses' abilities to perceive their partners' attitudes and feelings. However, there is no indication that the skills training and resultant increases in perceptual accuracy are related to increases in marital adjustment. These findings do not necessarily contradict the findings of other research. Rather, they suggest that skills training may be successful if the criterion for success is increasing the awareness of interactional patterns and communication skills. In some instances, however, increased understanding of one another through use of these skills may provide information to spouses that their own marital system is not functioning successfully and thus the spouses' estimation of their degree of marital adjustment may be lowered.

Behavioral Theory

Behavioral therapy is based on theory derived from experimental research. This research, designed to discover basic principles of learning, has resulted in such concepts as positive and negative reinforcement, conditioning, and shaping. An empirical approach views each intervention as an experiment to test and refine the principles of learning. The theory emphasizes behavior that can be explained by learning processes. "Behavior is composed of cognitive, motor, and . . . emotional responses. Behavior is seen as responses to stimulation, external and internal, therefore the goal of therapy is to modify unadaptive stimulus-response (S-R) connections and the methods, insofar as possible, are analogs from experimental psychology. Behavior therapy is marked by its adherence to scientific method in evaluating its results, and designating process variables" (Goldstein,

1973, p. 207). Behavior theory is compatible in some ways with a General Systems theory approach despite basic differences. Both view behavior as being adaptive to context and deny that individual behavior can be viewed as occurring in a vacuum (Gant, 1979).

In providing therapy or preventive services to marital couples, behaviorists have taken an educational approach, emphasizing communication and negotiation skills so that couples can change their behavior patterns themselves (Lazarus, 1968, 1969; LeBow, 1972; Liberman, 1970; Rappaport and Harrell, 1972; Wieman, Shoulders, and Farr, 1974). Stuart (1970, p. 172) points out the emphasis on behavior: "If 'loving' behavior is sought, such behavior can clearly be brought under therapist and spouse control in much the same manner as any other response can be controlled." The behaviors that produce marital satisfaction and happiness can be defined and the environmental contingencies that influence these behaviors can be systematically structured so that these behaviors occur. "A happy husband and wife are happy because of what their partner says and does. A behavioral approach is concerned with initiating and maintaining the behaviors which result in marriage happiness" (Knox, 1971, p. 3).

Behavioral therapists have also examined the dynamics of marital interaction that control spouses' behavior. Patterson and Reid (1970) define reciprocity and coercion as the two basic patterns in family interaction. Reciprocity occurs when spouses reinforce one another at the same rate, with positive reinforcers maintaining the behavior of each. Coercion occurs when aversive stimuli control the behavior of one partner and reinforcers maintain the behavior of the other (Patterson and Reid, 1970). In marriage spouses request changes in each other's behavior as they adjust to one another's differences. Conflict arises when one partner demands change from the other and the other is either unwilling or unable to change. Often the more frequently a partner must request the change, the more aversive the demand becomes. For example, if a wife is angry because her husband leaves his clothes on the bathroom floor, she may reveal her feelings and ask him to pick them up. The husband may put away his clothes for a few days and thus the wife forgets about the issue. She does not say anything further; she does not provide such positive reinforcement for the changed behavior as, "Wow, sweetheart, I really like the way you've kept your clothes picked up. I married the most thoughtful man in the world." However, if the husband slips once and leaves his clothes scattered about, the wife may become exasperated. Frequently, this kind of aversive attack is met with counterattack and the interaction is diverted away from the problem. Yet, because the problem still exists, it will probably precipitate the same kind of argument over and over again. As the husband promises to try harder in order to quiet his wife, both spouses are reinforced by the interchange—the wife, because she is promised what she requested; the husband, because criticism of him has ceased. Therefore, in each coercive interchange, the aversive behavior of one partner (the wife) is strengthened (Patterson and Hops, 1972); and the other partner (the husband) becomes more likely to use aversiveness, thus increasing the frequency of aversive interchanges and coerciveness in the relationship.

A partner who does not receive positive reinforcement from a spouse will view the nonreinforcing spouse as less attractive. Stuart (1969, p. 676) states: "It is seen that each partner reinforces the other at a low rate and each is therefore relatively unattractive to and unreinforced by the other." Therefore, only by using negative reinforcement (coercion) can spouses provoke the desired responses in each other. Each partner tries to minimize individual costs since each has little hope of receiving anything rewarding from the other. Consequently, spouses tend to withdraw from one another.

Behavioral marital therapy intervenes in these coercive interactional patterns in three ways: (1) to reduce the rate of aversive behaviors when spouses attempt to negotiate behavior change (Patterson and Hops, 1972; Weiss, Hops, and Patterson, 1973; Patterson, 1971); (2) to develop the power of each partner to mediate rewards for the other by increasing the frequency and intensity of mutual positive reinforcement (Stuart, 1969, 1970, 1974); and (3) to help the couple to develop a system that provides for a continuous readjustment of the reinforcers from their partner (Azrin, Naster, and Jones, 1973). The objective of intervention is to maximize the elements of this reinforcement interchange (Azrin, Naster, and Jones, 1973). Behavioral therapists assume that frequently couples have the usual problem-solving skills in their repertoire but need help in dissolving the barriers that keep them from using these skills in the marital relationship (Patterson, Hops, and Weiss, 1975).

Marriage Enrichment Programs. Behavioral theory has been applied less often than systems theory or Rogerian client-centered therapy to educational programs for nonclinical couples, and no standardized program such as the Minnesota Couples Communication Program or the Conjugal Relationship Enhancement Program has been established. However, several smaller-scale behavioral programs have been developed.

Fisher (1973) and Wieman (1973) directly applied the techniques of behavioral therapy to groups of couples. Fisher taught couples the principles of positive reinforcement; during the group sessions, spouses awarded points to one another for changed behavior. To develop greater understanding of their partners and therefore provide more positive reinforcement, spouses functioned as observers while their partner discussed marital problems in a small group. The three couples who accumulated the most points from the group each week and who were most accurate in predicting their spouses' responses on an attitude inventory were reinforced by group applause and a financial reward at the end of the program.

Behavioral programs have tended to emphasize teaching couples to contract for reciprocal behavioral changes. Dixon and Sciara (1977) adapted Azrin, Naster, and Jones's (1973) reciprocity counseling approach to a marriage enrichment group. "Reciprocity counseling is a set of procedures designed to increase the level of reinforcers exchanged by a couple" (Dixon and Sciara, 1977, p. 78). Exchanges anticipated to be mutually reinforcing are negotiated in the group setting and instituted in the couple's natural environment. Similarly, Wieman (1973) adapted Stuart's (1970) reciprocal reinforcement treatment to the group setting, teaching spouses to use reinforcing behaviors more effectively and to contract for behavior changes.

Harrell and Guerney (1976) designed the Behavioral-Exchange Program to teach groups of married couples cooperative negotiation skills, enabling them to deal more successfully with their marital conflicts. In this program didactic presentations and skill practice exercises train couples to employ a problem-solving process. The problem-solving skills, listed in sequential order, are: listening carefully (similar to the Rogerian skills), locating a relationship issue, identifying one's own contributions to the issue, identifying alternative solutions, evaluating alternative solutions, making an exchange, determining conditions of the exchange, implementing the behavioral-exchange contract, and renegotiating the behavioral-exchange contract.

Rose (1977) provides a comprehensive approach in his Communication Skills Workshop. He emphasizes teaching skills to improve communication rather than resolving specific problems. Three basic communication skills are taught: positive message exchange, behavioral specificity, and feedback. Participants also learn to rephrase negative messages in more positive ways. As couples master these skills, they then are taught a structured negotiation procedure for applying them to problems. This negotiation procedure is the familiar problem-solving process of gathering information, generating alternatives, evaluating alternatives, planning, contracting, and evaluating. In addition, techniques of intrapersonal communication are used to help couples confront relationship topics that arouse high anxiety (Witkin and Rose, 1978).

Evaluation Research. In their review of the literature, Gurman and Kniskern (1977, p. 8) report that "behavioral-exchange programs have not fared especially well, showing no difference from control groups in two-thirds of the studies reviewed. These results are largely consistent with the at best moderate gains found in studies of behavioral marriage therapy for more seriously distressed couples." Harrell and Guerney (1976) found in researching the Behavioral-Exchange Program that couples showed significant improvement in conflict management but showed no significant improvement in marital satisfaction. Couples with severe relationship problems had the greatest difficulty applying the skills.

Fisher (1973) has compared the program based on reinforcement principles and behavioral exchange with a "facilita-
tive-placebo" control group and a waiting list control group.
Spouses in behavioral groups had more accurate perceptions of
their partners although measures of empathic behavior showed
no significant differences between any of the groups.

More positive results have been found with the Communication Skills Workshop. Rose (1977) and Witkin and Rose
(1978) have found that couples participating in the workshop
showed substantial gains on self-report measures of marital satisfaction and communication. Participants also improved in the
exchange of positive verbal messages during conflict although
their use of negative messages did not decrease and their use of
problem-solving messages did not increase. Those demonstrated
changes were maintained for a six-week follow-up study. No
control group was utilized.

Similarly, Dixon and Sciara (1977) report that their reciprocity counseling approach resulted in increased ratings of
marital happiness on several dimensions and heightened commitment to and optimism about the marriage. Their multiple
baseline data support the contingency relationship between the
introduction of reciprocity exchange procedures and increased
marital happiness.

Finally, Wieman (1973) has compared his behavioral program with the Rogerian Conjugal Relationship Enhancement
Program. He found that both programs significantly improved
marital satisfaction, which was maintained through follow-up;
and he found no significant differences between the two programs. Wieman's study raises the possibility that programs are
more effective than no treatment controls not because of the
interventions themselves but because of extraneous factors in
the setting. For instance, couples may improve simply because
they have the opportunity to interact with other couples in an
environment conducive to learning and sharing.

Marriage Enrichment in the Church

Because marriage enrichment originated and is still rooted
and flourishing in the church, its leaders are predominantly pro-

fessionals in pastoral care (Otto, 1975, 1976; Clinebell, 1975; Hopkins and others, 1978; Mace and Mace, 1975, 1978a, 1976b). Marriage enrichment actually began in 1962 in the Catholic church in Spain. In the United States it rapidly gained momentum in the 1960s through the impetus of United Methodists, Roman Catholics, and Quakers (Mace and Mace, 1978a). The movement has since spread to a variety of religious groups, including Baptists, Catholics, Christians, members of the Church of God, Jews, Moravians, Mormons, Presbyterians, Friends, and United Methodists, and community groups, including family service associations, YMCAs, family life councils, public schools, community colleges, and universities (Smith, Shoffner, and Scott, 1979).

In 1973 the Association of Couples for Marriage Enrichment (ACME) was founded by lay couples who had participated in marriage enrichment. This association has four objectives: (1) to work for the enrichment of member couples' marriages, (2) to provide mutual support, (3) to initiate and support community services that foster quality marriage and family life, and (4) to improve the public image of marriage as an expansive rather than restrictive state (Mace and Mace, 1975). It is significant that ACME is not designed for professionals; they can, however, participate as affiliates. Part of ACME's philosophy is that couples who have achieved satisfying relationships should be put to work helping others, "in accordance with the evangelical doctrine that we are 'saved to save' " (Hopkins and others, 1978, p. 7).

Marriage enrichment in the church is based on the belief that persons who have learned to satisfy their basic needs should continue to grow by developing their creativity and their unused potentials (Maslow, 1968). This belief is translated into the hypothesis that "all persons and all relationships are functioning at a fraction of their potential and that, in every couple or family, there is the potential for growth in the relationship as well as the possibility of personal growth, leading to a more fulfilling togetherness. It is a further hypothesis that every union or family can be strengthened through the periodic regeneration and renewal offered by marriage and family enrichment programs" (Otto, 1976, p. 11).

The goal of marriage enrichment is not just to challenge individuals to grow as individuals and as couples. It extends to the societal level—the enrichment of marriages should result in strengthened families; the development of support networks among families, congregations, and communities; and an ultimate investment of self in others and the perpetuation of humankind (Clinebell, 1975). Grounded in this philosophy, church-related marriage enrichment depends on the knowledge and the assistance of helping professionals in such areas as communication, conflict resolution, anger management, gender role redefinition, decision making, spiritual renewal, and sexual enrichment (Mace and Mace, 1975).

Marriage Enrichment Programs. Because marriage enrichment is a philosophy rather than a theory, prescribed methods for achieving program goals do not exist. Professionals have sought theoretical approaches that are compatible with the philosophy, thus the eclectic approach found in many enrichment programs. Techniques, resources, and materials come from diverse sources. "About 80 percent of the programs have certain common elements, such as the use of group discussion, two-person structured experiences, and lectures" (Otto, 1976, p. 19). Many program developers draw from the theoretical bases of General Systems theory, Rogerian client-centered therapy, and behavioral therapy although other sources such as transactional analysis, sensitivity and encounter group approaches, Gestalt therapy, and conflict theories also provide frameworks. Most programs emphasize that change in a marital relationship is more probable when the couple can experience new ways of functioning, instead of passively listening to didactic presentations. Also, programs challenge the "intermarital taboo" (Hopkins and others, 1978) that demands privacy within the marital relationship and insulates couples from the interaction and input they need to develop and change their relationships. Breaking down this taboo allows couples to share their marital experiences and therefore to provide mutual support as well as to advocate for and support community services that strengthen marriages and families (Hopkins and others, 1978).

Church-related marriage enrichment is presented in three

ways: through self-help materials such as books, cassette tapes, pamphlets, and manuals; through conjoint counseling with qualified professionals; and through couple groups (Hopkins and others, 1978). Unquestionably, couple groups have been the most widely used alternative of the three.

Although group procedures vary widely, they can be broadly categorized by the three particular religious bodies that originated them—the Roman Catholics, the Methodists, and the Quakers (Mace and Mace, 1978a).

The Roman Catholic Marriage Encounter, known as Marriage Encounter, is usually a weekend retreat program held for couples in a residential facility. Other models, however, such as weekly programs and even do-it-yourself programmed materials are also available (Demarest, Sexton, and Sexton, 1977). The encounter weekend, beginning in 1948, was the first marriage enrichment program. Approximately 500,000 couples have participated in encounter weekends, and the number is increasing at the rate of perhaps 100,000 per year (Genovese, 1975; Otto, 1975).

The weekend retreat is led by a team of two or three couples who have attended encounter programs and a minister, usually a priest. Team members give twelve presentations on various marriage topics based on a sequence of themes: self-examination, examination of the couple relationship, examination of the couple's relationship to God, and finally, examination of the couple's ministry in the world. (Prepared materials for these topics are available from National Marriage Encounter, 1978.) Following the presentations, leaders ask open-ended questions, which participants meditate on and then write about, describing their feelings. Each couple then shares their written statements in private and discusses them so that spouses can better understand each other.

The program emphasizes learning about one another and sharing feelings, not learning communication skills. The group only interacts socially and during religious observances of the weekend. "The Marriage Encounter is designed to give married couples the opportunity to examine their lives together—their weaknesses and strong points, their attitudes toward each other and toward their families, their hurts, desires, ambitions, disappointments, joys and frustrations—and to do so openly and honestly in a Christ-like, face-to-face, heart-to-heart encounter with the one person they have chosen to live with for the rest of their lives" (Demarest, Sexton, and Sexton, 1977, p. 25).

Two organizations have developed in response to the marriage encounter movement. One, National Marriage Encounter, is an ecumenical organization that includes Jewish and Protestant leaders. It has also been adapted for the engaged couple, the single adult, and families with children (Demarest, Sexton, and Sexton, 1977; Bosco, 1976; Kligfield, 1976). The second, Worldwide Encounter, is a more fundamental group than National Marriage Encounter, with a much tighter structure. Leaders are required to use its manual.

The Methodists began the Marriage Communication Labs, a carefully structured program, which has been used by other denominations. Unlike the Catholic model, the labs consider group sharing an important component. In addition to sharing thoughts and feelings with one another, couples receive training in communication, such as the use of active listening skills and I-messages from Gordon's *P.E.T.: Parent Effectiveness Training* (1975). The emphasis is on helping couples to know how to deal with issues rather than tackling specific problems. It is experiential and inductive: "Most of the time we deal with specific items by asking couples to do a specific exercise, to reflect upon that experience in terms of what it says to them about their relationship, and then to determine what changes they may want to make, if any" (Hopkins and Hopkins, 1976, p. 229). In experiences and discussions deriving from exercises as well as in the skills training, partners share with other couples as well as with each other.

Similar to the Methodists' Marriage Communication Labs, but much broader in scope, is the Baptist Marriage Enrichment System, sponsored by the Sunday School Board of the Southern Baptist Convention. Although the system defines marriage enrichment as "any growth or new learning experience that enhances marriage" ("Baptist Marriage Enrichment System," 1981, p. 1), its format is primarily the weekend retreat. Participation in some marriage enrichment activity is supported by a broad spectrum of church literature. The Baptist system provides four levels of marriage enrichment retreats. The first level, the readiness level, offers self-taught resource kits, books, and abbreviated retreats. The second level is the basic level. It is a highly structured forty-one-hour program conducted in a weekend retreat format. Couples, some of whom may be helping professionals, are trained and certified to be leaders. This basic level is designed for couples who have had no prior exposure to personal growth or marriage enrichment experiences. Leaders work from a detailed transcript of the program content, which includes communicating, cultivating nurture and managing feelings, dealing with conflict, building trust and experiencing intimacy, and enhancing intercouple fellowship and worship. The theoretical basis for the retreat is transactional analysis although elements of behavioral theory and systems theory contribute to the framework. The third level of the Baptist system is the intermediate level, a less structured one which deals in greater depth with communication and the management of feelings. It is restricted to those who have already participated in a basic-level retreat. Finally, the advanced level is a retreat with a very loose structure; it does not follow any one model but rather "is tailored to the objectives expressed by the couples attending" ("Baptist Marriage Enrichment System," 1981, p. 4). The goal of the Baptist system is that by 1985 a total of 50,000 couples from at least 10,000 churches will have committed themselves to some marriage enrichment activity.

The Quaker model of marriage enrichment differs markedly from the encounter and communication models. In this model there is a minimum of organized structure. Exercises are used only sparingly as facilitative aids. Couples themselves decide what areas of marital growth they wish to explore and, in couple dialogues, share their own marital experiences with the group (Mace and Mace, 1978a; Mace and Mace, 1976a). This program is often used by couples who have previously been involved in a marriage enrichment weekend and who then want to become members of an ongoing support group or have another retreat as a follow-up to their first experience.

In 1975 Otto (1975) estimated that 180,000 couples had

participated in marriage enrichment programs. Participation in the Roman Catholic Marriage Encounter alone has far exceeded that estimate in the few years since 1975. Clearly, intervention into marriage relationships through growth experiences and communication skills training is widespread. Some of the church-related marriage enrichment programs available include: Clinebell (1975), Genovese (1975), Hinkle and Moore (1971), "Marriage Communication Labs" (1975), and Otto (1976). Other program models that are not part of church-related enrichment but which nevertheless strive to achieve similar goals are also available (see Clarke, 1970; Otto, 1976; Stein, 1975; and Sauber, 1974).

Evaluation Research. Because church-related marriage enrichment is more a philosophical approach than an application of theory and because many of its leaders are lay couples who have participated in the programs, little research has been done on its effects. Reports of program results frequently rely on testimonies from participating couples rather than on controlled examination of specific variables. These testimonies suggest that a marriage enrichment retreat "enables the couple to make an honest assessment of where they are in their marriage . . . to identify together the directions in which they want to seek future growth; and to learn at least a few new skills that will aid them in the growth process" (Mace and Mace, 1978a, p. 6).

Couples appear to obtain a vision of their relationship potential if they achieve the goals they establish in a program. Marriage enrichment thus seems to instill hope; whether or not it also provides the skills to make dreams reality has not been researched. Follow-up contacts suggest that couples need additional help if they are to achieve their goals (Mace and Mace, 1975).

Because few outcome studies have been done, particularly of the Roman Catholic Marriage Encounter which has had such spectacular success in recruiting couples and building the movement, Doherty, McCabe, and Ryder (1978) have raised some serious concerns. Their observations suggest that Marriage Encounter attempts to present a single definitive goal for all married couples. They further suggest (p. 102): "More serious, it claims divine sanction for this goal." This goal is complete unity in which aloneness, loneliness, independence, and individuality are viewed as harmful. Because the program uses a lecture format with little or no opportunity for feedback and discussion and because it is held in a retreat setting, participants cannot critically assess the changes they are encouraged to make.

Doherty, McCabe, and Ryder (1978, pp. 104–105) have listed the following potentially harmful effects of an encounter weekend: (1) the perceived benefits may be at best temporary and at worst illusory; (2) it encourages a denial of differences and of separateness in married couples; (3) the stress on the dialogue technique may lead to a kind of ritual dependency; (4) in fostering a return to the "breathless closeness" of early marriage, Marriage Encounter may be guilty of promoting the very syndrome it seeks to cure, namely, the illusion-disillusionment cycle of marriage; (5) couples who do not practice their daily dialogue technique may experience guilt which turns to resentment of each other; and (6) Marriage Encounter may also have separative or divisive influences on the couple's relationship with their children, relatives, and friends.

Most recently, Doherty and Lester (1982, p. 9) have reported on a ten-year retrospective study of 129 randomly selected couples who had participated in Marriage Encounter. They found that 19 percent of the couples reported more frustration because of awareness of unmet needs, 14 percent reported conflict over Marriage Encounter itself, and 9 percent reported greater discomfort in discussing feelings with their spouses.

DeYoung (1979) concludes from his experience with participation in a Marriage Encounter program that it is as much an initiation ceremony into a new adult status as it is a way of helping couples to communicate. This "encountered" status entails membership in the "encountered community" and responsibilities to recruit other couples and to build a stronger religious community.

Milholland and Avery (1982) have conducted the only other published evaluation of Marriage Encounter. In their study of forty couples in two weekend retreat groups, they found a significant increase in self-reported trust and marital satisfaction that was maintained during a five-week follow-up. They conclude that the lack of focus in Marriage Encounter on mutual understanding and problem solving does not exclude possible improvement in these skills. In fact, their findings suggest that whether because of couples' expectations of how Marriage Encounter will affect their relationship or because of actual changes in their interactions, couples achieve and maintain increased relationship trust and satisfaction through Marriage Encounter.

Furthermore, in spite of the criticism, the testimonies of many couples who have participated in Marriage Encounter should not be dismissed lightly. Proponents of the movement have suggested that the powerful dynamics at work cause significant positive change in the lives of individuals and couples (Regula, 1975; Koch and Koch, 1976). Stedman (1982) expresses agreement with the characterization of the retreat experience as an initiation ceremony, but does not agree that this is problematic—the "encountered" community that couples join challenges them to initiate changes that will effect a solid, lifelong marital relationship. He summarizes several unpublished studies that report significant increases in marital communication, adjustment, commitment, and self-disclosure (Stedman, 1982).

While some studies have been reassuring, the suggestion of potentially harmful effects to nearly 10 percent of participants—150,000 couples out of the estimated 1.5 million couples who have participated (Doherty and Lester, 1982, p. 9) documents the need to emphasize that individuality is not necessarily threatening to marriage and that marriage enrichment programs that focus exclusively on attitudes and values may lead to unrealistic expectations of marriage on the part of participants.

Other Theoretical Approaches

Although most of the major enrichment programs developed from one or a combination of the theoretical approaches discussed in this chapter, program frameworks have not been limited to these theories. Many clinical practice theories suggest approaches to preventive services such as marriage enrichment. Their concepts are applicable to developing the relationship potential as well as to remediating the problems of individuals and their systems.

Zinker and Leon (1976), for example, have developed a Gestalt marriage enrichment program that focuses on the processes of communication. Through awareness exercises, couples learn to express feelings and thus develop skills to restructure their relationships.

The concepts of transactional analysis have been applied to another marriage enrichment program (Capers and Capers, 1976) in addition to the Baptist Marriage Enrichment System. Verbal and nonverbal exercises are used to identify the ego states of nurturing parent, critical parent, natural child, adopted child, and adult. A main emphasis is on helping spouses gain control of their ego states.

Maslow's Self-Actualization Theory maintains that a basic need for and drive toward self-actualization exists in every individual. Because self-actualization occurs through relationships, "the marital relationship can be viewed as a vehicle which can move individuals toward self-actualization" (Travis and Travis, 1976b, p. 74). Self-actualization emphasizes individuality, self-respect, self-identity, and personal growth. Based on Maslow's theory, Travis and Travis (1975, 1976a, 1976b) have developed the Pairing Enrichment Program. This program uses a retreat setting where couples receive materials when they are in a group, but they experience all communication exercises and transactions privately, like in Marriage Encounter. Couples are then given booklets containing summaries of the weekend's sessions and suggestions for exercises to be done at home for three weeks. In one study using Shostrom's Personal Orientation Inventory, a group showed significant increases in self-actualization over a waiting list control group (Travis and Travis, 1976b). A second study reported significant increases on the Caring Relationship Inventory for couples who had participated in the program (Travis and Travis, 1976a).

Schmitt and Schmitt (1976) offer marriage renewal retreats that assume a model of marital development based on Rankian philosophy, or the Rebirth Theory of Psychology. The emphasis is on "emotional insight": "It is the experience itself that heals, not the rationalizing about the experience" (Schmitt and Schmitt, 1976, p. 110). Unlike many other models, this approach focuses on group process and the phases of group development as well as the marital relationship.

Maxwell (1979) has suggested incorporating Ellis's rational-emotive approach into existing programs of marriage enrichment. He has further suggested that it be used as a basis for a new model of marriage enrichment. Ellis's approach emphasizes the deliberate management of one's own feelings toward self, spouse, and the marriage. Hypothetically, "strong marriages are those where anger is seldom experienced or, at least, is constructively managed" (Maxwell, 1979, p. 111). To control anger spouses are taught to separate desires and preferences from demands on their partners to change their behavior. Once the distinctions are made, they can abandon the need to make demands and still maintain their individuality. "By not demanding that a spouse behave in certain ways, one is free to feel positively toward that spouse, regardless of what he or she does" (Maxwell, 1979, p. 114).

The Creative Marriage Enrichment Program (Hof and Miller, 1981) has been developed from well-defined theoretical roots. First, Rogerian theory emphasizes that participants learn to provide an empathic environment to express feelings, to increase self-acceptance and self-knowledge, and to learn to be accepted and to accept others. Second, a behavioral emphasis enables participants to learn and practice specific skills that will aid in changing their own behavior. Communication, contracting, and negotiation skills are also taught. Third, an emphasis on group processes allows couples to experience various curative and growth factors.

Although these three theoretical components form the basis for the program, Schutz's (1967) theory of interpersonal needs provides the overarching framework. Schutz describes three basic needs, inclusion, control, and affection, and the program is designed to meet these needs. The aim of the Creative Marriage

Enrichment Program is to teach couples skills to help them develop an appropriate and satisfying balance between partners' needs while taking into account individual differences. By achieving this balance, couples can have a fulfilling marital relationship (Hof and Miller, 1981).

In addition, the program's structured experiences vary to provide for individual learning styles. Thus activities include concrete experiences, reflective observation, abstract conceptualization, and active experimentation. Also, leaders can adjust the structure in the program in accordance with participants' needs, the setting, and time constraints.

Unfortunately, research results are not yet available to evaluate the effectiveness of the program.

Nelson and Friest (1980) have developed a marriage enrichment program called Choice Awareness. They have not indicated a particular theoretical approach on which the program is based but seem to have combined behavioral theory concepts and communication skills training with their emphasis on cognitive and affective change: "In sum, these workshops are designed to encourage more constructive *cognition* about personal interactive choices, to mobilize the positive *affect* which exists in marital relationships, and to elicit more positive interaction *behavior* through Choice Awareness" (Nelson and Friest, 1980, p. 405). Preliminary research indicates that couples who participate in Choice Awareness workshops perceive their marriage relationships as more closely approximating their own concept of the ideal marriage than do couples in control groups.

Epstein, Degiovanni, and Jayne-Lazarus (1978) have suggested that assertion training for couples is a useful approach. They found that compared with couples in a control group, couples who participated in a two-hour workshop in assertiveness showed significant increases in verbal assertion and significant decreases in verbal aggression. This success in such a brief program suggests that other communication skills training programs could include assertion training.

L'Abate (1981) has developed a didactic structured approach called Marriage Enrichment Programs for Couples. These programs (L'Abate and others, 1975a, 1975b) differ markedly from others in that they are administered to an individual couple by a leader or leader couple. The programs are constructed for specific purposes and situations; they can be developed to deal with assertiveness, equality, negotiation, conflict resolution, clarification of sexual attitudes, sexual fulfillment, and any other area of concern to couples (L'Abate, 1981).

Another approach, the self-help program, provides prepared materials for couples to use individually at their own pace and/or in groups. These materials have been developed by Bach and Wyden (1968), Broderick (1979), Calden (1976), Clinebell and Clinebell (1970), Kaufmann (1978), Knox (1975), Otto (1969), and Ruben (1980). Further, Clinebell (1976) has put programs on cassette tapes that can be used prior to marriage enrichment groups, as part of a self-help marriage enrichment group, and to train marriage enrichment leaders. (See L'Abate, 1981, for reviews of additional self-help programs.)

Approach Selection

The professional offering a marital education program can choose from an increasing variety of models and theories. Even the limited amount of available research has shown that any of the approaches summarized in this chapter are potentially effective in meeting specific goals. The key to making a selection is deciding on the purpose of intervention and the desired outcome. With particular goals in mind, professionals can choose one approach or a combination that provides the appropriate strategy.

General Systems theory approaches, Rogerian client-centered therapy approaches, and behavioral approaches have been effective in teaching a variety of communication and conflict negotiation skills. The church-related marriage enrichment programs appear to effectively increase marital satisfaction and instill hope and motivation to improve the marital relationship. Thus many programs, such as the Methodist Marriage Communication Labs, have combined a skills-oriented approach with a marriage enrichment program that focuses on couples understanding themselves and their relationship.

On the one hand, the danger in combining approaches is that resource constraints will force a watering down of both approaches, thus weakening the effectiveness of each one. On the other hand, using two models may enhance the effectiveness of each. However, no research has been conducted to determine what happens when approaches are combined. This limitation, along with the limited research available on all models, makes deciding whether to combine models particularly difficult. In Chapter Three some of the issues to consider when planning a marriage enrichment program will be discussed in further detail.

3

Designing
and Implementing
Group Programs

The practitioner who provides direct services and also evaluates treatment outcomes and the researcher who studies the effectiveness of service methods and also offers services to clients both begin program development in the same way—by establishing intervention goals. Their approaches to determining these goals, however, differ. The practitioner's goals develop out of clients' needs—clients desire more satisfaction from relationships, more effective communication, a better understanding of themselves and others, or solutions to specific problems. The researcher determines goals by testing theory or evaluating research.

Once goals are established, they must be translated into observable and measurable objectives. For example, the practitioner might formulate the following objective: Participants in the marriage enrichment group will score significantly higher on the marital adjustment scale after completing the group than they did before participating in the group. The researcher might decide on a different objective: Couples in groups led by a married couple will improve significantly more on measures of communication skills usage than couples in groups led by one leader or by an unmarried pair of professionals.

Having established objectives, both the practitioner and researcher follow the same process of program development; they must: (1) define a target group; (2) establish the time frame and schedule for meetings; (3) develop suitable content for the program; (4) recruit and screen participants; (5) determine appropriate leadership; and (6) determine how change will carry over to and be maintained in the natural environment. The program developers must keep in mind their objectives while performing each of these tasks. And, of course, the alternative strategies for each of these tasks may be the focus of research study.

In this chapter some significant points of each developmental stage are discussed. The literature on group dynamics provides additional information on each one. However, the dynamics in a group of married couples are different from those in a group of unrelated individuals who do not have ongoing primary relationships with one another. A marriage enrichment group really consists of subgroups, each with its own past, present, and future, established communication patterns, and interpersonal goals. A marriage enrichment group's goals are clearly subordinate to both the individuals' goals and the subgroups' goals. It is necessary to consider the impact of these differences on the enrichment group.

Determining Group Membership

Homogeneity/Heterogeneity. The selection of couples to participate in the program should be influenced by the group's objectives, despite temptation to ignore this criterion. When recruiting enough couples to start a group is difficult, the qualifications for group membership may be modified considerably. Sometimes this has no effect on a group, but at times it deters achievement of group goals. For instance, though a particular group requires that couples be married for no more than five years, the leader may decide to include a couple who is living together and plans to marry. Group cohesiveness and solidarity may be disrupted if this couple is included in a church-related program in which most group members object to cohabitation before marriage. On the other hand, their inclusion may have little consequence in a group of couples, some of whom also cohabited before marriage and thus may share the same attitudes about marital and premarital relationships.

The issue of homogeneity/heterogeneity becomes much less crucial when the group's focus is on intracouple dialogue with little group participation and discussion rather than on group discussion and intercouple dialogue that provide insight into others' marriages. For the kind of group trust and cohesiveness that nurtures intimate interchanges to develop, couples must be able to identify with one another and be in agreement with one another on such important issues as religious beliefs; education and socioeconomic status; stage of the family/marital life cycle; sex roles (traditional, reversed, or dual-career); marital alternatives (childless, open, traditional); and prior experiences with marital enrichment programs. Of course, issues that are deemed important will vary from group to group. Intragroup differences on one or more of these issues may provide some useful perspectives, but too many differences may weaken group cohesiveness. Couples within each group need to be compatible, and compatibility can only be defined with reference to one another, not to some absolute standard.

Stages of the Marital Life Cycle. A group that includes couples experiencing different life cycle stages can allow for some interesting complementarity. For instance, newlyweds may learn a great deal from observing the interaction of couples who have been married twenty years; the older couples can function as models for effective communication and conflict negotiation. Older couples may find that observing younger couples provides data for reevaluation of their own relationship —that is, they may learn to appreciate more deeply their years of skills development and shared experiences that resulted in self-understanding and understanding of each other. Heterogeneity, therefore, may be quite useful in a process-oriented group which emphasizes skills development and attitude change. However, homogeneity becomes more critical in groups with greater focus on specific issues in marriage than on processes of communication, issues such as sharing thoughts and feelings about new parenting, children leaving home, and retirement.

One of the most exciting services in marriage enrichment is preparing couples and families to deal with life crises so that they can avoid the potentially destructive effects of crises and use crisis experiences to make creative changes in their relationships. The limited research on the family life cycle has pinpointed critical life cycle transitions for which such intervention appears to be valuable. For instance, marriage enrichment services are often designed for premarital couples. These couples can examine their relationships for areas of potential conflict and can learn skills for resolving such conflict. It is helpful, before marriage, to learn more about one another, to consider each other's expectations, and to discuss rules for the relationship and how they enhance or limit intimacy and marital satisfaction.

Premarital couples in enrichment groups, however, may have difficulty predicting areas of conflict. They may be so caught up in wedding plans that they do not want to contemplate issues that seem distant and perhaps irrelevant. Therefore, marriage enrichment groups provide a significant service to newlyweds. The first few years of marriage are critical—divorce rates are higher in the early years than in any other stage and are highest among those who marry young. During the first year of marriage, the number of separations peaks, and the largest number of divorces is granted in the third year (Leslie, 1979). It is particularly important in the early years of marriage for couples to learn how to handle conflict constructively, to define roles and expectations, and to learn how to change the rules of their relationship to fit their needs.

Although some question exists as to whether the birth of a child creates a marital crisis with negative consequences (LeMasters, 1957; Dyer, 1963; Hobbs, 1965; Rhyne, 1981), certainly the addition of children to a relationship results in a reshuffling of responsibilities and priorities. Spouses' time and emotional energy become scarcer and increasingly more important (Rhyne, 1981), frequently causing a decrease in marital satisfaction, particularly for the new mother (Rollins and Feldman, 1970). Discussing ways to cope with these changes, assessing priorities, developing support systems such as co-op child care, and parent training are valuable marriage enrichment services. In addition, marriage enrichment can help couples structure time for themselves away from children and develop a value system that supports this priority, as well as provide a group that will listen to and relate to the difficulties of adjustment.

Marriage enrichment during the middle years is often neglected although it can be a valuable service during this stage of the life cycle. Programs can be designed to educate couples about the mid-life crisis and its ramifications on the marital relationship. For example, the importance of love and sexual gratification increases during the time a couple has children growing up in the home (Rhyne, 1981). Marriage enrichment programs can provide a forum for spouses to discuss life changes with each other and with other couples who are also experiencing them. These discussions can help establish a sense of normalcy and confidence in an individual's ability to cope.

Spouses' interaction patterns and roles change when grown children leave the home; along with these changes, spouses' dependence on each other for need fulfillment may increase. Sexual expression takes on particular salience for women during this period, and both partners experience an increased need for each other's friendship (Rhyne, 1981). The physical and emotional changes that come with aging may have a significant impact, which can be buffered by an environment conducive to sharing feelings with each other and with other couples going through the same changes.

Relatively few marriage enrichment services have been provided for couples in their retirement years, yet significant changes occur during the transition to this stage of the life cycle. Opportunities to explore alternatives and training for new roles are not generally available in our society to help couples prepare for the financial, emotional, and relational changes they will experience because of retirement. For example, spouses may suddenly find themselves spending almost all their time together, with fewer outside involvements to provide input and interest within their relationship. Some couples may also be attempting to cope with shrinking income, serious illness, significant decreases in physical strength and capabilities, a changing sexual relationship, and the prospective death of a partner. An enrichment program can provide an environment conducive for spouses to share their fears, hopes, and frustrations and can provide the information and the resources needed to cope with change. Enrichment services can also teach communication skills and educate couples about changes in sex roles and sexual performance that occur during the process of aging.

These are only some of the many kinds of services that can be provided in groups that are homogeneous as to stage of the marital life cycle. L'Abate and others (1975a, 1975b) have developed over fifty marriage enrichment programs, some of which are geared to specific stages of the family life cycle, for example, Three-Generational Families and Between Parents and Adolescents.

Levels of Marital Adjustment. A common stipulation for group membership is that both partners be committed to the marriage—neither partner can be seriously contemplating ending the relationship. However, the possibility exists that even troubled couples, if willing to suspend their decision about the future of their relationship, can benefit from such aspects of a marriage enrichment program as developing communication skills. Many couples who eventually end their marriage find that they must still interact on a regular basis in their cooperative attempt to raise their children. Their ability to communicate effectively continues to affect the outcome of their interactions. Couples mired in significant interpersonal conflicts can benefit from an educational group if they change their focus from their problems to their strengths. For couples experiencing such difficulties, however, it seems important to provide a group structure that will focus their attention on skills acquisition, understanding themselves and each other, and on other group objectives. In an unstructured setting such couples tend to continue their patterns of conflictual interaction unless they are specifically redirected. Thus the degree of structure provided by the marriage enrichment program is an essential component in determining whether troubled couples can be treated effectively.

Hof and Miller (1981) suggest that the more troubled the marriages are in a particular group, the greater the need for structure. The following elements can help provide such a structure: a limited, well-focused agenda, highly skilled and active leadership, conjoint crisis-intervention therapy offered concurrently with the enrichment program, small group size, and effective screening. During screening, problem identification and evaluation, and goal setting can be accomplished. "Such a procedure would permit the reduction of negative feelings which could block the couple's participation in a positively oriented program" (Hof and Miller, 1981, p. 49).

Even though couples experiencing marked marital difficulties should not, as a rule, be excluded from marriage enrichment, there are marital systems for which enrichment programs are contraindicated. L'Abate (1978, p. 263) has suggested three guidelines for determining couples who should be offered alternative services: (1) families in which there is an entrenched problem and a long-standing dysfunctional pattern of relating to one another are not amenable to enrichment. They are simply too disturbed and disorganized to be enriched; (2) an uncooperative family is also not enrichable. This kind of family may resist change as a whole or through individual members; [and] (3) They [members of an uncooperative family] are not motivated to change since change would involve for them giving up control of the family and accepting responsibility. These latter two points, however, refer not so much to the kinds of families to eliminate from marriage enrichment services as to the necessity for the individual participants and the group's leaders to agree on what the services will be and what they will expect from one another. Those couples with whom such an agreement has not been reached or for whom there is not enough structure in the intervention program are often called uncooperative, unmotivated families.

The key, therefore, in group composition is a screening process that allows leaders to perceive current or potential individual and/or relationship problems which would interfere with the achievement of the couple's objectives as well as the objectives of the rest of the group. In some cases, a thorough discussion of such problems or issues may result in establishing common expectations for all members of the marriage enrichment group, so that troubled couples can participate successfully. In other cases, providing a troubled couple with referrals for services more appropriate to their immediate needs will result. Hof and Miller (1981) suggest that as many as three sessions may be needed for evaluation, problem identification, ventilation and resolution of feelings, and setting goals for marriage enrichment or other services. Such a screening need not necessarily involve a diagnosis of the seriousness of a couple's difficulties, but it should lead to a decision about whether the enrichment experience will be a useful one for the couple at this juncture in their relationship, and if so, in what ways.

L'Abate and Rupp (1981, p. 101) have defined behavior as "the outcome of will plus skill (motivation and abilities)." In this framework, therapy is primarily directed toward motivation —dealing with feelings of frustration and despair about a relationship and engendering hope, when hope is realistic, that the relationship is worth risking time and energy to change. The skills marriage enrichment offers can be used to improve the relationship only when the couple is committed to making the effort. Because one of the major outcomes of enrichment is engendering a couple's excitement about the future of their marriage, inquiring into participants' faith in the value of their marriage can be useful in determining whether they can benefit from the program. If a leader chooses to include couples whose commitment to improving their relationship is questionable, he or she should do so with full awareness of the possible need for adjunct counseling and even crisis intervention.

Problems arise when screening is too superficial to indicate those applicants who are experiencing significant difficulties. The process is compounded when couples are either embarrassed by the difficulties they are experiencing and attempt to hide them from the leader, or when their communication is so disrupted that it is only when they begin to practice communication skills in the group that the seriousness of their differences becomes clear.

There are a number of criteria which will help the marriage enrichment leader assess the marital adjustment of a couple, whether their expectations for counseling in an enrichment group setting are unrealistic, and detect other indicators that their participation in the group would be inappropriate for them and might also interfere with the work of other couples. First, the leaders will most likely want to use standardized evaluation instruments as a part of the screening procedure, such as one of Olson's family inventories, known as ENRICH and FACES II (Olson, 1982) or Spanier's Dyadic Adjustment Scale (Spanier, 1976). The results of an inventory or scale not only provide a basis on which to evaluate the effectiveness of the service but are also invaluable in pointing out areas of marital difficulty.

Second, leaders need to be alert during the screening interview for indications that one or both spouses is seeking help for problems rather than an opportunity to assess the relationship and develop the relationship's resources. Of course, all couples have some problems, but when the major reason for participation is solving a longstanding issue, the couple should probably be referred for other kinds of counseling. Verbal clues, such as expressions of misgiving by one or both spouses that enrichment will not be "strong enough medicine," may indicate the couple is seeking an expert to tell them what to do. A couple may feel that they have already defined their problem, that exploring the relationship further will not help solve it, and that they want answers.

Bertcher and Maple (1974) suggest that one helpful strategy in flushing out these kinds of expectations is to give participants an opportunity to observe an effective marriage enrichment group in action. A videotape of a group in session or a reading that provides a brief background of marriage enrichment and some examples of what groups are like might suffice. In discussing these stimuli in the screening session, the leader should be alert for comments such as "too superficial," "threatening," "too open-ended," or "those people don't seem to have the same kind of problems we do." Such reactions need to be acknowledged and explored to determine whether they indicate that applicants' needs and expectations are not suited to a marriage enrichment program.

Finally, the screening process includes defining the prospective participants' specific objectives. This is a crucial outcome of the screening interviews because these stated goals are the basis for the contract between the couple and the leader as to what they expect from each other. These objectives provide a framework for the group's work by specifying in advance any issues that may be crucial to the couple but that need to be addressed in an alternate service modality, such as conjoint counseling.

Screening procedures are well and good when the leader has the opportunity to use them. However, when the leader is contacted by a church, a parent's association, or another group already in existence, and asked to speak or lead a program, there is frequently no opportunity for screening. This problem does not affect most issues of group composition; such a group is usually sufficiently homogeneous to be cohesive, for example. However, couples' degrees of marital adjustment are not usually generally known and therefore cannot be a factor in the cohesion of many kinds of groups. Thus there may be a wide variety of levels of adjustment, and possibly some couples whose relationships are in jeopardy. The group leader can impose considerable control in such situations by employing a structured approach, but even so, there are two factors that usually prevent serious problems from erupting in existing groups. One is the insight of the group's natural leaders—probably those who have contacted the marriage enrichment counselor. Leaders such as pastors are very likely to know which relationships are troubled and the general nature of the problems people are experiencing, and may thus be able to provide valuable consultation when formal screening is not possible. Second, the group's norms of appropriate behavior may be enough to prevent one couple from dominating the group with their problems. Couples are less likely to try to turn their Sunday school class, or other group with whom they have an ongoing relationship, into a therapy group. In fact, the leader will probably encounter the opposite problem and have difficulty getting members to disclose intimate aspects of their marriages to people with whom they have ongoing relationships. Again, the leader might do well to check with the contact people to get some idea of the group norms for self-disclosure. When these norms cannot be identified, the leader may need to give an explicit description of what participants can and cannot expect from the experience.

Clearly, when screening is possible, it is ideal to be able to use it to compose a group that can meet the objectives of its participants. In so doing the leader can help ensure that participants will benefit from the experience and can be alert to and provide adjunct services, such as crisis counseling or marriage therapy, to couples who need them.

Screening need not always be used to establish homogeneity in a marriage enrichment group. It may, for example, be useful to form a group of couples who report varying degrees of marital satisfaction. Troubled couples may find that better-adjusted couples can serve as useful models of interactional skills if the leader is adept at eliciting such modeling. The better-adjusted couples may find that less-satisfied couples can be good models of self-disclosure and risk taking in the expression of their needs to the group. Frequently, couples who see themselves as satisfied find it difficult to admit the existence of chronic conflict and dissatisfaction. If the leader is skillful in engendering group cohesiveness and mutuality, the disclosures of troubled couples wlll illustrate that such openness in the group environment is acceptable and, in fact, helpful.

For this kind of modeling to be effective, the group members must feel a sense of belonging and trust. If a couple is so enmeshed in their own difficulties that they cannot interact with the group or with each other, they may have an adverse effect on the other couples. Others in the group may become frightened by the intensity of the conflict and feel powerless to show the concern or offer the empathy that would be invaluable to the troubled couple. They may also be afraid to admit any of their own marital problems—they fear their own relationship may degenerate into such conflict. In this situation, the troubled couple may feel isolated and embarrassed, and become even further convinced of their own marriage's failure.

Though a group is to be heterogeneous in marital satisfaction, the different levels of satisfaction should not isolate one couple from another. Nor should couples fall into two distinct groups: the unhappy and the blissful. If we imagine placing couples on a continuum of marital satisfaction, with *unhappy* at one end and *blissful* at the other, the couples should *not* form the following group configurations: one cluster of unhappy couples and one of blissful couples; one isolated, unhappy couple and the rest blissful couples; one isolated, blissful couple and the rest unhappy; a few unhappy couples, a few clustered in the middle of the continuum, and a few blissful couples.

In an effective heterogeneous group, the couples will be spaced more or less closely along the continuum in one of the following configurations: all couples near the middle of the continuum; couples ranging from the middle of the continuum to the blissful extreme; couples spaced from the middle of the continuum to the unhappy extreme; couples spaced from the middle of the continuum to the blissful extreme.

Powell and Wampler (1982) have found that couples who request participation in a marriage enrichment group tend to cluster in the middle of the continuum; they are neither as satisfied with their marriages as those who do not participate nor as dissatisfied as those who request marriage counseling.

Group Size. The size of the group is a function of its goals and the program structures uses to achieve those goals. In models such as the Catholic Encounter model, in which there is no group interaction as such, size is not as relevant an issue as in programs in which group interaction is a primary tool.

In those programs emphasizing group interaction, appropriate group size may vary. Large groups (more than five or six couples) tend to provide members significant opportunities not to participate. Furthermore, they allow more room for differences among members and demand more skill from leaders. They also require a high level of maturity from participants who want to be active in the group (Vinter, 1967). To help eliminate member anonymity, a large group can be subdivided into smaller work groups, either led by one team leader or monitored by one leader who moves from group to group. Such smaller groups can have a stable membership, thus providing a sense of intimacy and mutuality among the couples. These smaller work groups can then all meet together for presentations, skills demonstrations, and discussions.

Smaller groups tend to have greater member participation, greater individual involvement, and greater pressures for consensus, and therefore are usually more cohesive. When the program remains constant, relationships tend to become more intense than those in a large group (Vinter, 1967). In addition, in a small group it is easier for the leader to handle any problems or marital crises that develop. However, the intenseness of a small group, the push toward consensus, and the inability to maintain anonymity may be so threatening to some participants that they either stop showing up for sessions or become defensive and refuse to participate. Some couples may first need to become comfortable in the less demanding and less intense environment of the large group before they can submit themselves to the self-disclosure and intimate relationships characteristic of a smaller group.

Recruiting Group Members. Marriage enrichment services can be offered in two ways. First, a helping professional who functions as a guest leader can provide a service for groups already existing in churches and other organizations. This type of group presumably has its own goals established. The professional then designs program content and activities to meet these goals. Of course, in this situation the professional frequently does not have the opportunity to control the participants' levels of homogeneity/heterogeneity, stages of the life cycle, and levels of marital adjustment. However, enough homogeneity among members will probably exist so as not to be a problem. The most serious potential problem in the preformed group is that very unhappy couples will either dominate the group or become withdrawn because they fear exposing their conflicts to their friends and acquaintances. Couples in such groups will probably be more heterogeneous on the dimension of marital satisfaction than couples who individually request marriage en-richment services.

The second way in which services can be offered is for the professional to establish objectives with appropriate pro-gram activities and then seek couples who can achieve their per-sonal goals through participation in the group. The professional may design the service specifically for one or two clients and then seek additional couples with similar needs to complete the group. In contrast, the professional may establish a service for a segment of the population whose needs are not being met and then recruit couples to participate in the program. In both cases, it is the professional who establishes the group's goals.

Couples for marriage enrichment groups, therefore, de-pending on whether they come from groups affiliated with an institution, may or may not be socially related to one another. For the professional who wants to develop a pool of potential participants from which to form enrichment groups, the follow-ing list of resources may be useful:

- Ministers and officials who marry couples—ministers are front-line professionals working with troubled couples in all stages of the marital life cycle and thus are good referral sources.
- Church and other religious groups—programs such as Sunday school leadership training and other religious educational programs recommend enrichment services.
- Obstetricians, pediatricians, and physicans in family practice —often they are willing to make information available to pa-tients in their offices.
- Media representatives (newspapers, radio, and television)—they may make public service announcements and may pre-sent special features about enrichment services.
- Helping professionals and agencies, including psychiatrists, social workers, psychologists, marriage counselors, family service and community mental health agencies, pastoral care agencies, and hospital social service departments.
- Public school systems and colleges—instructors of family

courses in local colleges may provide students information about enrichment services.

- Senior citizens groups, special interest groups such as Alcoholics Anonymous and Al-Anon, babysitting co-ops, civic groups, and clubs.
- Welcome wagons or newcomers clubs—they may be willing to distribute flyers.
- Childbirth classes.

Screening Prospective Couples. Many of the models of marriage enrichment allow the leader to control group membership and thus provide some method to screen prospective couples. It is during a screening that the leader finalizes decisions about group homogeneity and heterogeneity, couples' positions in the marital life cycle, and degree of couples' marital satisfaction.

When couples respond to an advertisement about a marriage enrichment group, the group leaders schedule screening interviews. During the interview the leader and the couple discuss in detail the group's goals and procedures to determine whether goals are congruent with the couple's needs.

The leader needs to understand the specific reasons the couple is interested in participating in the group. When the couple does not volunteer this information, the leader must elicit it. If they state or imply that they need help with specific problems, it is important that the leader demonstrate empathy, understanding, and acceptance. The leader must model the communication skills that are useful in the marital relationship and must also build client rapport and trust. It is essential for the couple to believe that the leader's concern for their needs is genuine. They must not think that the leader is trying to alter their needs to fit the group's goals.

Also during this interview the couple begins to establish a relationship with the leader so that they feel as if they know at least one person in the group. This process is, of course, most relevant for couples joining groups composed of strangers. Therefore, it is important that the leader initiate trust and self-disclosure, which will later enable the group to rapidly begin work on its tasks.

Although the leader may find that the interview helps to reveal a couple's marital satisfaction and also helps to determine their influence on the group, it is important that the couple not see the session as diagnostic. In other words, the leader must emphasize the strengths and goals of the couple rather than focus on difficulties requiring treatment. The leader may find that an open discussion about the couple's relationship helps to avoid a diagnostic atmosphere. To generate this discussion, the leader can administer one or several measures of communication skill or marital adjustment. Of course, these measures can be used as pretesting and can be compared later to posttest results. (Several such measures are included in Resource B.)

The leader needs to be alert both to verbal and nonverbal cues of uncertainty exhibited by either spouse. The leader must show respect for any doubt and discuss it as openly as possible. This respect for and open discussion of doubts facilitates the couple's assessment of their own needs and feelings, as well as their decision about participating in the group.

Once the couple has discussed their needs and concerns to the point that they and the leader sense mutual understanding, the leader can verify that the couple meets all the established criteria for participation in the group—length of marriage, degree of adjustment, and so on. At this point, if both the leader and the couple agree on the couple becoming group members, the leader provides them with an overview of the group's rules on confidentiality, attendance, right not to participate in a particular activity or discussion, punctuality, payment of fees, completion of homework, and participation in any postgroup or follow-up evaluation.

At any time before the first session, the couple or the leader can decide against the couple's participation. The leader can then help them to explore alternative resources such as counseling, self-help groups, printed material, communication courses, and other enrichment groups.

Couples who are going to participate in the group often sign a contract to finalize commitment to the group's rules and purposes. The leader may also want them to sign a release of information form so that evaluation instruments can be later used in research. Of course, these documents must be clearly explained and any concerns of the couple must be addressed.

Structure of Meetings

The format for marriage enrichment groups will vary, depending on a group's goals. Enrichment groups may meet weekly or they may meet over a weekend for a retreat or marathon. Sometimes a combination of these two formats is effective.

There are a number of advantages to a weekend retreat structure. The retreat allows couples to escape from the pressures of everyday life and hence focus more exclusively on their relationship. Confidence, trust, and valuation both of the group and of the marital relationship can build without the interruptions of daily life. Because of the impact of uninterrupted input, a weekend retreat or marathon is most useful in influencing attitudes and values. Pragmatically, couples are a "captive audience"; it is unlikely that they will miss sessions.

Weekly sessions have different advantages. They are most useful for skills training because couples can practice and generalize newly learned skills in the natural environment. Between sessions, they can reflect on and discuss group input; they also have more opportunity to evaluate program content and then provide feedback for the group. Davis and others (1982) have found that weekly sessions result in more improvement in marital adjustment than do weekend retreats. Pragmatically, some couples find it difficult or impossible to leave home responsibilities for an entire weekend. In addition, there is no unalterable end point (Hopkins and others, 1978)—the group may elect to stay together for an additional set of sessions.

A combination of the two structures can capitalize on the advantages of each and thereby be used to achieve particular sets of goals. For instance, a marathon session can be used to help group members develop a sense of cohesiveness and mutual trust while couples experience a newfound hopefulness and commitment to the marital relationship. This retreat (a full weekend with overnight accommodations or an all-day Saturday or Sunday session) can then be followed by weekly sessions that focus on preestablished goals, such as development of communication and conflict negotiation skills. Thus, the hopefulness and excitement engendered by the weekend experience motivates couples to learn the new skills that will enable them to make necessary changes in their relationship and adjust to any future demands. There are, of course, other combinations that can effectively be used to achieve a group's goals, including: weekly sessions interspersed with marathon sessions; weekly sessions of skills training concluded with a marathon session in which skills are applied to specific content issues; and a retreat followed by an ongoing support group. The particular goals and resources of the group will determine the most appropriate combination.

One of the most comprehensive marriage enrichment programs to date has been developed by Hof, Epstein, and Miller (1980). Their program involves the blending of three formats. First, a weekend retreat or similar extended format is used to create positive feelings between partners, positive attitudes toward the marital relationship, and motivation to continue work on the relationship. Participants are also introduced to relationship skills that are taught in the highly structured second component, the multiweek training program. Finally, the third format is an ongoing marital growth group designed to maintain positive changes and initiate new ones. Hof, Epstein, and Miller's (1980, p. 245) model is based on the theory that to be effective a marital enrichment program must: (1) increase couples' motivation to expend the effort required to produce change; (2) reduce resistance to change stemming from anxiety and advantages of existing interactional patterns; (3) build specific skills for communication, problem solving, and conflict resolution; (4) generalize gains from the treatment setting to the home environment; and (5) maximize longevity of positive gains.

The length of the sessions is a pragmatic consideration. Two or two-and-a-half hours for weekly sessions appears to be most widely used. Because of family and job responsibilities, couples cannot commit themselves to more time than that on a week night. Furthermore, they cannot focus on learning for much more than two-and-a-half hours when already tired from the day's activities. Compared to longer sessions, shorter sessions use a greater proportion of the meeting time getting started, ending, and dealing with group maintenance matters than focusing on the group's goal-oriented tasks. However, other factors may dictate the use of longer or shorter sessions. For instance, in a rural community where couples travel significant distances to participate in a program, longer, but fewer sessions are advisable. When an organization such as a church group requests marriage enrichment, it may be most feasible to fit the program to the group's already existing time period, such as fifty minutes.

The number of weekly sessions or the total number of hours actually devoted to the group's tasks should also be determined by the established goals. Generally, the more hours the group meets, the more it can accomplish. However, the greater the number of sessions, the greater the opportunities for schedule conflicts that result in couples missing meetings. Lapses in attendance affect program continuity. Also, because of holidays and vacations, couples find it difficult to maintain a high level of commitment and involvement to programs that stretch out over many weeks. Some problems of long-term commitment and involvement can be allayed by combining two or more sessions into four-hour "minimarathon" meetings. Thus the total number of weeks in a program is reduced.

Developing the Program

When the goals of the marriage enrichment group have been defined, the leader can choose a theoretical approach or a combination of theoretical approaches that purport to achieve these goals. For instance, if the group's goals are to increase spouses' understanding of each other and their ability to communicate that understanding so that intimacy and trust are increased, the Rogerian client-centered therapy approaches may be most appropriate. If the goal is to engender a sense of hope and recommitment to the marriage so that couples will be motivated to seek changes in their relationship, the church-related marriage enrichment approaches may be most suitable. A leader may choose a General Systems theory approach if the group's goal is to increase the capabilities of couples to generate changes dictated by individual needs or environmental demands. And of course, any combination of these with other theoretical approaches may be applicable to a group's particular goals.

The choice of a particular theoretical approach is important because it relates to the kind of group activities that will be structured to reach the goals. For instance, to increase communication skills, the Rogerian approach indicates activities associated with demonstrating and practicing skills; to change values, the church-related marriage enrichment approach suggests activities that challenge old values and generate new ones.

The goals need to be translated into specific learning objectives for the participants. The leader must be aware of the three kinds of learning: cognitive, skill, and affective. Cognitive learning may include gaining an understanding of the stages of the marital life cycle and typical crises of development, the stages of human sexual response including differences and similarities in male and female sexuality, and the nature of emotions and the ways they can be expressed, repressed, and suppressed. In skill learning couples develop communication skills, conflict negotiation skills, reinforcement skills, and others that change behavior. In affective (attitudes, values, and feelings) learning, couples may be taught to reevaluate sex-role expectations of spouses, to reevaluate designations of time and money resources, to develop a greater feeling of commitment and happiness within the marriage, and to experience greater hopefulness about the potential for change.

A marriage enrichment program may focus on one or more of these modes of learning, and perhaps the most effective program will include all three although one may receive more emphasis than the others. For instance, a program that emphasizes skill learning in order to increase communication skills will also need to involve both cognitive learning, to teach what the skills are and how they are used, and affective learning, to teach the value of the skills and of a commitment to practicing them outside the group setting. Hof, Epstein, and Miller (1980, p. 244) have suggested that programs must combine behavioral and attitudinal learning to be effective: "Enrichment programs that focus primarily on attitudinal/motivational change may not develop couples' relationship skills sufficiently, and positive attitudes developed in the absence of skills are likely to sour. On the other hand, skill training programs that lack sufficient grounding in attitudinal change may encounter significant resistance to change from participants. Couples who are not motivated to expend considerable effort are unlikely to change long-standing relationship patterns."

Learning in each of the three modes occurs in successive steps. Each step is briefly summarized here and an activity designed to illustrate mastery of the learning objective is provided where appropriate. The leader should become familiar with the process of writing instructional objectives, as adequately defined by the Program Development Center of Northern California (1972) and Mager (1962).

Cognitive learning occurs in six progressive steps (Program Development Center of Northern California, 1972):

1. *Knowledge*—the learner is able to define, recall, and identify that which has been taught. When learning about the marital life cycle, participants list the stages of development with some of the identifying characteristics of each.

2. *Comprehension*—learners are able to explain, summarize, generalize, and comment upon that which is being taught. Participants at this stage give personal examples of how the stages of the marital life cycle affected them in predictable ways.

3. *Application*—learners are able to apply what they have learned to new situations. Participants examine their own responses to past developmental crises and then predict how they may respond in future crises.

4. *Analysis*—participants are able to understand the elements of the new knowledge, to deduce, categorize, and compare.

Couples examine the processes by which change occurs in their relationship in response to the developmental life cycle and then compare these processes with those used by other couples.

5. *Synthesis*—participants are able to create new patterns and structures to develop, manipulate, modify, and plan. Couples construct ways of handling developmental changes and plan for and modify (or enhance) the impact of the stages of the marital life cycle.

6. *Evaluation*—participants are able to judge the value of what has been learned for a given purpose, to conclude, criticize, and appraise. Couples evaluate the usefulness of the concepts of the marital life cycle in understanding their own response to changes and also determine when to use these concepts.

Skill learning can be broken down into seven sequential steps. Middleman (1977) has developed a useful model that involves increasing integration of the skill into the behavior of the learner.

1. *Observation*—learners see and hear examples of the skill to be performed and discriminate good skill execution from poor skill execution. When listening skills are being taught, the leader demonstrates these skills through role play of a marital discussion and in another role play conducts a discussion without the skills.

2. *Conceptualization*—learners identify and analyze specific behaviors involved in utilizing the skill. Participants help identify aspects of listening skills—appropriate body posture, eye contact, gestures, and verbal behaviors such as restating the essence of the partner's communications to verify accurate understanding.

3. *Imitation*—the learner attempts to reproduce the skill, getting feedback regarding accuracy. In small groups couples attempt to employ listening skills and other group members comment about their performance.

4. *Precision*—learners focus on accuracy and mastery of the

skill. Participants continue to practice the listening skills as they discuss with their partners a variety of topics, some of which are conflictual and therefore tax the listener's skills. Participants continue to receive feedback from others about their performance of the skills.

5. *Coordination*—learners are sufficiently adept at the skill that they can begin to turn their attention away from their own listening behaviors and focus on their partners' communicative behavior.

6. *Habituation*—learners use the skill naturally and spontaneously. It becomes a part of the participants' communication patterns in settings outside the marriage enrichment group.

7. *Instruction and stylization*—the learner teaches the skill to others and is able to add individuality to the skill performance. The participants can adapt skills to the marital relationship as well as to other relationships.

In skill learning, two elements are of utmost importance. First, learners must have opportunities for practice and feedback so that they can develop precision in using skills. Second, couples must be motivated to learn the skills. Practice and feedback opportunities cannot produce positive results without motivation.

Some of the variables that increase couples' motivation to learn modeled skills include: positive verbal reinforcement of the modeled response; knowledge that the learner will be expected to perform and appropriately moderate anxiety; use of concise verbal labels for the behavior to be imitated; interspersing practice with modeling rather than modeling the total behavior and expecting the learner to imitate it; use of prestigious models, for example, the group leader; use of multiple models; and using repeated practice over multiple situations (see Bandura, 1971; Boies, 1972; Deci, 1971, 1972; Frederiksen and others, 1976; Janis and Mann, 1965; Kelly, 1955; Lazarus, 1971; Miller and Dollard, 1941; Rachman, 1972; Ritter, 1969; Thelen and Rennie, 1972; and Yates, 1970).

Based on these variables, motivation can be increased by

employing the following techniques to teach skills: training participants to give positive reinforcement, providing positive reinforcement for skill execution, allowing frequent practice of each of the skill components, inventing short, easy-to-remember names for each skill component, modeling segments of skill rather than the whole and allowing participants to practice each one before introducing a new one, using a variety of models such as videotapes of couples and leaders, and allowing practice on a variety of topics that elicit varying levels of emotional involvement.

There are five steps in affective learning (Program Development Center of Northern California, 1972).

1. *Receiving*—learners exhibit a willingness to attend to what is being taught; they choose to listen and find out. For example, when a group is exploring attitudes about marital sex roles so that couples can choose the roles most useful in their own relationship regardless of societal expectations, the learner becomes interested in listening to the effects of sex-role stereotyping on marital relationships. (This example of a group objective will be carried through the remaining steps.)
2. *Responding*—learners become interested and concerned. They actively participate in the discussion of how roles have been defined in their own relationship.
3. *Valuing*—learners demonstrate feelings of worth and appreciation for the value being taught. Couples demonstrate appreciation for sexual equality by examining and, if necessary, changing the role expectations in their relationship to meet their unique needs.
4. *Organizing*—learners apply their new knowledge in resolving any conflict involved in building a new value system. Spouses redefine their relationship and alter priorities so that they become congruent with newly accepted sex roles.
5. *Characterization*—learners develop a pervasive, consistent life style. Participants behave in ways congruent with acceptance of sexual equality.

A summary of the process of program development discussed thus far may be helpful. First, the goals of the marriage enrichment service are defined. Then a theoretical approach to achieve these goals is selected. The goals are next translated into learning objectives. They are examined to determine the most effective learning models (cognitive, skill, affective) and to decide the level(s) of accomplishment. From the learning objectives, the kinds of learning activities that will provide the opportunities to reach these objectives can be determined. This process is most obvious in the skill domain in which the learning activities involve skill demonstration and conceptualization, followed by a series of practice and feedback sessions. Chapter Four illustrates this process in more detail by presenting two marriage enrichment programs with explanations of how their learning activities are conceived to accomplish objectives.

Structured learning activities can often be the vehicle through which learning goals can be achieved. The learning activities to be used in a marriage enrichment program can be gleaned from a variety of sources. Resource A provides annotated descriptions and a listing of many such activities.

Determining Group Leadership

Many church-related marriage enrichment programs are led by specially trained couples not in the helping professions. At times, particularly in the Catholic Marriage Encounter, several married couples form a leadership team. Common practice in secular marriage enrichment programs is to have a married couple in which one or both spouses are helping professionals or two helping professionals—a man and a woman—who are not married conduct groups.

The use of couples who are not helping professionals by church-related marriage enrichment programs is clearly related to the programs' emphasis on growth, not remediation: "The leader couple should provide a *model*—not a model of perfection, but a couple already doing what the others are being encouraged and helped to do. . . . The role of leader is that of participating facilitator. This stands in contrast to the therapist role, which is that of a non-participating facilitator. These retreats, it must be clearly stated, are *not* therapy, and therefore not for couples with serious difficulties. . . . Leaders do not, therefore, have to be professionally qualified because they are not undertaking professional work" (Hopkins and others, 1978, p. 18).

No research exists to indicate the validity of the assumption that two leaders are more effective than one. However, the value of two leaders is obvious for modeling self-disclosure and other communication skills for the group. Demonstrating the application of concepts, the use of skills, and the values conducive to marital adjustment and happiness can be done quite effectively in role play by the leaders. Yet, there are techniques that one leader can employ to provide this kind of demonstration using videotapes, audiotapes, or films; coaching one of the participating couples to demonstrate the desired behaviors, or role playing with one of the participants.

When two leaders conduct a group, a significant factor affecting group dynamics is whether they are married to each other. A married couple can create an environment for openness and trust by sharing their own marital experiences with the group, in didactic presentations as well as in demonstrations. It is essential, of course, that they have come to an agreement on what they will disclose. In contrast to individual leaders and team leaders who are not husband and wife, leaders who are married to each other are able to participate as a married couple in group activities, which may be advantageous in terms of group cohesion and involvement.

Leaders not married to each other can also engender openness and trust by sharing their marital experiences as long as they both agree to use this technique and can feel comfortable using it. They may find themselves recreating marital situations with one another that typify their own marriages. This process can be useful if two dangers are avoided. The first includes betraying spouses' confidences, telling stories that can be interpreted as degrading to their spouses while self-exonerating, and in any other way modeling inappropriate spouse behavior. The second danger, resulting from the first, is group members

experiencing leaders as inappropriate in providing self-disclosures in the absence of their spouses (even if an absent spouse
would not actually feel betrayed). Group members' trust in
and respect for the leaders can thus be damaged. Such damage
hinders the leaders' ability to teach the desired values and skills
because their worth as models has been decreased. Therefore,
any self-disclosure must be done with caution. It is less risky
for leaders to share insights about their *own* behavior than to
share those relating to absent spouses.

A final issue to consider in selecting group leaders is
whether they should be trained in the helping professions. This
issue can be evaluated by two factors: the goals of the group
and the degree of marital adjustment of the participants. In general, leaders need special training to provide the learning experiences necessary to reach the group's goals, whether it is "professional" or specialized training in a particular model. Also, the
more troubled the marriages of participants, the more necessary
professional training is in dealing with possible crises and in providing remediation to individual couples. However, credentials
are usually less important than the individual's knowledge, expertise, warmth, and enthusiasm (Satir, 1975). Indeed, some
evidence suggests that nonprofessionals may equal or surpass
the effectiveness of helping professionals in groups in which
couples are not having serious marital difficulties. (For a summary of this research, see L'Abate, 1981.) Mace and Mace
(1976c) have suggested helpful criteria for selecting lay couples
as leaders and procedures for training them.

When helping professionals and their untrained spouses
conduct groups, it is important for each married couple to determine how they will function in the group—as coleaders or as
leader and assistant. An unequal leadership arrangement (helping professional as leader and untrained spouse as assistant) may
unintentionally model unequal marital role expectations for
group members.

Generalizing and Maintaining Program Content

When the marriage enrichment program ends will couples
use the skills they have learned in their daily interactions? How

long will the hopefulness and new commitment to their marital relationship last? Marriage enrichment services must address these issues. Everything couples learn in an enrichment program is useless if they do not generalize their new knowledge, skills, and attitudes to their home environment. Even if they do so, it may be even more discouraging if they cannot maintain the changes, but rather find themselves slipping into old patterns of thinking, feeling, and acting.

Giving couples assignments to complete at home between sessions can help them to incorporate learning experiences into the home environment and to evaluate their usefulness. Group discussions can help couples make their new learning more useful so they will be motivated to make it an ongoing part of their lives.

When the program is completed, positive changes in behavior can be maintained through follow-up sessions, reunions, and support groups in which couples meet to continue discussion and to reinforce their changes. Encouraging couples to develop social relationships with one another also proves beneficial; couples can often help one another continue to work toward the changes they have begun. Couples can also be encouraged to join groups such as Association of Couples for Marriage Enrichment. These groups send out monthly publications and hold meetings that focus on continuing the development of a satisfying marital relationship.

4

Leading the Group
and Achieving Goals

Once program goals have been established, sessions organized, activities selected, and couples recruited, the program must be implemented so that individual couples as well as the group have opportunities to achieve their established objectives. Even some of the best-laid plans do not achieve objectives when leaders are unable to generate excitement in couples to risk replacing habitual behavioral patterns with new ideas and new ways of relating.

Each group is unique in its composition, objectives, and development. Knowledge of group processes is necessary for sensitive, flexible, and effective leadership, and leaders must be able to adapt their style, strategies, and content to the needs of a given group. Those who cannot sense the changing needs of a group and respond by altering their plans for achieving objectives exhibit the kind of rigid behavior that can be problematic in a marital relationship. Similarly, leaders who are not skilled in directing a group back to its agreed-upon tasks when members persist in superficial discussions or activities that do not move the group toward its objectives are also ineffectual.

It is beyond the scope of this book to teach group dynamics and the skills of group leadership, but some characteristics of groups of married couples that make marriage enrichment leadership unique can be pointed out. Of course, group experiences vary widely, from the highly structured lecture format of the Catholic Encounter experience to the unstructured Quaker group. Likewise, effective leadership behavior varies— to implement the plans of different approaches as well as to meet the needs of different groups. However, to the extent that some basic similarities in marriage enrichment groups exist, this chapter will provide some guidelines that will help leaders translate program plans into accomplishments. Group norms and settings conducive to the achievement of marriage enrichment goals, guidelines for effective leadership, and the dynamics of group development will also be discussed.

Beginning the Group

The extent to which couples know each other and the group leaders is an important consideration in planning initial group sessions. If a group has been formed by the leaders, couples will have initiated a relationship with them in a screening interview. In groups established by a counseling center, couples may have obtained marriage counseling from the leaders. In an already existing group—a club or church group, a staff group, or a professional group—the couples are acquainted with one another.

No matter how well persons know one another in other contexts, the marriage enrichment group creates a unique setting, and the leaders should expect to find some degree of anxiety among group members. The participants in any newly formed group may be asking themselves a number of questions: Are these other couples having problems? Do I belong here? What are they going to think of me? Is my partner going to embarrass me or say too much? Are they going to try to get me to talk about things I don't want to talk about? Is this group going to be too superficial and never get to the issues that I want to deal with? Are they going to move too fast for me? Am I going to find out something about my marriage or myself that I don't really want to know? Am I going to like these people? Will they like me?

Even when persons in the group are already acquainted, it is important to remember that the degree of acquaintanceship between members varies. Some persons may be close friends; some may barely know the names of other members. Perhaps all the men know each other but the women do not know anyone except their spouse, or vice versa. Leaders often skip the vital stage of group building because they mistakenly assume the existence of relationships between members. Participants who know one another ask some of the same questions that a group of unacquainted participants would. In addition, they may ask: How is what happens in this group going to affect my job or my relationships with others in my church? When this group is over, am I going to be embarrassed to see these people? Are they going to laugh at me or tell others at church or at work things about me I don't want known? If I try to protect myself from embarrassment, are they going to see me as being aloof and uninvolved? Is my spouse going to be angry with me if I say the wrong thing or share something he or she doesn't want known? How much should we tell this group about us? The leaders must address these questions and relieve participants' anxiety so that couples can move beyond establishing their identity as a group and begin work on enriching marriages. There are two interrelated means of accomplishing this: by building relationships between members and fostering the development of group norms and by creating a physical setting conducive to relaxation and intimacy.

Building Relationships and Norms. Before discussing building relationships and norms as a method and a medium by which marriage enrichment goals can be met, it must be pointed out that not all programs emphasize group membership and participation. For example, marriage enrichment can be presented in a lecture format to a large university class or preached from a church pulpit to a whole congregation. Similarly, enrichment can consist of lectures followed by individual couple discussions, as exemplified by the Catholic Encounter. Even in the

programs in which formation of a cohesive group is deempha-
sized and perhaps even discouraged, a group nevertheless often
develops informally. Couples may talk to one another before
and after classes; they may talk during meals while attending an
encounter retreat; they may ask the lecturer questions and then
discuss responses with one another. If leaders choose to focus
on enhancing group development as a method of enriching marriage, they must begin by building interpersonal relationships
through member-to-member communication.

Relationship building to achieve enrichment goals can begin with very simple techniques such as having participants wear
name tags and having them give brief self-introductions. It is important that the introductions focus on the marital relationships. For example, leaders should ask members to include in
their introductions such information as the number of years
they have been married, an anecdote about the marriage, what
they love most about their partner, why they decided to participate in a marriage enrichment group, and what they would like
to have happen in the group. There are five other activities
listed in Resource A that leaders can use to begin building relationships in a group. In selecting relationship-building activities,
however, leaders must assess the group's anxiety level so that
they do not choose an activity that could heighten existing
anxiety. For example, in a group unfamiliar with experiential
learning, anxiety and ambivalence are predictable. These group
members would probably be uncomfortable if they had to risk
embarrassment by revealing intimate information. A relationship-building activity such as having members talk with each
other's spouses to learn enough to introduce one another to the
group would probably not be as appropriate for this kind of
group as each couple sharing a wedding picture with the group
and describing how they met.

Couples who have experienced a number of different
kinds of groups or have perhaps successfully completed marriage counseling may be somewhat comfortable with self-disclosure. Because of their lower anxiety level, leaders may choose to
use a risk-involving activity. However, this group is not more
"advanced" than the first; the groups' needs for group develop-

ment are different and thus require different activities. Couples in a group with minimum anxiety might find it helpful to chart a marriage "lifeline," indicating significant events in their marriages, with peaks and valleys to correspond with changes in their relationship. These graphs could be shared with the group.

The purpose of any activity is to build relationships between participants, which function as resources for couples as the group moves toward its goals. No progress is made when activities scare participants into noninvolvement or bore them into frustration. With the leaders' guidance, through the selection of appropriate activities, the group is establishing its norms. A norm is a "shared expectation of right action that binds members of a group and results in guiding and regulating their behavior" (Bormann, 1975). These expectations are important in alleviating participants' anxiety about what the group experience will entail. Establishment of group norms for participation begins during the first activity, when members participate voluntarily or because of group pressure. The group's expectations about sex roles are determined by who speaks for a couple (one partner or both). The leaders, for example, may ask a wife how she remembers the first date with her husband if he has recounted that episode without her input. The activities the leaders introduce and their methods of implementation indicate to participants the leaders' role in the group. The norms established from the first activity will have continuing influence on group development.

When the group first convenes, it is often helpful to discuss explicitly both the leaders' and the members' expectations and to establish some guidelines for the group's work together. To solicit group discussion, leaders may present a list of their own expectations, which may or may not be negotiable. In either case, leaders must answer all questions participants ask and resolve any conflicts about expectations. Norms established at this stage of group development are basic to the operation of the group.

The following nine norms are commonly outlined by leaders:

1. Confidentiality—the degree to which participants will be expected to maintain the confidence of group members.
2. Time of meetings—whether the group will start on time rather than wait for latecomers and whether meetings will end at the designated time or continue, to accommodate discussions.
3. Attendance—how much emphasis will be put on regular attendance.
4. Fee payment—when and to whom fees will be paid.
5. Evaluation—whether any evaluation tools or techniques will be used and if so, what will be done with the findings.
6. Homework—what kinds of homework assignments will be given and the group's level of commitment to completing these assignments.
7. Structure of sessions—how much structure will be provided by the leaders and how much of the agenda participants are expected to generate.
8. Voluntary participation and self-disclosure—whether the group and/or leaders will be expected to pressure members to participate in the group, or whether participation will be strictly voluntary.
9. Follow-up—how leaders will contact participants when the program ends.

Leaders will be most effective if they allow norms to be negotiated through group discussion. In this way, the group can reach a consensus instead of passively accepting what the leaders have presented. Participants will readily adopt behavior congruent with these expectations, once each member has made a verbal commitment to group norms.

A lengthier process for norm building involves having participants list their own expectations. The participants make individual lists that are combined and discussed; the group then decides on its own "rules of operation." The group as a whole may brainstorm expectations instead of individuals making lists. The leaders may add issues that the group does not include, but the leader-initiated issues are also subject to group discussion and modification.

Group-generated norm development is most useful when leaders are not certain that groups will accept leader-generated norms. For example, in a graduate course for couples, I presented my expectation that participants attend every class unless an emergency arose. Little discussion of this expectation ensued because students do not often question the expectations of professors, at least not in the initial class session. However, during the fifteen-week semester, each couple missed an average of one and a half sessions. Curiously, the unwritten institutional norm allows students two cuts per semester. At the beginning of the following semester, I asked another class to generate its own expectations for the group. As students listed their expectations on the blackboard, I added my expectation that students attend every class unless an emergency arose. In discussing this expectation along with all the others, the class reached a consensus to adopt it. As a result, each couple averaged less than one absence per semester.

Although this classroom experience hardly qualifies as conclusive evidence, it reinforces the belief that group members and leaders must discuss all their expectations and reach a mutually satisfying working agreement. Leaders should use the techniques they think will be efficient and effective. In groups in which initial relationships exist between members, and participants are not reluctant to question leaders, a discussion of a leader-generated list of norms is useful. However, in groups in which leaders are seen as experts with unquestionable authority, this discussion format will probably not be productive. In these groups, facilitating members' expressing and discussing expectations might be more effective. Then, as the group learns to formulate its own norms, it is more likely to adapt and revise these as the group's needs change.

Many group norms remain unspoken; they cannot be mandated—they develop over time. Yet, leaders can guide the development of a norm, for example, the norm that spouses are not allowed to speak for one another without verifying the accuracy of their statements:

> *Joe:*   Trying to find time for one another is really
> hard for us. Mary just doesn't understand how

much time graduate studies take, which makes me really angry.

Leader: Joe, you're speaking for Mary and it might be helpful to hear from her if that is how she sees it.

Mary: That's not really what I've been trying to say. I mean, I agree we have trouble finding time for one another. But I do understand how much time Joe needs to study. And I'm really not saying that he should spend less time on his studies to be with me. But understanding it and liking it are two different things. I'm angry at the *situation,* and I'm looking forward to it changing. I would like for us to plan a vacation or something so that I would have something to look forward to.

Another norm leaders may want to encourage is spouses' giving concrete, behaviorally specific feedback to each other. Often describing behavior rather than simply labeling it helps couples not only to resolve conflict but also to increase understanding of what they value in each other. A leader can help couples develop this ability:

Susan: One of the things I love the most about Bob is that he is so sweet.

Leader: Can you tell Bob what it is that he does that makes you think of him as sweet?

Susan: He sends me flowers sometimes on days that aren't special; he did the laundry last week when it wasn't even his turn but he knew I was swamped, and he even visited my mother when she was in the hospital, which I know meant a lot to her.

Finally, leaders may want to encourage relationships established between couples in the group to continue beyond the program. By maintaining relationships, couples can serve as a support system for one another and thus ward off a sense of isolation they may have experienced before the group, in addition to providing encouragement to one another in other changes they have made. To encourage ongoing relationships, leaders can suggest that couples share refreshments after sessions, go to a restaurant for dessert after sessions, or plan a reunion or celebration that will be held after the program ends. By establishing small, stable groups of couples within the larger group to participate in learning activities, leaders can also engender strong relationships among members. Even the group setting has a significant effect on the building of intercouple relationships.

Group Setting. The physical surroundings of the group's meeting place affect the development of relationships, the participants' initial anxiety level, and the accomplishment of group objectives. For example, a classroom with immovable desks arranged in rows facing a blackboard produces anxiety in many people who disliked school and severely limits the kinds of group activities and the number of relationships that can develop. Often in this setting, participants become acquainted with those sitting next to them but cannot relate easily to other group members. Chair-desk combinations create some difficulty because they severely limit a couple's physical closeness. These limitations also exist in a church sanctuary with anchored pews. The sanctuary and classroom greatly contrast to a "living room" type of setting in which comfortable furniture is arranged to promote conversation.

Furniture, therefore, is a primary factor in creating a positive group setting. Ideally, furniture in meeting rooms should be movable so that circle arrangements for group discussions and dyad arrangements for private intracouple discussions can be easily formed. For activities requiring movement, the center of the room should be cleared of furniture.

Because many groups are held in the evenings after the eight-hour workday, comfortable chairs may lessen the effect of fatigue on the group's work. People who are comfortably seated are more apt to concentrate on group activities and invest themselves in what is happening than merely to count the minutes until they can go home. Some groups may enjoy sitting on a carpeted floor, which may be a restful and rather intimate interlude but can become exhausting after several hours.

The structure of the room is also important. A room should be large enough for the group to work in various configurations but not so large that the members feel overwhelmed by the space. A useful meeting place is a facility with one room large enough for a circle arrangement and with other rooms available for couples to talk privately. One of the most ineffectual environments is a room so small that spouses cannot talk to each other without being overheard. Other aspects of the meeting place that are important to ensuring a pleasant atmosphere are good ventilation, a comfortable temperature, and adequate lighting. Too bright lighting should be avoided, however, as it can create the impression of a workplace or clinical setting and may make participants feel "on the spot." An attractive room with pleasant decor can be a significant factor in setting the context for group meetings.

Noise level is also an important consideration, but one that is often ignored. A group meeting in a room located beneath a basketball gym may be interrupted by cheers and the noise of pounding feet. On the other hand, other distracting noises include ringing telephones and children—or adults—wandering through the meeting room. Some sounds can be helpful. Soft music can set a mood. Music can also be useful when all group activities take place in the same room. When couples want to talk privately, soft music can muffle other conversations and thus enhance their sense of privacy.

Drinks and snacks not only help combat fatigue but also help establish a climate of relaxed sharing. Sharing food is a primary method in our culture of establishing relationships.

Changes in setting may have a profound effect on a group. A group that decides to meet in a member's home after having held meetings in a classroom may find both relationships and group norms altered. Even such simple changes as adding a break period to share snacks may significantly affect participants. Asking participants to sit in a circle on the floor rather than in their chairs may change their expectations for relating.

The leaders can therefore implement changes in the setting to increase the comfort of the group and the intimacy of its interactions. Similarly, members may be so relaxed that they do not have the energy to deal with uncomfortable issues, such as conflict. By changing the setting, leaders can indicate that their expectations for the group are changing.

Group Leadership

There are two leadership roles in groups: designated leadership and functional leadership. In designated leadership, a person becomes a leader through appointment, election, or simple consensus based on the person's expertise or position. Thus far in the discussion, references to leaders of enrichment groups have been to designated leaders. These people either convened their own group or were asked to lead an already-formed group because they had training (expertise) useful to the group's members. The group accords these persons leadership based on their reputation of having skill in leading marriage enrichment experiences.

In functional leadership, a member of the group, and often several group members, assumes a leadership role. Functional leadership is defined as any act that helps the group achieve its goals. "More specifically, leadership consists of such actions by group members as those which aid in setting group goals, moving the group toward its goals, improving the quality of the interactions among the members, building the cohesiveness of the group, and making resources available to the group. In principle, leadership may be performed by one or many members of the group" (Cartwright and Zander, 1968, p. 304). A definition of functional leadership is useful because it implies that a leader does not just assume a title or exhibit a set of personality characteristics but performs behavior that is responsive to the group's changing needs. This kind of leadership models interpersonal roles, which are continually changing and adjusting to members' needs—role behavior most effective in marriage as well as in enrichment groups.

Leaders must perform two basic functions: the task leadership function, or behaviors that move the group toward the attainment of specified goals, and the socioemotional leadership function, or behaviors that strengthen relationships between persons, making the group more attractive to its members and therefore more cohesive. Group cohesion is necessary if the group members are to commit themselves to achieving their goals. Particularly in a marriage enrichment group where the group's tasks involve strengthening interpersonal relationships, goals often overlap so that the functions may be performed simultaneously. For example, an activity in which spouses identify the strengths in their marriage and share them with the group is designed to increase the attraction of spouses to each other. This result is an objective of marriage enrichment and thus the activity serves a task function. Additionally, the activity serves a socioemotional function because risking self-disclosure in the context of the group results in increased cohesiveness among participants. On the other hand, these functions may not be fulfilled simultaneously. For example, a leader who suggests that each couple find a quiet corner to discuss a film they have viewed about sexuality is probably moving the group toward its marriage enrichment objectives but is not strengthening group solidarity. Task leadership in a marriage enrichment group focuses on intracouple relationships; socioemotional leadership focuses on intercouple relationships.

Functional leadership also implies that leadership is not permanently invested in one or even several persons—different persons may fill the role at different times. Therefore, leadership evolves as the group develops. The group may begin with most of the leadership responsibility invested in the designated leaders, but eventually the members themselves may be allowed to carry out an increasing number of the leadership functions until finally, the group becomes "self-supporting." The members establish their own group goals and move the group toward these goals while taking care of members' socioemotional needs. This group decides to meet without the designated leaders when the program ends. Of course, because of the relatively short life span of current marriage enrichment groups, few groups reach a level of competency that allows for elimination of the designated leaders. Nevertheless, they may evolve a leadership structure in which the designated leader is only one of several group members who perform task and socioemotional leadership functions. For example, some members may help others identify communication patterns in their marital relationship (task leadership function); other members may suggest and spearhead going out as a group for pizza after the session and some may draw quiet participants into the discussion (socioemotional leadership functions).

A functional approach to leadership postulates that there is no one best model of how to lead a group. The highly structured format of a lecture series allows little room for member leadership to evolve—the leadership roles are invested in the designated leader/lecturer. By contrast, the group of couples who meet to discuss issues relevant to their marriages has little structure, at least at first. In time, the group does develop a structure, consisting of norms indicating how to accomplish their goals, and roles, including leadership. If the group decides to obtain the leadership services of a helping professional, this person often serves as a consultant to the established group with its recognized leaders.

The amount of structure in the group and the degree to which member leadership evolves are integrally related to the leadership style (see Figure 1). The three styles most commonly assumed by the designated leader are laissez-faire, democratic, and authoritarian. Leaders use a laissez-faire style in the already established group in which the members have developed functioning leadership roles and are achieving their goals by discussing issues which couples consider relevant. The group has little or no structure imposed by the designated leader. The structure is developed by the group, and it may take many forms. In this type of group the leaders allow members to establish the agenda and usually do not try to direct the group. They react to what the members discuss and are ready to give short, didactic presentations, lead activities, or offer discussion questions as they fit the group's agenda; they are also willing to abandon a subject when the group decides to deal with another issue.

In a group governed by the democratic style, the leaders

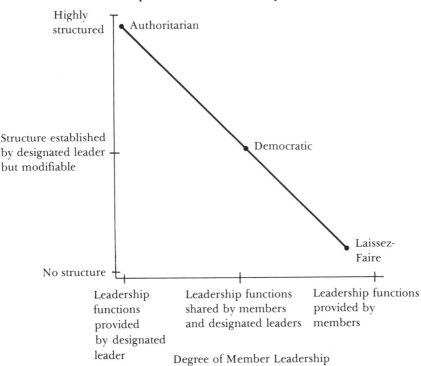

Figure 1. Designated Leader Styles in Relationship to
Group Structure and Leadership.

establish the agenda but couples interact with one another and
the leaders to influence the development of interpersonal relationships, the establishment of objectives, and the use of activities for achieving goals.

The group in which no structure or roles have developed
because members do not know one another is one that probably
needs a high level of structure to achieve its goals. Thus, the
designated leaders are more authoritarian; they are responsible
for establishing the agenda and for performing both the task
and socioemotional functions.

The prototype of authoritarian leadership in the marriage
enrichment movement is the Catholic Encounter, in which couples do not necessarily know one another; there is a high degree
of leader-established structure and adherence to leader-estab-

lished agenda and goals. Some communication training groups demonstrate democratic leadership; there is an established agenda, but through couple interaction, a leadership structure evolves which includes both professional leaders and group members. Couples influence how the group accomplishes its goals. Finally, the Quaker approach typifies laissez-faire leadership; there is little leader-provided structure and the leader reacts to the expressed needs of the members but does not take charge. Clearly, the terms *authoritarian, democratic,* and *laissez-faire* do not reflect the quality of leadership but rather a difference in style demanded by a group's composition and objectives.

Once established, a leadership style can be altered. If a group formed by leaders is allowed to develop its own roles and norms, it develops group leadership. The group and the leaders may begin to discuss the group's purposes and activities, and if the leaders allow and encourage this kind of interaction, the structure of the group will be modified. The leadership style then has moved away from authoritarian and closer to democratic leadership.

Similarly, if an established group involved in pursuing its objectives asks leaders to join as consultants, they may initially prefer the laissez-faire leadership style whereby they wait for the group to suggest issues and to solicit their involvement. However, when the group is having difficulty reaching its goals either because its member leadership is ineffective or because it has been unable to develop appropriate strategies for achieving its objectives, the professional leaders may be asked to assume more leadership functions—initiate structures and provide direction. For example, one group goal may be to examine role expectations in marriage. If members talk about their difficulties in resolving differences over role expectations but do not move beyond this discussion, they may ask a professional leader to help them examine ways to resolve conflict. The professional leader may assign readings, initiate some structured activities, share some information about research on this subject, or provide some problem-solving approaches to resolving differences. The group has therefore moved away from laissez-faire leadership, toward democratic leadership.

To summarize, no one best kind of leadership exists—the style of designated leadership must be determined by the situation. How effective a particular style will be in helping a group achieve its goals will depend on the degree to which the leader's behavior matches the requirements of the group situation (Fiedler, Chemers, and Bons, 1980). A leader's decision to assume all leadership responsibilities or share leadership functions with the group's participants should be based on the characteristics of the group and its objectives. There is a rich literature available for those wanting to explore the situational leadership model (see Bradford, 1978; Cartwright and Zander, 1968; and Hersey and Stinson, 1980).

Group Maturity. The focus of task and socioemotional functions should be derived from the group's maturity (Hersey and Blanchard, 1977). Hersey, Blanchard, and Hambleton (1980) define two components of maturity that affect leadership approaches: psychological maturity, or the willingness and motivation to do a task; and task maturity, or the ability to accomplish the task. Applying these components to a group is difficult, however, because they are based on individual characteristics. These individual characteristics interact to create group characteristics different from the summation of members' motivations and capabilities. An enrichment group's psychological maturity, for example, can be affected because some members are not committed to the program and are only attempting to weather the experience. To what extent, through the interaction of group members during activities, can the group sustain the motivation of some members and yet produce excitement and a sense of challenge in those who question the value of the group experience? It is this group factor, the *cohesion* which develops as members interact and establish group goals, that is the most significant factor in determining the designated leader's appropriate socioemotional leadership behavior.

Similarly, a group's task maturity is based on more than the competencies of its individual members. To what extent does the group have the complement of skills needed to accomplish its goals? A group may include a number of members highly skilled in relating interpersonally but may not have a single participant who can help the group set goals and communicate knowledge about such relevant issues as marital sexual behavior and attitudes, communication styles, values clarification, and role expectations that directly affect the ability of the group to achieve its goals. Therefore, it is important to emphasize that task maturity is a factor that not only involves pinpointing the capabilities of individual members but also *utilizing complementary differences to move the group as a whole toward its goals.* Dividing the group into the skilled and unskilled does not promote goal achievement.

To summarize, a major determinant of leadership functions in a group is the group's maturity. Group maturity is a different variable than the psychological and task maturity of an individual or a summation of these traits in a group. Group maturity depends on the group's ability to establish clear and realistic goals that it can pursue through its own resources and its cohesiveness, the "we-ness" of the group, or members' commitment to the group and its goals.

Ability. The ability of a group is a function of its members' capabilities to lead, to establish goals, and to obtain the resources needed to achieve those goals. Ability is also reflected in the nature of the tasks chosen to pursue the group's goals. The more able the group, the more likely members are to select or agree to group-oriented tasks—that is, tasks that must be accomplished in a group. For example, suggesting that a couple read and then discuss a book with each other may be an appropriate task for fulfilling a marriage enrichment goal, but it does not require the resources of the group. Groups with greater ability would explore the content and implications of the book through activities such as group discussions and illustrative role plays.

The greater the ability of the group, the clearer the goals it establishes for itself. Clear goals are specific and measurable. Thus a group with ability will establish indicators to signal that objectives have been achieved. For example, participants find it difficult to determine whether a goal such as "achieving greater marital happiness" has been reached because it defines neither *happiness* nor *greater.* A more specific goal for a couple might be: "to use the problem-solving method in a dialogue while the group listens and to reach a decision that they will implement to resolve a conflict." Of course, a group does not often spell out objectives as explicitly as a professional might, but members will clearly understand what they are attempting to accomplish in their group activities.

Finally, the more able the group, the more likely it is to establish realistic goals—goals which the group can achieve through its own resources. For example, members of a less able group may need a designated leader to explain and demonstrate the problem-solving method used to resolve conflict and then to guide them through its implementation. In contrast the more able group will use its own internal leadership structure; the members themselves explore the method together and coach one another in its implementation.

It should be noted that ability is not a characteristic that a group either has or does not have. No group is so able that it completely provides its own leadership, establishes its own goals, and relies on all its own resources to reach these goals. If it were, it would not come to the attention of a professional leader. Similarly, no group is so lacking in ability that it needs a professional leader to assume all these functions.

Cohesiveness. A second major factor in the maturity of a group is the cohesiveness, or we-ness of a group. No matter how capable the individual members are of achieving specified goals, the group must develop role structures, a sense of commonality, and the ability to work together, both to achieve group goals and to deal effectively with interpersonal relationships. Cohesiveness is reflected in group goals that result from a blending of individual needs. Cohesiveness develops as tasks become clear and as members begin to trust and care for one another. Another major factor in building cohesiveness is the motivation of individual members.

Motivation in a marriage enrichment group is almost always high although occasionally the group includes a reluctant spouse who has been "dragged along" by the partner. Generally, people participate in a marriage enrichment group because they want to; only the motivated risk participating in the anxiety-provoking experiences that enrichment programs often create. Also, in a society in which people must divide their recreational time between familial and social demands, most couples will be making sacrifices of some kind to take advantage of an enrichment experience. A high level of motivation becomes an important factor in selecting appropriate leadership style because members will exert themselves to provide leadership functions when they are interested in the success of their group.

Of course, some individual motivations may detract from group cohesiveness. Individual desires and needs to dominate, to advocate a certain position (for example, all marriages should be egalitarian), to absolve oneself of responsibility for marital difficulties, to remain uninvolved and detached so that the status quo can be maintained, and many others may interfere with the development of the group's cohesiveness. Lack of group solidarity affects the members' ability to reach consensus in group decisions, whether decisions determine group goals or meeting time.

There are also several group characteristics that can increase cohesiveness. Similarities among group members, previously discussed as group composition factors, help members to identify with one another. Activities that are both enjoyable and meet the members' needs also develop cohesiveness. The group's physical surroundings and size are important in providing the appropriate setting for group bonding. Finally, a style of leadership which allows members to participate in decision making increases cohesion (Bormann, 1975).

A Leadership Model. When examining the two factors of group maturity, ability and cohesiveness, the parallels with the task and relationship dimensions of group leadership become apparent. Therefore, these two maturity factors become important indicators of the style of leadership that can be effective in helping a group achieve its goals. Figure 2 illustrates how group maturity and effective leadership interact. This model is adapted from Hersey and Blanchard's (1977) theory of situational leadership, derived from their experience in organizations and management. Those familiar with Hersey and Blanchard's (1977) theory of situational leadership will find that this model is both similar to and different from theirs.

Figure 2. Effective Leadership as Defined by Group Maturity.

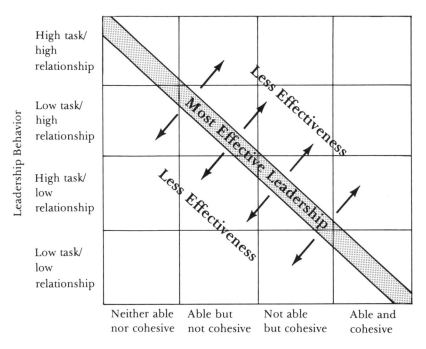

Four significant differences between marriage enrichment groups and other groups such as work groups demand that different models of leadership be used in each. First, as has been discussed, a marriage enrichment group consists of persons who are committed to achieving the group's goal—enriching marriage. Thus the relevancy of Hersey and Blanchard's focus on individual motivation decreases while the relevancy of the focus on group cohesion increases. Second, marriage enrichment groups exist only to meet couples' interpersonal needs, causing a greater overlap of task and relationship functions in enrichment groups than in other kinds of groups. Task functions refer to intracouple relationships. Socioemotional functions refer to intercouple relationships which should always serve to enhance

intracouple relationships. In the enrichment group both functions, however, concentrate on building relationships whereas in
a work group, the establishment of relationships may detract
from task accomplishment. Third, compared to work groups,
marriage enrichment groups often have limited time frames.

Finally, more than in other types of groups, in a marriage
enrichment group tasks are not completed when a session ends.
Spouses go home together to explore what the group experience
means to each of them. The hours spent in the marriage enrichment group are really a continuation of the couple's life together and only have meaning in the context of their relationship.
Therefore, how spouses interact between group meetings may
dramatically affect the group's task of enriching marriages.
Therefore, the enrichment group calls for leadership that will
enable couples, when away from the group, to work toward the
goals they have established for their marriage. In contrast, leadership theory based on work groups presumes that the majority
of work occurs within the group context.

In the model of effective leadership depicted in Figure 2,
the group that has neither ability nor cohesiveness needs a designated leader who can provide both task and relationship leadership. A group which has ability but little cohesiveness needs
designated leadership that concentrates on the relationship dimension—to help the group form relationships and role structures, and enable members to use their task abilities, which will
also help them begin to develop a sense of group identity. The
group that has cohesiveness but does not have a great deal of
ability needs a designated leader who will provide task leadership—to help the group formulate goals and guide activities designed to achieve the goals. The effective leader will reinforce
the cohesiveness of the group by not interfering with the group's
ability to care for the socioemotional needs of the group. Although the leader will still be personable and concerned with
the needs of the couples in the group, the leader will initiate
task activities that focus primarily on achieving group objectives
and secondarily on continuing the development of group unity.
Finally, in a group which is both able and cohesive the leader
should reinforce the ability of the group to fulfill its own task
and relationship functions. In this group the designated leader/

professional may assume the role of consultant rather than functional leader.

As Figure 2 shows, the continuum of leadership styles is also a continuum of group development. A group may begin with little ability or cohesion and develop these characteristics over time. Of course, actual boundaries between the categories as they appear in the figure do not exist: one style of leadership blends into the next and one level of group maturity blends into the next. Though a group often develops its abilities to establish and achieve goals before it develops a sense of unity (able but not cohesive), the development of cohesiveness may occur first. Members establish positive relationships with one another and then move toward establishing group tasks and goals. Very often ability and cohesion develop simultaneously— as the group develops its abilities, it also develops cohesiveness and socioemotional leadership skills. Also, it is important to realize that group changes occur gradually and that a leader's decreasing emphasis on either of the leadership functions does not signify that a function is being ignored. On the contrary, it signals that the group is satisfying its own needs.

Groups may move either direction on the continuum; they may become more or less mature at given stages of their development. They also may vary in the degree of change in ability and cohesiveness, as couples' needs change and as leaders adapt their behavior to fit group needs. Many groups may not have the opportunity to develop either ability or cohesiveness if they are limited by time or by task structures. Group movement on this continuum and thus the most effective style of leadership are highly related to the processes of the group's development. Two examples of how this leadership model can be used in planning and leading a marriage enrichment group are presented in Chapter Five.

Group Development

A major factor in determining appropriate models is the stage of group development. Leadership behavior which would be appropriate during the first hour a group meets would be extremely inappropriate weeks later when the group had developed its own history, structure, norms, and goals. Therefore, leaders need to understand the dynamics of group development in order to be truly effective in helping a group achieve its objectives. Some useful references for developing an understanding of group development include: Bradford (1978); Hare (1976); Hartford (1971); Henry (1981); Jones, Barnlund, and Haiman (1980); and Vinter (1967). An overview of the stages of group development is provided here with some suggestions for leaders on how to adapt their styles of leadership to the group's developmental needs.

Pregroup Phases. A marriage enrichment group becomes a group when its members meet and identify themselves as part of the same unit. Before that group identity even begins to develop important decisions will have been made that will influence the nature of the group.

The first phase of group development occurs when the organizer conceives the idea for a marriage enrichment group (Hartford, 1971). Initial thoughts about group composition and group purposes may shape the actual development of the group. The organizer then discusses the idea with colleagues or other significant persons, whose reactions may be critical to a group's ultimate formation. There are a number of important questions to be answered at this point such as: Who should be involved in shaping the group? Who should make decisions about group membership? Whose support will be needed to provide the resources to make the idea materialize? In this initial stage, the organizer must also decide how the group will be led. If the organizer does not assume leadership, discussions with those who may provide the service must begin. This step marks a critical juncture in the development process. For example, a pastor may decide that the church year should begin with a marriage enrichment retreat for church deacons and their spouses. The pastor probably has a perspective on the church's needs and has decided what the purpose of the retreat should be. If the pastor engages the services of professional marriage enrichment leaders, it becomes essential that the pastor and the designated leaders discuss objectives and plans. If possible, the leaders should involve the potential participants in this initial discussion. This method of preplanning differs from that often used by professional leaders of establishing a program without investigating the expressed and unexpressed needs of a particular group.

When possible, screening should take place during the pregroup phases. This process gives leaders the opportunity not only to determine whether the group experience suits the needs of potential participants, but also to modify or rework the program so that it can meet needs most effectively. In other words, screening interviews allow leaders to communicate their expectations to couples, and they allow couples to communicate their expectations and needs to leaders. Thus the most appropriate group experience can be developed.

Phase One: Dependence. The next stage of development begins when members meet for the first session of the marriage enrichment group. This stage is often characterized by undirected activity—members are trying to get comfortable, both physically and emotionally. Participants often talk without really listening to one another; some remain passive, waiting to be told what to do. The participants expect leaders to be in charge, to tell them what to do and how to do it. Some may become anxious or upset if the leader does not provide this kind of direction. Often, during this first session, one or two participants dominate the group, unchallenged by the others who wait quietly to see what develops.

Even the seemingly irrelevant small talk cannot be ignored in this stage because members are testing this new situation and making decisions about whether to participate in the program. They are determining whether they can relate to others in the group and whether the group (at this point, personified in the leader) is going to meet their expectations.

The leaders may feel a great deal of pressure from the group to perform. However, although the leaders convene the group, provide the structures, and actively work to help persons connect and identify common purposes, only the group can form itself. The amount of time spent in this stage will depend on whether the group was formed by a leader (members are strangers to one another) or was an already established group (members are acquainted with one another). The importance of

this stage may be underestimated for a group that is already in
existence. Although members have relationships with one another and may have even worked together as a group, this context, with new goals and objectives, requires an altered structure
of interpersonal relationships. Furthermore, the leaders are new
members who will alter the group's character.

To help a group through this phase, leaders should engage
all members in discussions on topics that are not risky and that
allow members to begin to relate to one another. Skills that
members already have need to be supported. For example,
when members voice their expectations for the group, they
should be encouraged to continue this kind of goal-oriented behavior. It is helpful for the leaders to clarify their expectations
and facilitate the development of group goals at this stage.
Knowing what to expect reduces participants' anxiety and increases their participation. Any leader behavior that helps
members establish their initial roles in the group and build relationships with one another will move the group on toward the
next stage of development. Such actions may include pointing
out that two members were born in the same state, asking a
particularly quiet member to write on a blackboard ideas about
the group's goals, and asking members to give a brief introduc-
tory talk about themselves or their partner. (Several other in-
troductory activities have been discussed earlier in this chapter
and additional activities are presented in Resource A.)

Phase Two: Group Conflict. In Phase One, a group will
develop some initial stability, including a stable membership,
an initial commitment to a set of expectations and goals, and an
implicit role structure. In this phase, group conflict, the members often begin to challenge the group's leadership and perhaps
even its objectives. This behavior is more explicit when the
designated leader does not impose a strict structure and shows
an openness to share leadership. If the group members are relatively comfortable with conflict, they may challenge the leaders
in many areas. These challenges may take the form of questioning the effectiveness of selected approaches to particular content or of questioning the leaders' use of certain learning structures. For example, the leaders may suggest that a particular

problem-solving method be used in marital conflict situations and one or more members may indicate that the approach is not applicable in their relationship. Other members may state that the leaders require them to spend too much time in couple dialogues and do not allow enough time for didactic presentations, or vice versa.

Of course, these challenges may always be well founded, but when the leaders begin to feel that no matter what they do, someone objects, the group has reached the "adolescent" conflict stage of its development. During the dependence stage, participants may have consented to group goals and structures that felt comfortable and were nonthreatening—obviously the decisions did not reflect couples' needs and expectations, which were more risky to consider during the group's formative period. Only when members begin to feel secure about the leaders' abilities to guide the group do they feel confident enough to risk voicing their relevant concerns. The leaders may congratulate themselves at this stage though praise seems inappropriate when they are being challenged and when their group is embroiled in conflict. However, the group has formed and no longer needs the tight leadership it required during the dependent phase. Couples want to be involved in deciding the course of the group—they want to take more responsibility for leadership functions. This process parallels the early turbulent stage of marriage beginning when couples admit that "the honeymoon is over." In fact, some couples may now be sorting out their own initial marital role expectations and reenacting the conflict on the group level. The leaders' ability to guide the group through this conflict thus becomes important modeling.

Unfortunately, in many groups, often in church groups, this conflict does not surface directly. When members are not comfortable with challenging a leader overtly, conflict becomes indirect. Subgroups may form that discuss the group between or before and after sessions. (The parallel in marital relationships is a spouse who "runs home to mamma" or complains to friends rather than confronting the partner with the conflict.) Members may agree verbally to group decisions about homework assignments or discussion topics, but then they do not complete their assignments and they do not participate in the group discussion. Some members even drop out at this point. Unresolved marital conflict heightens this group conflict. For example, participants may feel threatened by open disagreement between group members if they fear that allowing disagreement with their spouse to surface may destroy their marital relationship. Or a woman who is dissatisfied with the expectations in her marriage that she is responsible for all the housework may lash out at a male leader whom she sees as assigning tasks without group discussion and consensus. Although these marital conflicts complicate the group conflict, they provide fertile ground for learning alternative patterns of relating in marriage as well as developing a more cohesive, functional group.

Awareness of these group dynamics often helps alleviate defensiveness in leaders and allows more openness in the development of strategies for group learning. When the group is experiencing conflict that represents a challenge to its dependence on leaders for task and socioemotional leadership, leaders can facilitate the group's development of its own leadership and revision of its objectives to reflect more accurately the members' goals. During this group conflict phase the leaders should include all participants as often as possible in each group activity. Activities that acknowledge the conflict may be very helpful. For example, asking that the group reevaluate its goals or discuss its approach to task fulfillment gives members permission to voice concern and frustration. In groups threatened by open disagreement, leaders may ask participants to write down anonymously at least one suggestion for changing the group's structure. Then a list of suggestions can be compiled for discussion, which can effect constructive group changes.

Leaders must serve as facilitators and clarifiers during this second phase of development. It is important that they remain open to group challenges and encourage differences to surface. Learning to handle conflict in ways that strengthen rather than cripple relationships is important for both the group and individual couples. Often this is the single most important skill for married couples to develop in a marriage enrichment experience. The leader may or may not decide to point out the parallel between couples' experience with group conflict and their experience with marital conflict. In either case, it may be appropriate to change the group focus to constructive marital conflict.

During this time of change in the group's structure, however, the leaders may find that working on the group's task is difficult. Some members may be angry at the leaders while others are angry at those who display annoyance with leaders; this upheaval and resulting anxiety at the group level make it difficult for participants to risk conflict with their spouses. Leaders can ease anxiety by using group-oriented activities rather than couple-oriented activities—to focus on the socioemotional functions of the group. When group conflict has been resolved, a firm basis will exist that allows couples to focus on their marital relationship.

Examining the dynamics of the group during this second developmental phase may intensify the conflict but also shorten it. This phase, as well as others, may last only part of one session in a short-term program or may continue through several sessions in a program of longer duration. Groups unable to resolve the conflict may never progress to other phases. However, most groups complete the phase, especially if the leaders use it as an opportunity for members to examine the group's commitment to its purposes and the benefits conflict can bring both to the group and to marriage. Thus leaders may enable the group to control some of its experiences and reduce the threat of change.

Phase Three: Interdependence. The group that successfully moves through conflict displays new characteristics. The role structure has been altered; a number of participants may now provide leadership and the designated leaders may have changed their styles of leadership. Also, the group may have modified its goals and be ready to begin working to achieve them. Balance is evident in members' work toward task accomplishment and their enjoyment and ease in relating to one another. Members are developing the ability to find humor even in crises. Members are comfortable with their group roles and understand them, and they are developing friendships with one another that exist outside the group as well.

At this stage of development the designated leaders become more facilitative and exercise less control. The group has developed cohesiveness and accepts idiosyncrasies of both members and leaders. Norms established during the period of conflict now provide the structures for moving toward group goals. For example, one norm may dictate that partners bring up an issue only after their spouse verifies that it can be discussed with the group. Another norm may establish that designated leaders provide members with an outline of the session's activities so that participants can decide how much time to spend on each issue or to discuss issues not included on the outline. The group develops and modifies norms throughout its development —norms that are unique to this group rather than the basic expectations established by leaders in many groups as basic ground rules. However, even ground rules may have been challenged during the developmental stages. For example, members may have decided to change their meeting time or to eliminate or add homework.

Many groups flounder during the interdependence phase because leaders have difficulty giving responsibility for the group to its members. This is an extremely important process because it parallels one necessary for marital development. Couples must be capable of developing norms and roles unique to their individual needs, their situation, and their expectations of the relationship. Couples must challenge the rules that operate in relationships with parents and friends; these cannot be carried over into marriage unchallenged if the relationship is to meet the unique needs of the spouses as partners. Couples must learn to feel comfortable with changes in their marital relationship, if the resulting relationship truly meets their needs. The criterion for evaluation in each relationship is whether the marriage works. Similarly, in the interdependent phase of the marriage enrichment group the leaders must be able to recognize the function of the group's own structures and norms and to accept its independence—they must not try to regain control so that the group becomes more dependent on them again. During this phase leaders can trust group members to fulfill more of the group's socioemotional needs. Members can show concern for one another, solicit the involvement of those who are quiet or those signaling nonverbally that they want to participate, share their own experiences to provide new perspectives on the problems or issues with which others are dealing. Therefore, the leaders can focus primarily on intracouple tasks. They can provide more couple activities and fewer activities to develop group cohesiveness. Also during this phase the group accomplishes its objectives.

These stages have been presented as phases having distinct starting and termination points. However, as a group's needs change, it may move in and out of a number of stages in one session; it may stall in one stage, or may move to a previous stage; for example, from the interdependent phase into conflict again. Much of this movement depends on the length of the program, the opportunity for the members to function as a group instead of as a collection of individual couples who passively listen to lectures, and the style and skill of the leaders.

Phase Four: Ending. The greater the cohesiveness of a group, the more time and energy it needs to spend in the ending phase. In short-term programs groups having shared few experiences may only need a brief discussion about what they enjoyed about the enrichment program and what their plans are for their marriages. Groups that have been together for many weeks and whose members have developed intimate and functional relationships that satisfy personal and marital needs may need to prepare for termination many weeks in advance through a series of special activities. Leaders often make the mistake of giving group endings short shrift as they try to fit in all the material not yet covered. Members who want to learn the most may encourage this. Leaders may not realize the intimacy of relationships that often develop in a marriage enrichment group as couples reveal experiences that they may never have discussed with their partner, much less with another couple. For couples who will continue relationships with other couples once the program has ended, termination takes on a particular import. They have to decide how what they have learned about one another and how the changes in their relationships will affect their interactions.

If the group experience has been both useful and enjoyable, participants may deny its end by clinging together and voicing intentions to continue the group although they are making no concrete plans to meet again. Of course, some groups may opt to continue as a support group, but even these groups need to discuss the ramifications of the ending of the structured program and how they will continue. Some members may experience regret that they were not as committed to the group as they could have been. Others may avoid the ending by not attending the last few sessions—an increase in absenteeism is common.

The designated leaders who functioned peripherally during the interdependent phase now need to assume a more central role. They should plan rituals and activities that explicitly deal with ending or modifying relationships. Having the group make a list of what it accomplished and what it failed to accomplish is a useful activity. Leaders can also use other structural activities to help participants say goodbye to one another. For example, each couple may prepare a symbolic gift for every other couple. These gifts may be brief written messages or objects that symbolize their feelings about one another. Through structured activities, participating couples can show appreciation for one another's contributions, to give some vision of what they each will continue to work toward, to say goodbye.

While leaders are helping couples part with one another, they should also provide increased time for spouses to interact privately with each other. It is useful for a couple to have a chance to solidify changes they have made, make plans for the future, and, in general, assess what the experience has meant for them. Some groups use a reaffirmation of wedding vows to cement symbolically the decisions made during the program. Through such a ritual, a couple can say goodbye to the group and then begin their changed relationship with one another and with other couples in the group.

This stage of a group's development may take on added meaning for some members who are experiencing a termination of relationships at a number of levels. For example, couples who have recently launched children, who are facing retirement or dealing with recent retirement, or who are anticipating the death of a partner may have particular difficulty moving through this phase. These participants need additional time and activities to help them deal with feelings of loss. Such activities can provide modeling of approaches to loss which help couples and individuals develop useful coping strategies.

In summary, Figure 3 suggests how effective leadership and the stages of a group's development are related. During the dependent phase, a group has little cohesiveness and is not capable of accomplishing its tasks. The leaders therefore, are

Figure 3. The Relationship Between Effective Leadership
and Stages of Group Development.

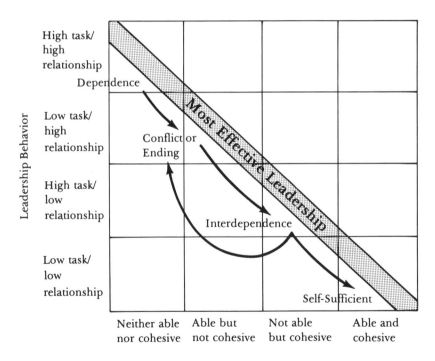

very active in both the task and relationship dimensions. As the group begins to challenge its initial structures and goals, and the resulting conflict, the leader becomes more active in the relationship dimension, focusing on group relationships rather than marital relationships. The crucial factor during this phase is the lack of group cohesiveness. As the group resolves conflict and develops a new role structure and norms, its cohesiveness is significantly increased and the group is ready to focus on enriching marital relationships. During this interdependent phase the leader is most active in the task dimension, developing members' abilities to enhance their own relationships and one another's marital relationships. The group may then decide to continue as a support group without professional leadership, thus moving into a self-sufficient phase, or it ends. When the group decides to end, the leader again becomes active in the relationship dimension, helping couples to deal with feelings of loss and to say goodbye to one another. The "able but not cohesive" classification of the group's maturity is applicable at this point; the group has accomplished its tasks or has developed the skills to accomplish them (ability), but its cohesiveness is not sufficient to keep it together—other commitments and interests have become more important.

Marriage enrichment leaders, therefore, are constantly monitoring two interrelated processes: group development and the development of marital relationships, which includes couples examining their attitudes and values, learning new concepts of relating in marriage, and developing interpersonal skills. These processes can at times be at cross-purposes, but it is the leader's responsibility to integrate them so that the objectives of marriage enrichment can be achieved. Examples of two marriage enrichment experiences in Chapter Five illustrate this integration of couple learning and group development.

5

Examples of Group Programs and Activities

The discussion in Chapter Three of how to develop a marriage enrichment program suggests that once the goals of the service have been defined, leaders can use a series of sequential steps in cognitive, affective, and skills learning to help determine appropriate learning activities. (A number of such learning activities can be found in Resource A.) It becomes apparent, however, in examining all the variables involved in leadership behavior and group development (discussed in Chapter Four), that leading a group is more than choosing the appropriate activities and implementing them. Leaders need to be flexible, recognizing when activities—including lectures, structured activities, informal and formal discussions, couple dialogues, demonstrations, films, and homework—should be modified, amplified, postponed, or eliminated. A group will respond to a given activity not only according to its appropriateness but also according to the leader's skill in introducing it and guiding the group through it.

With these factors in mind, two marriage enrichment programs are presented here to illustrate some of the issues involved in implementing program plans: the use of structured

109

activities, the processes of leadership, and the dynamics of group development. One program has been designed for a leader-formed group meeting once a week and the other for an already-existing group meeting for a weekend retreat. These programs should not be construed as models of *the* way to provide marriage enrichment services in these two contexts; they are included because they illustrate some important issues, not because they are inherently better than other program models. In fact, because all groups are unique, and therefore need programs designed especially for their particular couple and group goals, group maturity, and structures, the two programs presented here are appropriate only for the two specific groups described.

A Marriage Enrichment Group Focusing on Communication Skills

A social worker in a counseling center is counseling individual couples in crisis. Listening to them talk with one another the social worker observes that often they do not understand each other's thoughts or feelings. Although the worker has been able to help the couples resolve differences and become more committed to their relationship, the professional thinks training in communication skills would help avert future crises. Learning how to listen should help couples develop better mutual understanding. The social worker and these couples then determine that a marriage enrichment program designed to meet this learning objective should be developed. From referral sources the worker finds additional couples who would like to participate in the group.

Through the interaction with couples who will participate in the group, the social worker defines the learning objectives for the group as follows:

1. Participants will learn the skills of active listening. In a discussion with their spouse, participants will use the skills in responding to their partner's communication accurately. (This involves behavioral learning at the level of coordination.)

2. By increasing their ability to listen to each other, spouses will be more accurate in their understanding of each other's needs and expectations of the marital relationship. (This involves cognitive learning at the level of comprehension.)
3. Participants will use the listening skills not only during the marital enrichment group but also as they interact at home and in other relationships. (This involves affective learning at the characterization level.)

Theoretical Approach. A Rogerian approach emphasizing learning listening skills is most appropriate to achieve these objectives. The overarching goal is that through increased capacities for understanding each other, couples will be able to adjust to changes in their relationship and the environment caused by events such as the birth of a child, a grown child leaving home, loss of a job, or a move to a new city. A Rogerian approach works well with the General Systems theory premise that the greater the variety of information provided to a system and its components, the more capable the system is of adjusting to changes that occur within as well as outside it. Thus spouses' perceptions of their partner's attitudes, feelings, and behavior should be more accurate if they listen more effectively. More accurate perception of each other means greater understanding, which allows partners to meet each other's needs, resulting in a more satisfying relationship. Therefore, the program not only uses skill training approaches but also provides opportunities for spouses to examine their attitudes, feelings, and behaviors about a number of topics (sexuality, role expectations, time management, and so on) that are relevant to their understanding of each other and their relationship.

Group Membership. Once the social worker has identified couples who understand the group's goals and who think that the enrichment service would help them, additional couples who will benefit from the program must be found.

The objective of developing communication skills is appropriate for couples in any stage of the marital life cycle. Because of the emphasis on listening skills, couples need to be willing to express themselves verbally and to discuss some aspects of their marital relationship with the group. In forming a compatible group, member characteristics such as socioeconomic status, sex-role preferences, and age should be considered because they affect group cohesiveness, but couples heterogeneous in reference to these characteristics can benefit from the group. Because group interaction will be emphasized, the number of couples in the group should be limited to eight.

Group Meetings. Primarily, the group goal is to learn a set of skills; therefore, weekly meetings give couples time between sessions to integrate the skills into their interactions in the home environment. Six, two-and-one-half-hour sessions are adequate to achieve the group's purposes.

Group Leadership. Ideally, two people, not necessarily married to each other, should lead this program because of the planned use of role-play demonstrations. Because the couples involved in the group have had significant marital difficulties and some may still be receiving counseling, the use of helping professionals as leaders is advisable. In the program presented here, the social worker decides to lead the group and to ask a female colleague to work with him.

Generalization and Maintenance. Homework assignments must focus on using the skills being taught in the group. It is also helpful to plan a follow-up session to encourage participants to work on maintaining changes in interactional behavior.

Learning Activities. Activities designed to achieve the group's objectives are selected for each session. The following descriptions of the six sessions include references to numbered activities, which are explained in detail in Resource A. The rationale for each activity indicates the targeted level of cognitive, behavioral, or affective learning. The sequence of activities is derived from the assumption that learning builds from one activity to the next until the program's objectives are reached.

Session 1. Because group members are strangers to one another, the first session is crucial for helping participants become acquainted with one another and for developing a sense of group identity and purpose. The leaders introduce themselves to the group and ask participants to introduce themselves and tell how long they have been married.

The leaders then begin pretesting. They first explain that participants will be asked to complete some written evaluation measures in order to identify couples' current needs and provide information that leaders will use to shape the program content. The measures will provide a baseline from which the leaders and participants can later evaluate the effectiveness of the enrichment programs. Leaders also suggest that these measures may help couples crystallize some of the issues they would like to address during the marriage enrichment experience. Care is taken to assure participants that the measures are methods to identify issues and areas of strength, not tests with right and wrong responses. Confidentiality is also assured.

Measures of marital adjustment, communication, and skill usage are chosen to reflect the objectives of the group. Although testing may create some anxiety, it is important to administer these measures as early in the group's experience as possible in order to get indications of each couple's thoughts and attitudes about their relationship and their skill in interacting with each other. These measures also will lend a sense of purposefulness and direction to the group, as they focus on marital experiences of couples and help them identify what they would like to change in their relationships.

Because the pretesting session contributes to the initial anxiety, and does not promote activity that builds group identity, the other activities must be less stress producing and must focus on group building. The establishment of group cohesiveness is essential for reinforcing the value of the group to its members and in developing the group's capability to reinforce skill development and practice. The leaders therefore select the exercise titled Getting Acquainted (A-1). In this activity individuals are asked to list five distinctive personal characteristics, discuss their lists with their spouse and form one list that describes their relationship, and then share their description with the group. This activity will help couples know one another as couples and usually evokes a great deal of laughter and responses such as "You're like us." It also helps couples conceptualize how they function as a system.

For participants to learn one another's names so that they can begin relating personally, leaders introduce the Naming exercise (A-2). In this activity each person identifies every other group member by name (of course, members remove their name tags). The leaders should perform this activity first in order to lessen member's anxiety.

Finally, during this session it is important for the leaders to outline briefly the content of the other sessions. At this time leaders can present their expectations for the group about attendance, participation, fees, and make other suggestions about group norms as discussed in preceding chapters. Leaders must elicit discussion about each expectation. They should also ask the group to make other suggestions or to raise any issues of concern.

Session 2. Skill learning begins in earnest in Session 2. During the first thirty minutes leaders present some of the concepts of verbal and nonverbal communication. Some suggestions for this presentation are given in the Attending exercise (B-1). In this presentation as well as others, it is important that leaders use as many modes of communication as possible. In addition to talking to the group about the concepts, leaders should write them on a blackboard or on a handout, and demonstrate them through role plays, videotapes, or films. For example, outlining the main ideas, giving some kind of demonstration of the concept, and then leading a group discussion about it increase the participants' ability to understand, remember, and integrate what they have learned. Providing opportunities to be informed about a concept, see it in operation, and then try it out experientially recognizes that individuals have different learning styles and promotes maximum learning.

The leaders next introduce the attending skills. It is important for leaders to model the skills *before* asking couples to demonstrate them. The principles of modeling and skill learning introduced in Chapter Three should be used. The skills should always be named, explained, and demonstrated in steps small enough for participants to use each skill successfully and thus receive reinforcement for their efforts from the leaders. As couples see and discuss how the skill can be useful, they should become motivated to master the techniques.

Two leaders, Bill and Sue, might explain and model the attending skills as follows:

Sue (leader): In improving our communication ability and in learning to understand one another better, one of the first things we have to do is listen to each other. A common complaint is, "You just never listen to me." Now, how is it that we decide that our partner isn't listening to us? How do you know when your husband or wife isn't listening to you?

Kate: When he never looks up from the paper while I'm talking.

Doug: When she starts lecturing the kids right in the middle of what I'm trying to say.

Sue (leader): What is it that your partner does, then, that makes you feel like you're being listened to? Have you ever had the experience of saying, "You're not listening to me?"—only to have the other reply, "Yes, I am, . . ." and then go on to repeat back verbatim what you said? (Heads nod in the group.) What does that feel like?

George: I still feel dissatisfied somehow. She may have heard my words but that isn't all I wanted. I wanted her attention.

Sue (leader): Right! Listening is not just recording in our brains the words of another. It is giving that other person our attention, focusing on what they are saying not only with their words but also with their gestures, posture, and facial expressions. It means we aren't just hearing, but we are trying to understand. Hearing is passive, but understanding is active; it requires that we try to make meaning out of what we are hearing. How do you know you are giving that kind of attention or that you are getting it?

Doug: She looks at me.

Barb: He stops what he's doing.

George: She doesn't walk out of the room or start doing something else.

Sue (leader): Good! Listening involves a lot of things. It is looking at someone. It is moving physically close enough so that we can see their nonverbal communication as well as hear their words. You can't listen when one is in the kitchen and the other is upstairs in the bedroom. We call this skill *attending*—we look at one another, we position ourselves facing the other and slightly leaning toward them. (Sue writes these on the blackboard.) This communicates: "You are important to me. I want to understand you." It also helps us focus our attention on what is being communicated. Bill and I are going to demonstrate this for you.

Bill (leader): What's that you say? (group laughter)

(Bill and Sue sit down with their chairs at a forty-five-degree angle to one another and their bodies approximately three feet apart. Sue leans slightly toward Bill and looks at him.)

Bill (leader): Well, I certainly feel like I have your attention. There are some things I have been wanting to say to you. It helps to feel listened to. I just balanced the checkbook and I'm furious!

(Sue leans back in her chair and looks away.)

Bill (leader): I really think we need to look at the way we've been spending money lately. I think you've become very careless.

(Both laugh and get up from their chairs.)

Bill (to the group): What did you see happen?

Doug: At first she seemed to really be listening to you. She was leaning toward you and looking at you. But when you started with that "Now I'm going to really tell you," she pulled away.

Sue (leader):   Yeah. It's often difficult to give someone our attention when what they're saying is something we don't want to hear. We almost physically protect ourselves by turning our eyes, moving physically away. Unfortunately, that often becomes a way of responding all the time. We have to work consciously at attending to the other. Now we want you to experiment with this skill, called *attending.* Each person take a chair and move with your spouse to your own place in the room, and then we'll tell you what to do next.

The leaders now begin to give the directions for the Attending exercise (B-1). In this exercise by assuming different body positions, participants experience the difference between communicating with attending skills and without them.

Because leaders function as models whenever they work with the group (whether or not they and the group are aware of it), they should examine their behavior for its effects beyond those related to the immediate task. For example, when a participant disagrees with the leaders during a discussion, leaders model conflict management in their response to the disagreement. By accepting that opinions may differ and recognizing that a relationship still continues and in fact is enriched by this difference, the leader models tolerance for differences. By looking for areas of agreement and by emphasizing group achievement, the leaders model placing an emphasis on strengths rather than on chronic problems in a marital relationship. Leaders who are willing to forego some planned activities in order to pursue the interests and needs of the group model time management that focuses on building relationships as well as on task accomplishment, a needed emphasis for many couples.

During the next hour leaders explain the listening skills of paraphrasing content and asking for confirmation, using materials from Gordon (1975) and Miller, Nunnally, and Wackman (1975). In a role play the leaders demonstrate the skills. The leaders need to be comfortable with the content of the role play. In addition, the content must center around an issue relevant to but not threatening to participants. In this way couples are not so preoccupied with the issue of the role play that they cannot concentrate on the skills being demonstrated. The leaders may role play as follows:

> *Bill (leader):*   Because listening that is really meaningful in a relationship is not just passive hearing, we like to call this listening that we do with one another *active* listening. It is active—it is an activity in itself, not just the absence of doing something else while our partner is talking to us. There are several skills involved in active listening. The first is attending, which we have been talking about. Two others are paraphrasing content and asking for confirmation. *Paraphrasing content* means that we repeat back to our partner what we have understood them to be saying. *Asking for confirmation* means that we ask them if we are correct. "Have I understood what you are trying to say?" is the message we are conveying. To make this clear, Sue and I will demonstrate these for you. Sue, let's pick up where we left off.
>
> (Bill and Sue assume attending positions.)
>
> *Sue (leader):*   OK. What you are saying to me is that you are upset about the checkbook and angry because you think I've spent too much money. Is that right?
>
> *Bill (leader):*   Yes!
>
> *Sue (leader):*   I know I've spent a lot lately, but we talked about it last winter. I thought we agreed that we really needed to be careful for a few months until we had paid off Visa. So I didn't buy anything for myself or for the kids in terms of clothes. But the bill is paid off, and they were having this great preseason sale on coats and school clothes, so I decided to take advantage of it. I thought I had told you that we were going to have

to spend some money on clothes before school starts.

Bill (leader): So you're saying that you thought we had an agreement that once the charge bill was paid off, you could buy the things that you and the kids need.

Sue (leader): Well, you're partly right. But it isn't just the things *I* think we need. You agreed that my winter coat was pretty scruffy, and both kids have outgrown their stuff from last winter.

Bill (leader): So you're saying that you thought *we* had agreed to make those purchases.

Sue (leader): Right!

Bill (leader): I remember talking about it. It just really caught me by surprise because you hadn't said anything about it and I didn't know what that big bill was for.

Sue (leader): (Turns to the group.) What did you see?

Doug: Both of you tried to repeat back what the other one was saying.

Barb: You were attending the whole time.

Lou: When one of you didn't think the other was understanding you, you tried to say it another way.

Bill (leader): You're good observers!

George: It sounded really artificial to me. I don't need my wife to be a parrot.

Sue (leader): Oh, I agree. This is not helpful if all you are doing is parroting what is said. But there are a lot of times, especially on important issues or when there is a disagreement brewing, that it can help everyone to be clear. But you are right. This is certainly not something you are going to do every time someone says something.

Kate: So you're saying that this is to use when we're afraid there is going to be trouble?

Bill (leader):   Not necessarily just then. It's useful any time there is the possibility that you might not understand or be understood. It is also a great way to communicate to your partner that what they are saying and how they feel are important to you.

Sue (leader):   Like all skills, this has to be practiced. I hope you will try this out and give yourself some time to experiment with it before you decide whether it will be helpful for you. We are going to spend some time now practicing these skills.

The leaders initiate the Active Listening exercise (B-2) in which members practice the skills in small groups. This exercise provides the opportunity for skill learning at the levels of observation, conceptualization, and imitation. For this and subsequent issues that teach these skills, each couple is paired with another couple who will observe their interaction and give them feedback on their use of skills. Observing couples are given a handout that provides brief definitions of the skills. In this and in any other activity in which individual couples or small groups are expected to proceed without the leader, it is extremely important for leaders to give clear instructions and to have members illustrate active listening by repeating the instructions and raising questions about the assignment. The leaders should also emphasize that upon request they will consult with a couple or small group during the activity. The exercise is then processed in the group.

When the couples have completed the activity, the leaders may begin a group discussion with such questions as What did you find difficult? and In what ways was active listening helpful? By encouraging participants to share their experience and involving them in evaluation of the learning, leaders can correct any misperceptions and can reinforce the learning that has occurred. Also, this kind of discussion aids affective learning—as couples respond to their experience, they begin to see the value of the skills. Therefore, leaders should encourage discussion of applicability. Also, all group members need reinforcement for their participation in the discussion. Participants should be encouraged to talk with one another instead of directing all their comments and questions to the leaders in order to facilitate group formation and develop the norm of acceptance of the contributions of all members. Discussion should also focus on the *process* of using skills, not on the *content*—that is, not on the particular issue being discussed. Furthermore, it is important to remember that the members, not the leaders, should dominate the discussion. It should not become a minilecture or a question-and-answer session in which the leaders function as the central figures. The group will, of course, be most comfortable in this initial phase of development if the leaders provide structure and leadership in both task and socioemotional dimensions. However, the more the leaders can involve participants in these leadership functions, the easier it will be for the group to move through the transitional conflict stage of its development.

A follow-up discussion may proceed as follows:

Jan: This was really hard. It felt very fake. I felt like I was just saying the same words over again that George had just said to me.

George: That may be how you felt, but I liked hearing what I just had said. Maybe I'm just egotistical. (group laughter)

Bill (leader): I think what you're saying is really important, Jan. Any new skill feels very awkward at first. I can remember when I was trying to learn to drive a stick shift and the car bucked and jumped and finally died. Awkward was hardly the word for it! (Heads nod in the group.) Communication skills are the same way. It's only when we know them so well that we don't have to think about them any

more, that we do them naturally—and then they
are really helpful. I hardly ever think about letting
the clutch in and out while shifting gears any more.
Does that make sense? (nods) Did anybody else
feel like George did?

(Bill is here trying to urge members to talk to one
another. He responds to Jan's observations, but he
also wants group members to respond to one another.)

Kathryn: I don't think you're egotistical, George,
just because you want your wife to understand
you. It means a lot to me when I feel like Bob understands me. It even helps me not be so mad when
I know he disagrees with me if he at least understands where I'm coming from.

(Sue and Bill are nodding, agreeing, leaning toward
Kathryn. She is discussing the value of the skills,
and she is talking to George; thus members are beginning to interact. Leaders want to reinforce this
group interaction.)

During the final hour of the session, leaders introduce
skills of paraphrasing of feeling and suspending judgment in
conflict. For this introduction, it may be useful to paraphrase
the following quotations from Rogers (1961, pp. 333-334):
"(1) If you really understand another person in this way, if you
are willing to enter his private world and the way life appears to
him, without any attempt to make evaluative judgments, you
may run the risk of being changed yourself; you might see it his
way. . . . (2) It is just when emotions are strongest that it is
most difficult to achieve the frame of reference of the other
person or group, yet this is the time the attitude is most needed,
if communication is to be established." (Additional materials on
these skills can be found in Otto, 1976; Gordon, 1975; and Bernard, 1964.) The leader should avoid dealing with conflict
management per se but should present the two skills as providing those interactional patterns conducive to handling conflict
constructively.

Bill and Sue would therefore first define *paraphrasing of feeling* and *suspending judgment in conflict* and then move into a demonstration role play:

Sue: (With her hands on her hips, she is shouting, and walking across the room away from Bill.) How could you do this to me? I have said over and over how tired I am, how rough things are at work, so you take it upon yourself to invite the Smiths over for dinner tomorrow night without even checking with me first. And now I'm supposed to fix some delicious meal and entertain people I hardly know.

Bill: I'm hearing from you that you are really angry with me for inviting them, and that you feel really ignored. You have been telling me how much pressure you have been feeling and now you feel me just adding to it instead of trying to help you.

Sue: (Moving back toward Bill, she is still angry but speaks in a lower tone.) That's exactly right! So if you understand so well, why did you do it?

Bill: (looking at Sue) I know you have felt really under the gun lately, but the result has been that we haven't done anything for fun—it's just been work, work, work. I think it would really help me, and you too, to try to get away from it for an evening. I know you don't know them very well, but I really enjoy John's friendship at work. He is a great guy and really easy going. I want you to loosen up, and I think you will really like them. I didn't intend for you to cook; I thought we would just order a pizza and I'll toss a salad.

Sue: So you've been feeling a lot of pressure lately, and part of it is there's been no letup. So to help us both, you planned what you thought would be a fun escape kind of evening, and now you're feeling attacked because I jumped down your throat.

Bill: (to the group) What did you observe?

Doug: She's hot! (laughter)

Jan: You really pulled a fast one. It seems to me like you should have checked with her first.

Sue: How did you hear our discussion? Did we seem to be using the skills we've talked about?

(Sue is trying to direct the group toward a discussion on the process of communication rather than on the content.)

George: You weren't just parroting what had been said. Bill, you seemed to be reaching beyond her anger to the hurt and frustration she was feeling and mirroring that for her.

Bob: Instead of trying to explain yourself, you first let her know that you understand that she was angry. And was she ever!

Bill (leader): Beyond telling me she was angry, how did you know she was so mad?

Doug: She just *looked* it!

Bill (leader): What do you mean? How did she look?

Doug: It's those hands on the hips, that wagging head.

Jan: Yeah. And she got so far away from you—almost like to give herself room to yell.

Barb: But when you paraphrased her feelings, she began to move back closer and lower her voice. You kind of took the wind out of her sails when you were so understanding.

Bill (leader): So me paraphrasing her feelings came across as being understanding? (nods and yeahs from the group)

Sue (leader): So active listening involves not just paraphrasing words but also putting words to—describing—what we see the other doing. But we do this *tentatively.* Sometimes the meaning of non-verbal behavior is pretty clear—like hands on the hips. Other times, we may think we understand, but the feeling is not what we think it is. For instance, a scowl on the face may be interpreted as anger when we are really thinking hard about something. Have you ever had one of those frustrating arguments where you try to convince someone you're not angry when they think you are? This happens when we *assume* we understand our partner without checking out our inferences first.

This activity provides for skill learning at the levels of observation and conceptualization, and affective learning at the responding level.

Once the skills have been explained and demonstrated, and the group has analyzed its use in the role-play situation, couples are engaged in the Understanding One Another exercise (B-3). In this activity a couple chooses an issue which has caused conflict between them and by using active listening skills attempts to learn each other's thoughts and feelings about the issue. At the same time the couple receives feedback on their skill usage from observing couples. This activity provides for skill learning at the level of imitation. When couples are choosing some aspect of their relationship to discuss with the group leaders must emphasize that *both* partners agree on the appropriateness of a particular issue. One spouse should never be coerced into sharing an experience or discussing an issue that he or she considers private.

During these small group practice sessions, couples are not only learning skills but also are sharing their marital experiences with one another. They are developing intercouple relationships, discovering that they share common stresses, and learning methods of coping that others have used. Thus, the group cohesiveness is continuing to develop. In terms of the skill learning, leaders should move from group to group during the practice sessions to model helpful skill-oriented feedback. Feedback must be concrete and specific, and leaders should help couples develop the ability to provide this kind of feedback from the beginning of the program.

For example, Bill might move from group to group as couples practice the active listening skills; he may join a group while one couple, Lou and Jim, are talking and another couple, George and Kate, are listening and providing feedback:

> *Jim:* I know what you want—you want me to work all day and then come home and cut the grass, take care of the cars, and then do half the work in the house, too.
>
> *Lou:* Sometimes, I don't even think you try to understand. If you don't understand, then you won't have to do anything.
>
> *Kate:* I think you're getting angry instead of trying to understand what he's saying.
>
> *Bill (leader):* (talking to Kate) Kate, instead of trying to figure out Lou's motivation for saying what she said, why don't you try helping her use the active listening skills she's learned? Can you help her rephrase what she says to Jim?
>
> *Kate:* OK. Instead of telling him that you think he doesn't want to understand, why don't you see if you can understand what he's saying? Can you paraphrase what he just said and what he's feeling?
>
> *Lou:* (to Jim) What I'm hearing is that you think you are supposed to work and do the outside chores and then do the inside stuff too, and you are feeling really pushed and like I don't appreciate what you are already doing.
>
> *Jim:* Yeah.

Lou: But I don't *want* you to do more. I just want us to be more flexible . . . .

(Bill moves to another group.)

At the end of the session, leaders assign homework: each couple is to take home and complete the Fill in the Blank exercise (D-3) and then discuss their answers. During their discussion they are to concentrate on practicing the skills of active listening. To give the leaders some information on the spouses' use of the skills in everyday life, each participant is also asked to complete six Daily Rating of Spouse's Communication forms (see Activity B-2 in Resource A). Each spouse completes one of these handouts each day, preferably at the end of the evening. The form, which can be done quickly, helps participants focus on the skills throughout the week. This activity encourages skills learning at the level of precision, and when performed in later weeks, at the levels of coordination and habituation. It also encourages affective learning at the level of valuing, and later at the levels of organization and characterization. Spouses may or may not choose to share their ratings with each other although sharing may provide useful feedback on skill usage. Leaders should point out, however, that the ratings are not negotiable—that is, spouses are not to argue about whether they have been rated unfairly. The ratings are indicators of spouse *perceptions,* which may or may not correspond with how spouses view themselves.

In making homework assignments, leaders need to keep in mind the many other demands on couples' time and be realistic about the amount of time and energy couples can devote to homework. Therefore, the assignments should be structured. They should have identifiable limits, such as a set amount of time to work on a particular issue, and should result in an identifiable product—a discussion, a written assignment or filled-out form, a note, and so on. What participants are expected to do should be clearly specified; having participants repeat what leaders are requiring helps to ensure that they are being understood. Finally, assignments should be described as experimental—"try this for a week" rather than "from now on do this." Couples are more apt to try an activity if it is introduced tentatively; it thus becomes less threatening. If certain behavior improves the quality of their relationship over one week, they can then implement the change for a longer period.

Session 3. The content of this session will focus on conflict management and decision making, and the use of active listening skills as they enhance these processes. Leaders will first ask for a discussion of the homework assignment, including the rating forms. This will give participants an opportunity to ask questions and raise issues that need to be addressed.

During the first forty-five minutes, the leaders will role play a marital conflict, not always using the active listening skills. The group will be asked to give feedback to the leaders on their use of skills. This allows the leaders to help participants develop useful feedback skills. An abbreviated version of leaders' role play follows.

> *Bill (leader):*   I am sick and tired of your pulling the weeds out of the flower beds and throwing them on the lawn after I've cut it. Not only does it look awful, but the seeds get in and I end up having to fight a weedy lawn.
>
> *Sue (leader):*   Well, that certainly is an important issue! Shall we call the lawyer now?
>
> (The leader looks toward the group, nonverbally asking for input.)
>
> *George:*   You are blasting him out of the water again. You need to paraphrase his message.
>
> *Sue (leader):*   OK. It sounds like you're really frustrated when you work so hard on the lawn, and then I don't seem to take it seriously enough to pick up the weeds.
>
> *Bill (leader):*   Yeah.
>
> *Sue (leader):*   But what am I supposed to do with

the weeds? It's not like I do that on purpose. But I've got the baby to watch, and it seems to me if I get called away in the middle of it, you would understand. I was going to pick them up, but he woke up from his nap. And the last time, the phone rang and it was your mother.

Bill (leader): So you're saying you try, but other things are more important than my needs. (turning to the group) How are we doing?

Kate: You sound like you're trying to understand, but you are really using your rephrasing as a way to get in another dig. I think you need to say something like, "So what you're saying is you didn't do it on purpose and you wish I would quit bugging you."

Sue (leader): That is really good feedback. You're focusing on how skillful we are in communicating, and giving us some good ideas of how to understand one another better.

Leaders then ask for a volunteer couple to replay the scene using active listening skills. Again, the group is asked to give feedback. This feedback particularly needs to emphasize the positives so that volunteering behavior in the group is reinforced. If the leaders are not able to obtain two volunteers, one leader may replay the scene along with one volunteer. In this way, without making couples feel that their marriages are on the spot, the leaders can guide the group to take on more responsibility for leadership and direction of its learning. Participants can begin to increase their involvement in the group's activities.

The continuing focus on group activities and group involvement is also important because the group may be moving into the conflictual stage of development during this session. The leaders are encouraging this growth by focusing on marital conflict and by emphasizing group interaction rather than intra-couple activities. Throughout this session and the following sessions, the leaders should be sensitive to the group's need to discuss or challenge its role and its normative structures. These discussions will provoke an examination of marital conflict; leaders may need to point out the parallels between group conflict and marital conflict.

In the next thirty minutes, leaders present the effective use of I-messages, based on material from Miller, Nunnally, and Wackman (1975). To demonstrate this technique, leaders first role play a marital discussion using you-messages and ask participants to share their observations. Next, leaders replay the same issue using I-messages. Again, the participants are asked to share their observations.

These two role plays may be presented as follows:

Bill (leader):   You constantly harp on picky things. If things aren't done to suit you, you just get mad. What difference does it make if I don't pick up the Sunday paper when I'm through reading it? It's not the end of the world. If it bugs you so much, pick it up, but quit nagging me about stupid stuff.

Sue (leader):   I can't believe you are so selfish, so uncaring. It's not just the Sunday paper, it's your whole attitude—like I'm just hired help to run around and pick up after you. You don't care how I feel, or how tired I get of living with a slob. (turning to the group) What did you observe?

Kate: That hurt! You can be really nasty! You called one another a lot of names. And it sounded very hurtful.

George: Neither of you was really trying to understand the other. You weren't listening.

Lou: But it's really hard to listen and say, "I hear you saying that I'm a slob." Who wants to paraphrase that?

Bill (leader):   I think you're right. In order to be listened to, we have to say things in a way the other can hear. Did you hear all the "you's" in what we were saying? We did a lot of blaming and very little sharing of our own thoughts and feelings. It's really helpful if instead of talking about "you," I can talk about myself—"I feel . . . I think . . . I want . . . ." Let's play it again so you'll see what I mean.

Bill (leader):   I am really tired of your being angry about papers in the living room. I don't understand why I can't leave the paper on the floor without your getting upset. A neat house is not very important to me, and I don't understand why if it bothers you, you can't just take care of it without getting angry.

Sue (leader):   If it were just the Sunday paper, it wouldn't bother me. But I spend so much time every day picking up toys, clothes, and dirty dishes. I really don't care if the house is neat all of the time, but I don't like being the only one who does the picking up. I feel unappreciated, and I wish that you would recognize that I feel really cared for when you put your stuff away. I know it sounds silly in a way, but I feel loved when you do something like put the Sunday paper away when you really don't care if it's on the floor or not. (turning to the group) What was different?

John: You still weren't using active listening, but you didn't sound as angry.

Lou: Instead of blaming, you were telling one another how you felt and what you wanted. You weren't attacking one another.

With these role plays, members begin to learn how to use I-messages. The activity also helps the group to examine communication styles, which either manage or heighten conflict. This set of expression skills is complementary to the listening skills being emphasized in the group. The I messages also may help participants present their thoughts and feelings about the group.

At this point, the group is ready to focus the remainder of the session on marital conflict. Leaders explain the various causes of arguing such as the misplacement of anger (spouse is the focus of anger generated by another person or event), a disagreement about the facts of an issue, or a conflict in attitudes and values (Garland, 1978). Leaders stress that couples need to define the causes behind their arguments.

Leaders next introduce the Win/Win Conflict Negotiation activity (C-1). Leaders illustrate these skills using a role play and group discussion. In small groups couples practice the model using personal issues while other participants coach and observe. Leaders stress that couples are to continue to practice the active listening skills and that the other participants are to provide feedback on these skills. Thus couples approach the levels of precision and coordination as they use these skills in more difficult discussions that focus more on content than on skill practice per se.

In activities that allow couples to try out some new skill and/or discuss a particular aspect of their relationship, it is essential that all couples have equal opportunity for participation and learning. To ensure this involvement, leaders may have to structure time and be strict in its management. This direction may anger the group and thus provide a situation in which the group can express conflict and begin to restructure the roles of leaders and participants.

For example, Bill and Sue may structure the time they allot for a small group activity so that each of three couples in a group can have time to practice the win/win model on a conflict situation of their own. When each couple's allotted time has elapsed, they may announce, "Time—move on to the next couple." When the large group reconvenes to discuss the activity, the following conversation, which exemplifies the process of conflict development, may take place:

> *John:*   It really bugs me when you call time and
> expect us to just drop where we are and move on

to the next couple. One of the couples in our group was in the midst of an important discussion and you just cut them off.

Kate: I agree. It seems to me that what we are talking about is much more important than staying on your time schedule. After all, I thought we were here to help one another.

Bill (leader):   So I'm hearing from you that you don't like us monitoring the time—that you're angry that we are trying to be in charge too much. Are you saying that you would like to have more input into how we spend our time?

Bob: I think so. I don't think we need you to tell us what time it is. Sometimes, I would like just to forget about what you have planned for us to do and do what is important to us.

Sue (leader):   So you are saying you want to have more say in whether or not we stick with our agenda?

George: Well, I, for one, want to hear what you all have to say. We get off on tangents, and I want you to call us back.

John: But, George, I don't think they are tangents. I think we were talking about some important issues in our group and we got cut off. (several nods and yeahs in the group)

Sue (leader):   So you would like for us to check with you to see if you are ready to move on rather than enforcing some time constraint on you. I am comfortable with that. What about you, Bill?

Bill (leader):   That's OK with me. There are some issues we agreed to cover as a group, but we can always be open to changing our goals to allow more time for discussion. What do you think, George?

As homework, couples should discuss for twenty minutes a minor conflict using the win/win steps. Couples are to be aware of the use of active listening skills in their interaction. They are also assigned to complete the Daily Rating of Spouse's Communication form for another week.

Session 4. The content of this session focuses on sexuality and how the use of active listening skills aids sexual adjustment in the marital relationship. Again, leaders begin the session with a discussion of the homework assignment, including the rating forms.

Leaders introduce the Inside and Outside Circles exercise (E-1). In this activity the men are seated in a circle, with their wives seated directly behind them; the male leader leads the men in a discussion of their experiences of sexual development. Men and women then switch places. This activity helps couples to begin to develop some ease in discussing sexuality and an awareness that their spouse and other group members have had similar experiences. Spouses often learn a great deal about one another in this activity. This exercise can be an effective group-building tool because it often involves a great deal of self-disclosure and group discussion, which are important if the group is moving to new role structures and expectations and is in transition from the conflictual to the interdependent phase of group development. New roles are being tested and affirmed, and emerging group leaders will begin to perform more of the socioemotional and task functions in the group.

To feel increasingly comfortable about discussing sexuality and to prepare couples to talk with one another about their own sexual relationship, the group spends the next twenty minutes on the Brainstorming About Sex exercise (E-4). In this exercise participants are asked to brainstorm words that relate to sexuality, including sexual anatomy. Often this activity produces laughter, which can help release tension resulting from group conflict and can also reaffirm group cohesiveness.

During the next hour the group views and discusses the film *Sexuality and Communication.* The movie enhances the cognitive learning about sexuality and encourages examination of sexual development and current attitudes and feelings about it. It also provides the basis for a discussion between spouses, in which the listening skills can be practiced. Thus spouses are being given another opportunity to put the skills to use.

Couples should find a private place to discuss their own sexual relationship, using the Assessing Our Sexual Relationship exercise (E-3) and incorporating active listening skills. Leaders should respect each couple's privacy; they may announce that they will be available for consultation if any individual couple would like to talk with them during the exercise.

Leaders should reconvene the group near the end of the session so that it can address issues that were raised in the dialogues and can discuss reactions to the evening's session. By this time, leaders will be taking less of a leadership role in the group's discussions. Now they will be focusing on eliciting the participants' responses, connecting members with each other by commenting on nonverbal behavior exhibited during the discussion, and asking questions that generate involvement, which all supplement the leadership generated by the group itself. The group's focus at this point will probably have turned away from the group's development and the development of roles and norms—the socioemotional dimension—and moved toward the goals of enriching couples' marriages—the task dimension. Members will have developed the ability to work toward group goals, to give feedback to one another and the leaders, and to discuss together what they have and have not accomplished in the group.

For example, the following discussion might take place when the group reconvenes after completing the Assessing Our Sexual Relationship exercise:

George: Now don't expect us to tell you what we talked about! (group laughter)

Bill (leader):   No, but *how* you talked is something we might want to look at. Were the communication skills we have been working on helpful here?

Kate: I think so. I don't think we have ever really

sat down and put into words what we have been trying to say to one another nonverbally all these years. I certainly understand my husband a lot better now.

Sharon: But it was hard! There are some things that are really hard to talk about!

Kate: Oh, I think so, too. But how else can we really understand one another?

Bob: I personally feel kind of relieved. I can't believe how hard it is for us to talk about sex when we talk so openly about other things and when we are really pretty comfortable with our sexual relationship. Now some things have been put into words, and I think it's like a dam broke. I think the words will keep flowing now.

Sue (leader): Doug, you started to say something.

Doug: Well, I'm not sure how to say it, but it really helped me to talk about this, because a lot of times I don't know what I am thinking or feeling myself until I put it into words. I not only understand my wife better, but I also understand myself better. (several yeahs in the group)

Session 5. The content of this session focuses on roles and values and the use of active listening skills in these areas of marital adjustment. After discussing any unresolved issues from Session 4 and the week's experiences using active listening skills, the leaders introduce the topic of how the roles assumed in marriage affect decision making. The participants are asked to participate in the Decision Making exercise (C-2). In this activity couples fill out a questionnaire about decision making in their relationship. Spouses then discuss their responses with each other while another couple observes and gives feedback about their use of the skills. Finally, couples as a group discuss their experiences with this exercise.

During the next forty-five minutes the members participate in the Priorities exercise (D-5). In this activity leaders describe a hypothetical situation: each person in the group has six months to live and must plan how to spend that remaining time. In the discussion of their plans with spouses and with the group, leaders ask participants to identify values they are not currently enacting that they would like to develop more fully. The group then moves into the Couple Time exercise (D-2). In this activity members chart their daily schedules during a typical week and identify periods of time spent alone, with the family, with a spouse focusing on their relationship, and focusing on household management. By examining the concept of time in both of these activities, spouses discuss with each other the current state of their relationship and expectations for their relationship. This interaction provides an important opportunity to use the active listening skills, thus moving closer to the coordination and habituation levels of skill learning.

Because the next session is the final one, the group is approaching closure. The activities should now focus on couples rather than the group and provide the opportunity for each couple to begin to develop goals that extend beyond the marriage enrichment group. The leaders need to discuss explicitly the ending that is approaching. They may want to facilitate plans for having a celebration in the final session—a potluck dinner or special refreshments. The homework assigned in this session is the Sharing My Feelings with You exercise (E-2). Again, couples are reminded to practice the skills and complete the Daily Rating of Spouse's Communication forms. By this time, participants should feel comfortable about both assignments.

Session 6. This is the group's final session. It is important to discuss the homework and complete any unfinished discussion from the previous session. Also, an hour should be allotted during this session to administer the posttesting. Then the group can discuss the testing and participants' reactions to the group experience. Leaders should ask participants to describe the program activities or discussions they deem the most meaningful and the least meaningful. Leaders should also solicit feedback on what members consider the most helpful and least helpful leader behavior. During this discussion leaders should refrain as much as possible from giving direct input. Their role should be to facilitate the responses of others rather than to respond directly to either participants' praise or criticism. This discussion serves a dual purpose: it provides the leaders with useful information about how participants have experienced their leadership and the group itself and it helps participants to summarize their experience for themselves and feel a sense of closure.

During the final hour of the session, each couple meets with another couple to evaluate their progress on the skills and to establish some goals to work on in the next six weeks. Leaders then ask couples to share these goals when the entire group reconvenes. The couples should be advised before beginning this activity that they will be asked to share with the group but may decline if they so desire. It is always important for leaders to warn couples that they will be asked to discuss with the entire group or with a small group work done privately with spouses; thus they are not caught by surprise and can avoid embarrassment about sharing a private issue or about not participating.

The goal-planning activity is a method of carrying over the group experience to couples' lives outside the group. It is often helpful for couples to discuss factors that will interfere with their goals and how they plan to deal with these. During this time, several couples may agree to meet to reinforce the group experience and to continue the sharing they found useful. At this point, the group no longer needs professional leadership, although the leaders may still function as consultants to the support group.

The group and the leaders plan to meet again in six weeks. That session will serve two important purposes: (1) to provide a session for evaluation testing to measure the durability of skills learning and (2) to give couples an opportunity to encourage each other in continuing to work on their established goals.

A Marriage Enrichment Retreat

The marriage enrichment retreat presented here is somewhat different from the program just outlined: in this example,

an existing group engages a leader to help it achieve marital enrichment objectives.

In a local church, Sam Davis, the teacher of a Sunday
school class of young married couples, decides that a retreat focusing on some of the issues relevant to young couples—and on
constructive ways of addressing those issues—will be very useful
to class members. In addition, he thinks such an event would be
ideal for establishing relationships that would help the group
develop more cohesiveness and mutual support as they tackle issues of young marriage and as they address other class goals.
When the teacher proposes to the class that they go on a retreat,
the idea is met with enthusiastic approval. The class and teacher
talk about their objectives for the retreat. The members want to
learn some techniques for coping with marital conflict, they
want some time as a group to get to know one another; they
would also like to spend some time alone with their spouses in a
relaxing environment away from the demands of home and
work.

With the group's approval, the teacher then contacts a
counselor from a church counseling center. Together the teacher and counselor explore the group's objectives for the retreat.
They agree that the counselor will lead the marriage enrichment
portion of the retreat; the teacher and the group will use the remainder of the time for unstructured sports activities, relaxation, and socializing.

The counselor suggests that the focus of the retreat be
on making good marriages better; couples will not feel as threatened as they would if the focus was on solving problems or if no
focus was provided. This theme also helps provide an emphasis
on learning and relationship enhancement rather than on remediation. Together the teacher and the counselor (retreat leader)
define the following objectives for the retreat:

1. Participants will develop an attitude of acceptance toward
    conflict in a marital relationship. They will recognize that
    conflict is both healthy and typical and that it provides the
    basis for continual adjustment to changing needs. (This in-
    volves affective learning at the level of valuing; couples will

demonstrate feelings of appreciation for the outcomes of constructive conflict.)
2. Participants will learn that certain skills help handle conflict and will be introduced to some of those skills. (This involves skill learning at the conceptualization and imitation levels. The affective learning at the level of valuing however, is more important; participants learn the value of skills in handling conflict. A retreat provides neither the time nor the structures for participants to learn the skills adequately. However, this new appreciation for skill learning can prepare the group for additional learning later.)
3. Participants will build relationships with one another through which they can be mutually supportive. (This objective involves affective learning at the level of valuing. Couples learn to value a support group in which members share struggles and victories.)

The teacher agrees to present these objectives to the class for approval or modification. The class agrees that the objectives reflect its goals, and the leader therefore plans the retreat around them.

Theoretical Approach. The objectives for the retreat primarily involve affective learning and are clearly in the domain of the church-related marriage enrichment approaches. The group hopes to engender a belief in the continuing growth and change that produce a viable marital relationship. The group is also attempting to challenge the intermarital taboo (Hopkins and others, 1978), which insulates married couples from one another. Finally, through the church, the group is attempting to develop an ongoing support system for marriage. Therefore, the program needs to include activities that explore attitudes and values about marriage and about participants' own marital relationship, that engender a sense of hope and excitement about the potential for change and growth in participants' marriages.

Group Membership. The counselor who has been asked to lead the retreat has little control over who will participate in it. This retreat group consists of ten couples who already know one another and have established at least an initial group identity. The group is homogeneous in age and stage in the family life cycle, and the members share a common belief system. However, the leader does not know the marital adjustment levels of the group members. The teacher may know whether any of the couples are having significant adjustment difficulties, and the knowledge may be helpful. However, the leader must be prepared for a variance in levels of adjustment. Selecting the theme "making good marriages better" helps to establish the expectation that this experience will not focus on individual problems. Nonetheless, during the unstructured periods of the retreat, the leader may talk privately with couples who request consultation. Such conferences should not be construed as the beginning of marital therapy. The leader should be brief in these sessions and serve as a referral source if couples desire counseling. Establishing a therapeutic contract at this time with a couple would be a violation of the group's objectives and might interfere with goal achievement—the couple might find it difficult to distinguish between the counselor's roles in therapy, where the focus is on solving problems, and in the group, where the focus is on enhancing relationship strengths. Of course, the leader might agree to work with a couple after the retreat weekend or can make referrals.

Because the group members already have established initial relationships with one another, the dependence stage of the group will probably be shortened. Activities during this phase should focus on developing the group's relationship with the leader and deciding how the group will function in this retreat context, which is different from the one-hour Bible class that meets on Sunday mornings.

Group Goals. A retreat setting is ideal for learning attitudes and values. Though the group initially wanted to include skill learning in its objectives, members had to modify the goal because of limitations inherent in the retreat format: limited amount of time, limited opportunity to try out new learning in the home setting, and lack of opportunity for group feedback and skill refinement. In addition to the retreat setting's capabilities for developing attitudes and values, it is also conducive to building the group as an ongoing support system.

Group Leadership. As was decided, the counselor, Sue, leads the group. The group's program focuses on attitudes and values, which do not require the close monitoring and feedback needed in skill practice. However, the class teacher, Sam, who is already a designated leader, becomes involved too. Sue asks the teacher to help her with demonstrations and other presentations and activities that require two leaders. Because of the nature of this group, a nonprofessional trained marriage enrichment leader rather than a helping professional may have been chosen to lead the group.

Generalization and Maintenance. Participants in a retreat often find it difficult to generalize and maintain their learning in the home and work environments; the retreat is removed from the everyday setting. Furthermore, it usually does not provide for a follow-up session. However, because the participants belong to an ongoing group, the class itself, strengthened by group-building activities, can encourage its participants to maintain and build on changes that result from the retreat experience.

Learning Activities. Many of the activities selected for the retreat are those used for the groups working on communication skills. However, they are organized differently and have different emphases and objectives. Activities are, after all, tools to be used and modified according to needs; they are not ends in themselves.

The retreat is held in a lodge in a nearby state park. The group does its own cooking. The program begins with the supper meal on Friday evening and ends late Saturday evening. Shortly after Friday's evening meal, couples are asked to fill out a brief attitudinal questionnaire about marriage in general and their marital relationship specifically. The leader explains that this survey, taken again at the end of the retreat, will be used both to adapt the learning activities to meet the group's needs and to provide information about the effectiveness of the weekend. The leader assures couples that their responses will be held in complete confidence.

The leader continues this first session by having spouses share how they met each other and what had attracted them to one another. Thus in a nonthreatening way, the counselor directs couples into an examination of their marriage. Sharing these stories usually generates a great deal of laughter in the group and helps participants to feel comfortable with one another in their new format. This activity also sets the ground for the support group, which it is hoped, will develop. Sue, the leader, decides to share how she met her husband and why she was attracted to him. She is brief because her husband is not present, and furthermore, she does not want to dominate the group. However, her interaction helps the group to know her better and makes her part of the group. She also tells a story about "the funniest moment in our life together" and then asks the group members to share their own stories. Again, this activity relieves a great deal of anxiety as the group laughs together and shares with one another. The group's mood is characterized by sharing, ease, and excitement about knowledge members are gaining of one another.

The leader next begins to introduce active listening skills. She explains that often couples have difficulty understanding one another because neither spouse really listens. The leader uses the Active Listening exercise (B-2) and asks the teacher to demonstrate the skills with her. This role play is similar to one used in the marriage enrichment group whose focus is communication skills. Couples practice the skills in small groups of three couples, discussing the topics "what I think you contribute to our relationship" and "what I want to see happen in our relationship during the next year." These topics serve a dual purpose: couples learn skills, and begin to share positive aspects of their relationship. The group has moved from recounting the past to discussing the present and future. The emphasis is still on strengths of the relationship and couples are continuing to share with one another. Therefore, skill learning is occurring at the levels of observation, conceptualization, and imitation. Attitudinal learning is occurring at the levels of receiving and responding. Participants are choosing to be involved, and are becoming interested both in finding out more about one another and in learning skills that can be helpful to them.

As the final planned activity of the evening, the leader introduces the Sharing My Feelings with You exercise (E-2). Having moved from large-group sharing to small-group skills practice and significant disclosures about their relationship, spouses now discuss privately their feelings about their marital relationship. This activity provides time for couples to practice the new skills while discussing positive aspects of their marriage. It also creates a sense of intimacy. The formal structure of the evening session ends with this activity. Couples now begin their late evening recreation and informal sharing. The positive experiences of the evening have presumably set the stage for sharing that is enjoyable and that builds group cohesiveness.

The Saturday morning session begins with work on marital conflict. Beginning with this topic provides sufficient time to work on it and allows couples to discuss it before becoming fatigued from the day's activities. The Win/Win Conflict Negotiation activity (C-1) is introduced along with a discussion of conflict in marriage. In small groups couples are given the opportunity to practice the negotiation procedure by working through an actual conflict agreed upon by both partners. Participants are now being directed not only toward a discussion of their current relationship but also toward some problematic areas of the relationship. This may take a great deal of time; the leader should be particularly active in helping the groups focus on their task of practicing the conflict management techniques.

For example, the leader, Sue, may move from group to group to listen to couples discuss conflictual issues using the model presented in the activity. She may join a group in the midst of John and Kathy's discussion of where they want to go for Christmas:

> *Kathy:*   So you want to stay home and I want to go to Missouri to see our folks. It seems like an either/or issue to me.
>
> *Jake (observer):*   These issues never have an answer. It's really tough.
>
> *Barb (observer):*   I personally think you ought to go visit your folks. After all, John, she wouldn't even be here if it weren't for your being in school.

Sue: Before you all choose up sides, perhaps it would be helpful if you see where you are with the model. It sounds like you have the issue pretty well defined and you've expressed your feelings about it. Maybe you could help John and Kathy to move to the brainstorming step, generating possible solutions. Remember, don't evaluate the ideas. Just think of as many as you can.

James (observer): You could go to Missouri this year and stay home the next.

Martha (observer): You could stay home this year and go to Missouri next year.

Kathy: I could go to Missouri and you could stay here.

Jake (observer): You could go someplace else, like on a cruise.

(Sue leaves the group; members are back to the task.)

At this point group members are providing support and skill guidance for one another—an objective of the retreat. The couples are also learning that these skills are valuable in dealing with important issues in their marital relationship. Before ending the morning session, the leader should reconvene the group for a discussion of couples' reactions to the exercise. A portion of this discussion follows:

Sue (leader): What kinds of reactions do you have to this activity?

John: It was really surprising to me that an issue that seems in some ways not very important, and I thought was being blown all out of proportion, is a problem for others, too.

Sue (leader): So you found that you were not alone in some of the issues that create problems for you.

(Instead of going into a lecture about the normalcy of conflict, she encourages the group to realize this through discussion.)

David: We found that, too. When Becky and Bill were talking, it could have just as well been Diane and me.

Karen: I never heard another couple disagree until today. My parents never fought—my Dad would just get very quiet. It has always scared me when Darrell and I have argued because I was afraid he would leave or something.

Darrell: And so we never really finish an argument. It gets started, and then we just drop it. I really would like to be able to learn how to reach some kind of conclusion so the same old issues won't keep coming up.

This discussion is key in crystallizing the new concepts that marital conflict is normal, that there are skills that can help it become constructive, and that the group can be instrumental in marital growth.

Group discussion is important now because the group is beginning to make changes in its own role structures and challenge the existing norms. For example, participants may be interacting in new ways. The new norm of risking a discussion of marital conflict with other couples demands a reorganization of how the members work together as a group. The group is probably also developing new leadership. Those participants who are skilled in facilitating sharing become increasingly important to task accomplishment.

An already-formed group such as this retreat group, in which the professional leader is involved for a relatively short time, will not usually experience overt conflict with the designated leader in this stage of its development although the possibility exists. The designated leader is probably viewed as an outsider, one who is consulting with the group but who will not stay with it. Therefore, challenges to current structure may occur more in relationships between members than in interactions with the designated leader. They may also occur in decision-making group contexts *outside* the planned retreat sessions: which recreational activities to engage in, whether the group will play together as a group, whether the group will divide into subgroups to go hiking, play cards, or go swimming, or whether couples will spend time on their own. Therefore, the designated leader should observe these group decisions so that the structured group sessions can complement the group's development and propel it toward interdependence. For example, Sue might observe that during the Friday night recreation time, the class teacher and Jake are instrumental in organizing the group for singing and charades. However, during the Saturday afternoon recreation time, when Jake tries to organize some softball teams, no one seems interested. Darrell and Karen suggest that members go for a hike instead. Several couples decide to go hiking and others choose to spend the afternoon swimming, hiking, or talking and sunning themselves on the front porch. Darrell says, "I think it would be better if we didn't all feel like we have to do the same thing. I think we have different interests and that is OK." The morning session's focus on the function of differences has been translated into the ability of group members to acknowledge their differences and to express conflict overtly (even though the conflict may be mild). Members are challenging the structure of the group, which has emphasized participation in a large group, by forming intimate small groups within the larger group. The leader's focus on conflict has facilitated this development in the group and observation of these changes will influence the leader's subsequent plans for and with the group.

Lunch and recreation time provide a needed break to relax after an intense morning and to assimilate what has been learned. At four o'clock the leader reconvenes the couples for an examination of changing roles of men and women and how these changes have affected their marriages. The Home Responsibilities exercise (D-1) is the guide for this investigation and it usually generates a great deal of discussion. It is important that the leader now function in a facilitative role, helping the group members talk with one another rather than to the leader. This discussion further establishes an awareness among the participants that they share similar difficulties and experience similar processes of changing demands, both within and outside the marriage, to which they are continually adjusting. An example of such a discussion follows:

> *Fran:*   I am amazed at how much frustration and resentment I was aware of when we did this activity. I think most of our arguments are about who does what.
>
> (long pause)
>
> *Sue (leader):*   Does anyone else feel the same way Fran does?
>
> (At this point, rather than talking directly to Fran or providing additional information to the group, Sue asks a question to generate group discussion and encourage the group to provide its own resources.)
>
> *Bob:*   I think we experience some of the same things. And it really isn't Barb's fault, but I get really frustrated with her just expecting me to do certain things because her dad always did. Why should I be any more responsible for checking the oil in the car than she is?
>
> *Joyce:*   I think that's it for me. It's not so much that I feel overly burdened or anything, but it's just the assumption—both mine and Tim's—that I do some things and he does others because that's the way our folks did it.
>
> *Bill:*   How can we be different?
>
> *Tim:*   Well, it seems like this little exercise is a start. There are some jobs I would like to negotiate with Joyce about; I want to take over some of the cooking and give up some of the yard work. I mean,

can you believe it? I'm the one allergic to Bermuda, yet I just assume that I have to endure and cut the grass.

At this point in the retreat, participants should feel comfortable with one another. The group should be in or rapidly moving toward the interdependent phase of its development. Once in this phase the group itself can provide support and encouragement to members as they work through marital issues. It should be noted, however, that this is the ultimate goal of interdependence. A group may not be able to make a complete transition from dependence to interdependence in a short weekend retreat in which significant amounts of time are devoted to couple activities rather than to group exercises. It thus may be more helpful to view the retreat as one experience in the group's existence, one which does not have to accomplish all the objectives that facilitate its development.

After dinner the group views the film *Sexuality and Communication* and is introduced to the Assessing Our Sexual Relationship exercise (E-3) in which each couple has private discussions. This activity is based on the assumption that sexual adjustment in the marital relationship is necessary and continuous; again, the objective of engendering a sense of the normalcy of conflict and adjustment is being addressed.

As the final activity of the evening, participants write love letters to their spouses. The leader provides paper and envelopes. This activity gives individuals an opportunity to examine the experiences of the retreat and their own feelings and attitudes about their marital relationship and its future. Thus changes that have occurred can be crystallized. The leader collects the sealed letters after assuring participants that the letters will not be opened and explains that they will be mailed the next week. This exercise helps to transfer the learning of the weekend to the home environment. Participants anticipate the arrival of their letters; their content serves as an impetus for couple dialogue at home and as a reminder and reinforcer of what the retreat meant to each partner. To further reinforce learning, the teacher agrees that a portion of the group's Sunday

School class the next week will be spent discussing couples' experiences and thoughts since the retreat. This discussion serves both as a reminder of the attitudes and feelings created at the retreat about a marital relationship, and as a method to continue the group's role as a support group and a forum for discussing growth in marriage.

The group adjourns for refreshments and a short recreation period before leaving for home. At this time, the participants complete the attitudinal questionnaire again so that the leader can determine what changes, if any, occurred during the retreat.

The two programs discussed in this chapter illustrate some of the principles involved in conceptualizing and conducting a marriage enrichment service. They are presented as models not because they are better than other approaches but because they point out essential components of a program and their relationships. The group objectives, its composition, and its structures (time and setting) determine the leadership style and activities that are most effective in reaching the group's goals. Structured activities, group discussions, and powerful leadership are only useful if they accomplish what they are designed to do—enrich marriages.

6

Common Problems in Marriage Enrichment Groups

No matter how well a group's program is planned, how dynamic the leader, and how committed the participants, inevitably the group will face problems—either an individual or couple will not be participating effectively or will experience a personal or relationship crisis, or the group as a whole will encounter barriers to reaching its objectives, such as lack of participation or disagreement with the leader's approach. It is not possible to address here all the problems that an enrichment group leader may face, but I will discuss those that are most likely to arise.

Because the group's focus is the marital relationships of the participants, it is inevitable that couples may face issues they have previously ignored in order to avoid conflict. Recognizing, for example, basic value differences may precipitate a marital crisis, which the couple may express to the group through argument, tears, or stony silence. However, it is not such overt signs that designate the situation a crisis so much as it is the spouses' feelings that an unavoidable crossroads has been reached —that they must face some decisions or changes and that they do not know how to proceed.

The ability of a marriage enrichment group to give definition to problems and crises is an important (but at times painful) advantage of participation. L'Abate (1981) has suggested that one of the fundamental functions of marriage enrichment is its ability to provide a context for the evaluation not only of a couple's strengths but also of the couple's need for other services. Leaders can obtain a great deal of understanding of a couple's relationship dynamics by observing their participation in group discussions and structured activities; that understanding can be useful in determining appropriate therapeutic strategies if the need for them arises. Although it is obvious that such an evaluative function is not a primary purpose of marriage enrichment, it can be extremely important to a leader who must cope —and help couples cope—with problems that arise in the group.

Choosing Leadership Strategies

There are several strategies that can be used when the leader becomes aware that a couple is in difficulty. In determining which strategy is most appropriate, the leader needs to address two factors simultaneously: what will be best for the couple and what will be best for the group, with the emphasis on maintaining goal-oriented processes for both. If a point of crisis is reached when a couple is working alone in a couple activity, the leader may ask if the couple wants his or her involvement at this point to help them deal with the crisis. This is usually only possible if there are two leaders, one of whom can continue to work with the rest of the group. In any case, a leader's involvement with such a couple should not extend beyond the time the rest of the group is spending on individual couple activities. Working with one couple while the rest of the group is engaged in a group activity not only identifies the couple as "troubled" but also defeats the marriage enrichment aim of dealing with crises as normal points of change and growth in a marital relationship.

If a couple needs more time than is available and appropriate in the session, or if the leader is working alone and cannot give individual attention, it may be best to schedule time after the session when the leader can meet with the couple. However, unless the contract between couple and leader is reevaluated, any time the leader spends with the couple should be limited to brief crisis intervention.

If a couple evidences a crisis during a group discussion or while other couples are observing that couple in dialogue, the leader can help by encouraging the group to identify with this kind of crisis through their own experiences. If the couple is willing, the leader can work with them to identify the basic issues and develop a plan for dealing with them in the group. Again, the leader is reinforcing the normalcy of crises and helping couples learn to deal with them. Of course, a crisis does not always occur when the leader has planned for the group to deal with conflict or values clarification, but to set aside a planned agenda may well be worthwhile.

Groups are often very uncomfortable with such open expressions of feelings as hostility, tears, loud voices, even when they are controlled. They violate the norms of expected behavior and generate the group's defensive mechanisms, mainly signals of withdrawal, which are designed to bring behavior back into an acceptable range. Members may express discomfort through silence, avoiding eye contact, and other nonverbal or even verbal expressions of embarrassment. If the behavior continues, the cohesion of the group is threatened. The leader therefore needs to actively take responsibility for the situation rather than wait for the group to handle it. Particularly when participants appear to be losing control—yelling, sobbing, or making threats—or if a spouse walks out, the leader needs to intervene to reverse the process, stabilize the group, and arrange to discuss the issue with the couple privately later. In such instances, the leader needs to call upon his or her skills as a therapist to accomplish this stabilization. Behavior that challenges the norms of the group usually should be regarded as a signal from the individual or couple that further intervention is needed, either through counseling with the leader or a referral source.

Let us look at an example of how a retreat leader might handle such a crisis. Let us imagine that after an exercise on home responsibilities, participants Cheri and Jim, in responding to the leader's question about what they experienced, develop the following interaction:

> *Cheri:* This has been very upsetting. I really didn't want to do this exercise, because I knew it would cause problems. Jim and I have some basic differences here, and he is simply unwilling to compromise. I realize that I haven't worked since Josh was born six months ago, but I plan to go back in another year or so, and he has used this to opt out of doing anything at home, including fathering his son.
>
> *Jim:* You're being unfair! She expects me to work all day, and some evenings, too, so the overtime can make up some for her not working. Then I'm supposed to come home and do everything at home. I know she's tired and doesn't want to be mother twenty-four hours a day, but I need to have some time for rest too.
>
> *Cheri:* And that's the way it goes over and over—like a broken record. I've threatened to run away from home with Josh—at least then I would just have two people to care for instead of three! I don't really want to, but honestly, I don't see any way out. We can't seem to work this out at all. [*At this point Cheri begins to cry and Jim is embarrassed, staring at the floor. The rest of the group is uncharacteristically quiet, avoiding eye contact with one another.*]
>
> *Leader:* So you both have had to face some significant changes in the past six months—decreased income, Cheri—you lost your involvement in your career, which you enjoyed; you are trying to adjust to some changes in how the two of you handle the home chores now that you are home more; and both of you have to adjust to another person in your family who demands a great deal of time and attention. All this has caused significant shifts in

how you handle the resources you have. Would you be willing to talk about this further in front of the group? And would the rest of you see this as something useful for all of us to focus on for awhile—how to handle changes that demand dramatic shifts in the ways we relate to one another? [*Cheri and Jim look at one another, nodding agreement.*] Do you need some time to talk about it privately?

Cheri: I don't think so. We've already told you a lot about it.

Jim: Yeah, we could sure use the help the group could offer us, although I'm not sure there's any way out.

Leader: All right, then what I would like you to do is to pull your chairs out and get where you are comfortable to talk together about it.

[The group moves chairs, gets set up.]

Leader: Now it seems to me we have a significant crisis that has generated several problems here, and it might be helpful to use the problem solving process we've already discussed. Perhaps the place to begin is to see if the two of you can really define what the problem is.

Jim: Josh is wonderful, and I love being a daddy, but the change in our home life has been overwhelming. There just is never a break.

Cheri: That's true. But I don't think that's the major issue. I think most of it is the change in how Jim sees me now that I'm home—he thinks I should have time to do everything at home, including the chores that used to be his. And it's not only that, but I guess it's partly how I feel about myself, and even more, how I think Jim feels about me. I liked being equals—taking turns cooking and cleaning up and so on, and it's almost like being lowered a notch and him being over me to have to do all those things we used to share. And I worry, too, that I want Josh to grow up just as attached to his daddy as me—I want Jim to share in the responsibility for him not only so I won't have to do it all, but also for his sake.

Leader: Whew! There certainly are a lot of issues involved here. It sounds as if it isn't just a matter of sharing house responsibilities, but some basic definitions of how you relate to one another are involved.

Jim: Yeah. I guess I really wasn't aware that Cheri was having trouble with feeling equal. I sure don't see her as any less equal. But I miss her. We used to have more time together. Josh takes a lot of her time, and she's tired, too.

Cheri: But if you'd—

Leader: [*Interrupting*] Just a minute, Cheri. Before we go on discussing that issue, perhaps it would be helpful to see if others in the group have faced problems like these.

As the group members discuss similar crises they have experienced, other new parents, specifically, say they share some of Jim and Cheri's feelings about fatigue, interruptions of sexual intimacy, lowered income, and additional expenses that contribute to conflict.

Leader: Jim and Cheri, you've been listening. What do you think?

Jim: I think we need to look at this some more. I think it's more than who empties the garbage and who changes the diapers.

Cheri: I agree. I think we're both under a lot of

pressure, and we need to figure out how to handle the different demands on us and still be caring with one another.

Leader: It does sound like there are a lot of things involved here. We can talk about it further right after this session if you want to. But I really appreciate your sharing your experiences with us. I think it has helped the group identify some of the struggles we are all experiencing, and maybe some of those who aren't parents yet will know to be alert!

After the session ends, the leader moves toward Jim and Cheri and asks if they would like to take a few moments to talk. She asks whether they were satisfied with the way the group session went, and whether they would like to talk further another time or work through some of the issues on their own, now that they have been identified. Jim and Cheri concur that they would like to talk further with the leader. Since there is not enough time during the retreat, the leader makes an appointment to talk with them during the following week.

If the couple had been uncomfortable or unwilling to deal with the issue in front of the group but wanted help with the problem, the leader would need to indicate to the couple and to the group that marriage enrichment often brings to the surface a number of matters that will not be solved in the group. The couple's discussion may have uncovered one such issue; others in the group may be dealing with similar situations but may not discuss them openly. The leader can then indicate to the group that he or she will be available for private discussions about such issues, if anyone so desires. The leader would then make it a point to check with the couple later to determine the most appropriate intervention strategy or give them a referral for counseling outside the group. Even if the couple had wanted to deal with the issue in the group, the leader may have decided otherwise. The leader may have concluded that turning the group's focus to this couple's issue would deter the group from reaching its objectives, perhaps because the issue was too complex or too threatening to be dealt with in the group context. In this case, the leader needs to share his or her assessment with the couple and recommend an alternative strategy for dealing with the matter, which may involve counseling for the couple outside the group.

Since one of the qualifications necessary for a professional marriage enrichment leader should be skill in marriage counseling, often a couple in crisis will want to contract with the leader for counseling services. Although this can be a useful strategy, to develop a counseling contract with a couple in the group is to risk confusion over appropriate behaviors in each setting, as well as to identify a particular couple as "special" in the eyes of other group participants. The couple and the leader may choose to wait to reevaluate their contract at the close of the marriage enrichment experience, at which time a counseling contract may be established, or the leader may choose to make a referral.

Identifying and Coping with Problems

Conflictual Couple. Loud argument, tears, and stony silence may indicate a sudden crisis. They may also be a sign of chronic conflict in a marriage. A couple who has difficulty resolving any conflict in their relationship may dominate the group, overwhelming other couples with their problems. Often the inclusion of a single conflictual couple may be the result of a mistake in the selection of group members. Also, couples in conflict may already be members of a group into which leaders have been brought as consultants. In these circumstances, it is too late to make changes in the group's composition. The leader needs to take a very active role if one couple is dominating a group. This may involve creating a number of small work groups so that there are fewer people to dominate; using structured activities that focus the discussion; and setting time limits on role plays or other activities in which couples explore their relationships in the group.

These are useful strategies, but they will not necessarily resolve the problem posed by a conflictual couple. That is, the couple may still dominate the small group, turning structured activities into new contexts for their old agenda or continuing their customary style of interaction within the new time constraints. These strategies should therefore be paired with some direct intervention aimed at diverting the focus from the couple's interaction, at least within the group setting. The leader may do this by referring directly to the group's expectation of a focus on growth and relationship potential rather than on problem remediation.

For example, Jim and Cheri's initial dialogue in the previous section may indicate more than a relationship crisis; it may indicate the couple's chronic inability to adapt to changes in the marriage and a habitual tendency to blame each other for the changes and resulting discomfort. The leader would make this distinction on the basis of the following criteria: Has the couple indicated that most areas of their relationship are conflictual or is there a basic cohesion and satisfaction pervading the relationship? Do they identify each other's strengths and the positive aspects of their relationship or do they focus on weaknesses and problems? If the leader had determined that Jim and Cheri's problems with home responsibilities were part of an overall pattern of conflict, she might have responded as follows:

Cheri: This has been very upsetting. I really didn't want to do this exercise, because I knew it would cause problems. Jim and I have some basic differences here, and he is simply unwilling to compromise. I realize that I haven't worked since Josh was born six months ago, but I plan to go back in another year or so, and he has used this to opt out of doing anything at home, including fathering his son.

Jim: You're being unfair! She expects me to work all day, and some evenings, too, so the overtime can make up some for her not working. Then I'm supposed to come home and do everything at home. I know she's tired and doesn't want to be a mother twenty-four hours a day, but I need to have some time for rest, too.

Cheri: And that's the way it goes over and over —like a broken record. I've threatened to run away from home with Josh—at least then I would just have two people to care for instead of three! I don't really want to, but honestly, I don't see any way out. We can't seem to work this out at all. [*At this point Cheri begins to cry as she has done twice before in the group. Jim is staring at the floor in embarrassment. The rest of the group is also avoiding eye contact.*]

Leader: It sounds as if you have a lot of problems in this area. I wonder, though, what has been positive about all the changes you have had to face? Jim, has there been anything about having Josh these past six months that you have experienced positively?

Jim: Well, [*long hesitation*] I've been proud of Cheri. She's tired and grumpy a lot—

Leader: [*Interrupting*] Yes, but just focus on what has been positive.

Jim: She's a good mother. I like to hear her singing to him, and being so tender with him. And I wouldn't trade being a daddy for anything.

Leader: What about you, Cheri? What have you enjoyed about the past six months?

Cheri: He's right. I get awfully tired. But I really enjoy being needed, knowing that I am so important to someone. And when Jim plays with Josh— *when* he does—

Leader: [*Interrupting*] Be positive!

Cheri: He really delights in him, and I feel proud that I could give him Josh. I know that sounds crazy, but it's almost like Josh is my present to Jim.

Leader: Jim, did you know that's how Cheri feels?

Jim: No, that isn't crazy at all. Cheri, it makes me feel good.

Leader: You each have been able to identify some significant positive feelings about the past six months in spite of all the conflict, and that's a good place to begin. Sometimes we need to begin with the good before we have the energy to deal with the problematic. I know we haven't addressed the problems yet, and we really don't have the time to do that in the group today, but perhaps we can talk afterward about some resources for helping you do that. I hope that the problem solving process may be of use to you, too, when you get ready to make some changes.

The leader would then need to follow up on this by discussing with Cheri and Jim possible resources for them: counseling with the leader or a referral to another counselor or appropriate service.

If such an intervention is not effective in returning the group's focus to strengths rather than the remediation of problems, the leader may need to make a more direct approach. The leader may decide to talk briefly with the couple in private to express concern over their problems and remind them of the contract that states that the group will not focus primarily on individual couples' conflicts. The leader can help the couple make plans to get other help if the couple so desires.

If the leader decides that the group will not be too threatened by participating in such a discussion, he or she may ask the group to respond to the couple, focusing on the processes they have observed rather than the content of the couple's disagreements. This discussion may involve responses of group members to the couple's conflict and ways the group and the couple would choose to cope with these thoughts and feelings. In fact, this kind of discussion can serve as a central format for a group in which a number of couples are coping with chronic conflict; a group may even be composed with this focus in mind.

Continuing with the example of Jim and Cheri, the leader might take the following approach:

Leader: One of the things we are trying to do is to identify the ways we see ourselves communicating with one another. Jim and Cheri, would you like some feedback about how the rest of the group is hearing you talk about this problem?

Jim and Cheri: Sure [*looking at one another and nodding*]

Leader: [*Scanning the group*] What similarities or differences can you identify in how Jim and Cheri are talking about this as compared with other times you have heard them discuss their relationship?

George: They're using a lot of "you" messages. Jim, I heard you say "you're unfair," and Cheri, I hear you say "you're unwilling to compromise."

Emily: Let's focus on the positives, too. [*Group laughs.*] I think you're both very open, sharing your feelings with one another, even though you may not do it in the best of ways.

Bob: Things sound so hopeless to me, like you can't find a way out.

Leader: Maybe we can put Emily and George's suggestions together and at least take a first step in building some hope that there is another way out. Jim and Cheri, would you mind talking about this again and letting the group coach you to use "I" messages?

[*The leader would follow through on the replaying of the discussion, and then proceed to direct the group's attention to the overall process.*]

Leader: I think this has been helpful to spend more time in looking at how we communicate with one another.

Jim: Yes, but we've still got the problem, and I'm not sure what to do.

George: Well, for one thing—

Leader: Just a minute, George. Excuse me for interrupting, but before we start looking for ways Cheri and Jim can resolve this issue, I wonder if this is the way we want to spend the rest of our session today. We had planned to let some of the rest of you have some time to talk about your own relationships, and to move on to some other material.

Nancy: I want us to help Cheri and Jim all we can. I think that's more important. But I want to cover the material, too. [*Several people nod.*]

Leader: So you want to help, but you also want to stay with our plan for the group and really don't want to have to give that up.

Cheri: I think we take too much of the group's time. I really would like to move on.

George: Well, you use a lot of time, but maybe you need it more than some of the rest of us! [*Group laughter*]

Leader: It sounds like there is agreement that we do spend a lot of time with Cheri and Jim because they have been willing to share themselves so openly with us. Perhaps we need to encourage some of you that are more shy to talk more. What do you think, Jim?

Jim: I think you're right. It's not just the time, but I think sometimes some of you are kind of uncomfortable when we're talking about our problems, and that makes me uncomfortable.

Betty: It does make me a little nervous. I want to help and don't know what to say. We all have problems, but you are so open about yours. [*Nods of agreement*]

Leader: So I'm hearing the consensus of the group, that Cheri and Jim have encouraged several of you to want to share more in the group although sometimes the asking for specific help with specific problems is not what you think we can best give one another. I know I certainly was excited by looking at *how* Cheri and Jim interact and replaying the discussion using the skills we've been working on. I'd like to know how some of the rest of you experienced that last activity.

The ground has thus been laid for the leader to focus at any time on how the group feels about Cheri and Jim (or others) claiming time for discussion of their own relationship, and to talk with Cheri and Jim privately about some additional counseling to help with the problems they are experiencing.

Member Aggressiveness. Persons who have had previous group experiences, such as group psychotherapy, sensitivity training groups, or even other educational groups, often bring with them expectations of how members and leaders should relate to one another that conflict with the norms most marriage enrichment group leaders try to establish. Often these are resolved as the group develops its own relationship structures and norms and members adapt to these expectations of the group. However, in almost all groups there are times when one or several members challenge the leader-established norms. Such challenges may create problems if they take the form of pushing others to relate differently; for example, insisting that others need to disclose more to the group. If the expectation of the group is that all participation is to be strictly voluntary, even the good-natured volunteering of someone else in the group for a role play, or coaxing of someone else to take a turn in answering a question, can be construed to be aggressive and inappropriate. Often, this breaching of the voluntarism norm leads to other more direct confrontations that may create feelings among group members of being betrayed or of being expected to participate in different ways than they had contracted for in the first place. It is important, therefore, that the leader be alert for this kind of breach of group norms and call the group back to its expectations for participation.

This does not necessarily mean that all confrontation should be avoided in all marriage enrichment groups, although some of the most respected leaders in the field insist that confrontation is inappropriate (Mace and Mace, 1976a) and it is certainly useful for many groups to adopt nonconfrontation as a norm. It does mean, however, that any behavior that breaches a group norm needs to be dealt with by the group and its leader, whether that norm is voluntarism or nonconfrontation or both. If a group agrees to use confrontation as a process of interaction between couples, it is important that guidelines for good confrontation be discussed and that the leader ensures that they are adhered to. Such guidelines include checking to gain agreement of the confrontee that he or she wants to receive the feedback, confronting strengths as well as problems, taking the confrontee's need for protection and privacy into consideration more than the confronter's need to "unload," focusing on specific behaviors rather than global personality characteristics, and keeping confrontation on the basis of enhancing possibilities for growth rather than on punishing.

When a leader observes someone breaching a group norm, it is often helpful to call it to the person's attention. This gives the group a chance to reaffirm or alter its norms. For example:

> *George:* Susan, Bob is always telling us about your marriage, but we never hear anything from you. Why don't you tell us what it's like for you instead of just letting us hear from him?
>
> *Leader:* Whoa, George. I hear you really being concerned about Susan. I think it is really great that we are getting to the place that we want to know more about one another's relationships. But our agreement is that we won't put anybody on the spot—

that it will be up to everyone to say what he or she wants without feeling that they have to.

George: Well, I guess that's true, but Susan doesn't have to answer if she doesn't want to.

Leader: So you're saying that you think it would be better if we ask one another what we want to with the understanding that we don't have to answer if we don't want to and no one is going to push?

George: Yeah!

Leader: What do the rest of you think?

Marsha: I suppose it's true that we don't have to answer, but gosh, if Susan says "I don't want to talk about it" then we're all probably going to think that there is something awful going on! [*Group laughter*]

Susan: I think you're both right. That's okay, though, because if no one ever asked me, I probably wouldn't say anything.

Bill: I'd like to go with George's suggestion, and just agree to be careful not to push too much.

Leader: So what we're saying is that we can certainly ask one another questions, but we all have the right to not answer and not think that others are going to keep bugging us about it or think there is something wrong. [*Several in the group nod.*]

At times, one member may persist through several exchanges in attempting to change the group's expectations even after the group has clearly restated them. Such a member may complain that group members are not sharing enough of themselves, the group is slow in "breaking down barriers," or in other ways simply that the group is not measuring up to the member's standards. It is the leader's responsibility to protect other group members from this kind of pressure. The leader

may do this by interrupting the aggressive member and redirect-
ing the group, pointing out the breach of the group's norms,
and implicitly or explicitly asking for a group consensus about
maintaining or changing the group's interaction behaviors. The
choice of strategy depends on how developed the group is, the
degree to which such a confrontation will enhance or detract
from the goals of the group, and the willingness of the member
to receive leader or member feedback. (The confrontation should
meet the criteria of appropriateness mentioned earlier.) For
example, early in the group's development, the leader most likely will take responsibility for dealing with the breach:

> *George:*   Everyone has had something to say so
> far, but you [*looking at Carol and John*]. It's time
> you said something!
>
> *Leader:*   Wait, George. Remember, everyone has
> the right to talk or not talk, as they are most com-
> fortable. We've talked about this several times, but
> I think you are so interested in everyone and want-
> ing to make sure everyone gets included that it
> keeps coming up.
>
> *George:*   Yeah, I guess so. I'm afraid Carol and
> John won't get as much out of this if they don't
> contribute something.
>
> *Leader:*   But I think they have contributed a great
> deal by their support of others. And I think it's up
> to them what they want to share with us about
> themselves. But I hear your concern that we all
> learn as much as we can. Why don't we move on
> now to consider how we manage all the different
> commitments we have that pull us away from hav-
> ing time together as a couple.

If the group has developed an easy style of communication in
which it is able to examine its processes as well as the content
foci of the group, the leader might choose instead to turn the
issue to the group:

George: Everyone has had something to say so far, but you [*looking at Carol and John*]. It's time you said something!

Leader: Wait a minute, George. I think some of the other members might have some reactions to what you're asking of Carol and John. Would it be all right if I asked them to share that with you?

George: I suppose. I guess you're going to say I'm pushing again.

Pat: You're right! [*Group members laugh nervously.*] I think you want to be sure to include everybody, but asking questions like that just makes them more uncomfortable—at least it does me.

Carol: Thanks for your concern, George, but don't worry. I'll speak up when I'm ready.

This kind of strategy demands more of the group, but when the group is ready to handle its own maintenance in this way, it is a powerful, effective approach that builds the group's capabilities rather than emphasizing the leader's continuing responsibility for the group.

If neither of these strategies is effective in controlling the aggressiveness of one or several members, the leader may need to talk privately with the member about conflicting expectations, referring back to the original agreement and emphasizing its role in the group. It is rare that the leader would have to have this kind of private conversation. If the member has needs that are not being met in the group, however, it may be that such a discussion can be used to examine ways of getting these needs met other than continually—and frustratingly—going against the group's norms.

Another form of aggressiveness is one group member being overly self-disclosing, embarrassing other group members, threatening them with the idea that such disclosure might be expected of everyone, and taking up too large a share of the group's time. For the most part, this can be handled similarly to the conflictual couple that demands too much group time and energy and deflects the group from its objectives. The leader should attempt to change the focus of the person's self-disclosure, looking for ways that the discussion can be turned to a focus on marital growth rather than on an individual's issues. If the leader determines that the demanding member is coping with some private troubles, the leader may choose to talk privately with the person about alternative sources for help. Whatever strategy he or she chooses, the leader needs to be active in stemming this kind of development early, rather than allow it to develop before attempting to intervene.

If the group is comfortable with the idea, the leader may ask them to respond to the member's self-disclosure, not so much to the content of the self-disclosure but more to the appropriateness of the sharing and how the group wants to handle this kind of sharing. However, it is only in the most advanced group, functioning virtually independently of the leader, in which members can be expected to respond to this kind of focus on process.

A third form of member aggressiveness is the tendency of one or more people to advise other members as to what approaches they should take to various issues. An important norm that can be developed and reinforced to deal with this problem is the expectation that members will not diagnose or analyze each other, nor will they offer opinions or suggestions. Rather, they will share their own experiences. For example, the following situation could have developed from the discussion with Cheri and Jim:

> *Marge:* It sounds to me, Cheri, that you've just about had it. If I were you, I would just lay out some ground rules. Like, whenever Jim comes in for the evening he is in charge of diaper changing and baby rocking while you fix dinner.
>
> *Leader:* It sounds like you've got some ideas of things that have worked for you, Marge. But I think it would be more helpful to Cheri and Jim if you

tell them about your own experience rather than assume that what worked for you will work for them. After all, none of us can know what will be best for Cheri and Jim but them. Maybe hearing about our experiences will give them some ideas, though.

Marge: I just know what Cheri is feeling. I tried to be supermom when Ashley was a baby—took care of the house and the baby and had supper on the table when Bob came home. And so I was always tired and he really didn't get a chance to be with Ashley because I was so busy proving that I could handle it all.

If the leader is alert for and intervenes when norms such as voluntarism, appropriate and requested confrontation, reasonable limits to self-disclosure, and sharing experiences (rather than opinions) are violated, the group will follow suit and develop its own policing processes to keep its interactions within these bounds. If the leader allows such incidents to go unchallenged, however insignificant they may seem at the time, the group may become confused about what the expectations are or a subgroup may develop norms of its own. This can lead, for example, to one relatively shy couple being pressed by the whole group to talk more and share themselves. Intervention becomes more difficult at this point, but it is nevertheless the responsibility of the leader since the leader has a service contract with that couple as well as with the other members of the group. The leader will need to protect the shy couple from the group's pressure and ask the group to reexamine its goals and norms and see if a mutually agreeable set of expectations can be reaffirmed. Again, the leader will not have to deal with this kind of group confrontation if he or she has been alert to the group's development throughout its history.

Resistance to Participation: The Dragee. David and Vera Mace (1976a) have used the term *dragee* to refer to the reluctant person who has been dragged into a marriage enrichment group by his or her enthusiastic spouse. Often, for these less-than-willing participants, initial discussions focusing on the positive aspects of marriage are sufficient to decrease reluctance and increase commitment to the purposes of the group. The Maces suggest that during the first session a general word of appreciation and gratitude be spoken by the leader to those less willing participants; for example, "It's a very loving act to attend a marriage enrichment retreat, even when you are not strongly motivated to go, just to make your partner happy. If you have done that, I want to pay tribute to you" (Mace and Mace, 1976a, p. 90). This definition of their presence as care and commitment to their spouses often reframes these participants' involvement as something positive. As such, it may contrast with conflict that may have occurred over the couples' involvement in the group, with the "draggers" blaming the "dragees" for not being more excited or committed to the experience.

Sometimes, however, a participant's initial resistance to participation is not overcome by early experiences in the group. There are at least three possible issues that can be considered in addressing this problem: The participant may have come only to avert marital conflict; other issues or concerns in his or her life may have more salience at this time. A person may be quite uncomfortable with speaking in a group. A person may be new to the experience of a group with an interpersonal relationship focus and may be uncertain how to participate. Yet another reason for nonparticipation may be a person's fear of the ramifications of looking at the marital relationship; I will look at that problem in the following section.

Let us first examine ambivalence or lack of interest as a cause of nonparticipation. Often identifying the specific ways a person is expressing ambivalence can provide the basis for group discussion or couple-leader discussion of goals and expectations for the group and for the marriage. Feedback about expressions of ambivalence may include observations of consistent tardiness or absence, incompletion of homework assignments, or frequent comments that content is inapplicable. Such violation of the group's norms may indicate that the person really does not want to be a member of the group or that the group contract does not fit the person's needs. A leader may present these tentative interpretations to the couple or group. It is important that the leader be nonjudgmental in this kind of confrontation; there are, after all, many other interests and concerns that can very well be more salient for some persons and in some situations than participation in a marriage enrichment group. The leader also needs to provide this kind of feedback as a question to which an answer is sought, not as proof of a person's ambivalence. The leader may be in error in assuming ambivalence; it may be that the person is not participating because he or she is fearful or uncomfortable in a group.

As in choosing a strategy to handle any problem, the leader needs to decide what will be the least confrontive and most supportive approach for effective intervention. For example, offering a brief aside to an individual—"I'm wondering why you've had trouble completing home assignments. Maybe this group isn't being very helpful to you."—is much less confrontive than making the same statement in the group. Calling attention in the group to tardiness, lack of preparation, or a person's comments that the group is not helpful and asking the group what to do about it is an extremely confrontive strategy and should be reserved for only the most cohesive and sophisticated groups. The leader needs to keep in mind that the purpose of addressing the nonparticipation of a member is not to coerce that member into compliance with the group's expectations. Rather it is to determine what the barriers are to achieving that participant's objectives for the enrichment group and how best to address those barriers, always balancing the needs of each participant and couple with the needs of the rest of the group. If the leader's strategy is too confrontive, the participants will become defensive and, perhaps, unwilling to engage in a mutual examination of barriers. The following conversation might occur after a weeknight group meeting between a participant and a leader concerned about her frequent tardiness and lack of participation in the group:

> *Leader:* Susan, I've been concerned that you have had a hard time getting here on time, and when you get here we don't hear much from you.

I'm afraid that you're not getting as much out of the group as you had hoped.

Susan: I always have trouble getting places on time; that's one of the sore spots in our marriage. As for my not talking, I've just had a lot on my mind. My parents are going through a divorce and my mom is pretty torn up. We spend a lot of time talking, and I'm just really exhausted by the time I work all day, listen to her, and then try to meet Tom here.

Leader: If being late a lot is an issue for the two of you, maybe it's something you would like to focus on next time as we talk about negotiating change with one another. I've noticed that Tom seems pretty steamed when you come in late, and I think that other group members may be picking up on it too. I'm not saying that you should necessarily be on time, but it might help to talk about it if it's a pattern and not just something about this group. But that's a different issue from your having a hard time concentrating on what we're doing. I know when I'm having some serious problems elsewhere in my life it is very difficult for me to focus on something else. Is there anything I can do to help you with that?

Susan: I'm not sure. Just telling you about it helps. I really wish the group had been at another time—it has just been so hectic. But I didn't know that it was so obvious I was distracted. I don't want my parents' problems to wreck something good that might happen for Tom and me. As for being on time, it just seems like the madder Tom gets the later I am, almost like I'm getting back at him for bugging me about it. And we just go in circles about this like we do some other things. I would like to get some input from the group if you think it would help.

If the leader determines that either discomfort with speaking in front of a group or lack of exposure to group experiences is a factor in members' lack of involvement, the leader may need to take on stronger task and socio-emotional leadership functions. That is, the leader may need to be more active, not only talking more but reaching for group members' thoughts and feelings and making connections among them. Also, more structured activities and discussions provide people with greater security about what is expected of them than do freefloating discussions.

When there are several members who are quiet, or when the whole group is not participating, and the leader feels compelled to urge responses from group members, it is most useful to focus on the group on the nonparticipation and try to determine what it means. Of course, there may be a lack of consensus on the goals and the objectives of the group, in which case these need to be discussed again. This is more likely to occur, however, in a group where members had been participating and then become less involved. When the group has never "clicked," when the leader continues to feel that the group is overly dependent on his or her leadership, it may be that the leader's expectations of participation have been unrealistic. The leader may need to model group participation through role playing, through self-disclosure, and/or through discussion of how the members can best participate in the group. A structured activity, such as "tell us about the funniest moment in your lives together," helps shape participants' sharing behaviors, focusing on positive disclosures about the relationship. It is important, also, that the leader expect progressive, not sudden, involvement in the group, and that he or she try to ensure that members will experience their involvement positively and want to repeat it. While the leader can do this by providing positive reinforcement, eliciting it from group members is often the most powerful incentive for continued participation. For example,

> *Leader:* Jan, I wonder if you would be willing to share with us what it was like to hear Edward talk about his concern about how you divide up respon-

sibilities at home and his willingness to try to change his orientation despite how hard that is for him.

Jan: I don't think I had ever heard you say some of that before, Edward. I know how hard it is not to expect me to do for you like your mom did. I feel really encouraged just knowing that you see it's a problem too.

When only one person or a couple is not participating, the leader may need to provide selective leadership, allowing the group members to lead as they are able but providing group experiences that will involve nonparticipating members in a comfortable way. The leader may do so by breaking the group into smaller work or discussion groups so that everyone has the opportunity to participate, selecting activities in which nonparticipants excel so that they can take on more group leadership, and/or providing those persons with such roles as recording ideas on a blackboard, organizing refreshments, or reporting on small group discussion. The leader should be careful not to force participation but to encourage it by providing the kind of session content with which these persons are comfortable and the kinds of group processes and roles that enhance their participation.

The leader should prevent a member being cast by the entire group into the role of refreshment-fixer or blackboard-writer. These roles are only useful if they stimulate the involvement of the person in the group. The leader should watch for and reinforce other signs of group involvement, such as head nodding ("I see you agree, Edward. John certainly needs some support right now!"). In such ways the leader can elicit greater participation by that member over the life of the group.

Resistance to Participation: The Fearful Couple. A silent spouse or couple may be signalling fear of the ramifications of looking at the marital relationship: fear of one another's anger or hurt, and/or fear that the base of the relationship is not sturdy enough to bear examination. While they may have come to the enrichment experience hoping to find some answers to their difficulties, they may also be reluctant to uncover their problems for fear that the group will not help and they will leave in worse difficulty than when they came. For participants who are worried about whether their marriage can stand examination, an accent on marital strengths in learning activities, an explicit normative stance by leaders that the group is to enhance positive aspects rather than diagnose problems, and at least initial avoidance of activities that encourage couples to explore the dynamics of their marriages in front of the group can be helpful. It is also possible, however, that such a couple may despair of finding help. The focus on enrichment rather than remediation may be disappointing when, despite their reluctance, they wanted to focus on their problems. This is more likely to occur in a group that has contracted with the leader to provide marriage enrichment rather than one formed by the leader. In such an already existing group, the leader usually has no chance to screen couples, to learn their expectations ahead of time, or to educate the group as to the purposes of a marriage enrichment experience.

Reluctance to participate often dissipates when the norms of the group are made clear or later, when other couples begin to share their experiences and the reluctant participants find that their relationship and troubles are not so different from others'. With such revelations, participants frequently voice a great deal of relief: "I didn't know anyone else ever felt like that!" is a common response.

It may be helpful to talk privately in an informal way with the couple who remains reserved in the group environment after the group has begun to develop. The purpose of this conversation should be to determine what is blocking the couple's participation. The leader should be careful not to violate the couple's right to voluntary participation, but rather to facilitate the couple and leader's mutual examination of any difficulties that may exist. If there is a disturbance in the relationship that one or both spouses are fearful of disclosing to the group, brief intervention may be in order, either by the leader or by an outside counselor.

Additionally, the leader may want to work with the couple, if there is mutual agreement to do so, to increase their involvement in the group. The leader may suggest or help them to rehearse privately ways of participating that are comfortable to both of them. The leader may even use structured role-playing with a prepared dialogue so that the couple can participate in the group in a controlled fashion rather than risking, at least initially, a spontaneous response to the group's discussion. With a group member's previous consent, the leader may also ask the group member to role play with the leader in a demonstration. In this way, a couple can begin to participate without having to talk about their own relationship. Of course, one of the more obvious ways of drawing such a couple into the group is to use a nonthreatening discussion or activity that does not involve disclosing intimate information about themselves. Whatever strategy is used, the leader needs to ensure that it is a positive experience for the participants, increasing the probability of other involvement in the group.

It should be emphasized that although some reluctant couples can adjust to the expectations of the group and can greatly benefit from the marriage enrichment experience, there are a few who need to postpone the enrichment experience and deal with significant difficulties in their relationship. This may or may not mean continued involvement in the group; the issues of the leader providing professional intervention or referral to another marriage counselor have already been discussed.

Differing Values. There are a number of explicit beliefs held by most marriage enrichment leaders—that there needs to be flexibility in sex roles, that egalitarian marriage is most functional, that anger and its expression can and should be constructive, and that the marital relationship can and should be the basis for individual development and growth. It is not unusual for some participants to disagree with one or several of these values, either overtly or subtly. The overt differences are usually not too difficult to identify; members may argue with the presentation a leader is making, apologize for their own beliefs if they place a lot of expert power in the leader's position, become angry, or even—if there is some role distance between leader and members (such as young leader working with retired couples)—laugh with more or less good will at the differences between their expressed values and those of the leader.

Subtle expressions of disagreement with the leader's value base may be more difficult to identify. These expressions may take the form of breaking the norms the leader and/or the group has established by being tardy, not following through on outside assignments, showing lack of interest, diverting attention from the topic, engaging in disruptive side conversations, or silence. It may take some expert group leadership skills to bring to the surface the value differences that are generating the deviance from the group's work. Often, however, open recognition of the difficulty through a careful examination of the group processes, both through review of the group's development and, perhaps, also by discussion of the leader's observations, will reveal the value issues.

If the leader is able to identify value conflict with one or several participants, an open discussion can be the basis of a helpful demonstration of values clarification and conflict management. This may be difficult because group participants often assume that there is a "right" way to approach marriage, which supersedes compromise—and leaders usually make the same assumption about their own values. It is crucial, therefore, for the leader to keep the process, rather than the content of discussion, in focus, identifying value clarification and conflict management as they happen.

> *Leader:* We have been focusing on how conflict develops in marriage and you all have talked about some of the disagreements you have. But you've been awfully quiet while I talked about fair fighting strategies, and no one has been willing to try it out in a role play. You haven't been reluctant to talk or try things out before. So I am wondering what's going on.
>
> *Ann:* We just don't have anything in our marriage that's worth fighting about. I'd rather live with the little things than make a major issue out of something that's not worth it.

Bill: My parents fought constantly. I can remember hearing my mother throw things at my dad and him threaten her. I swore I'd never treat my wife that way, no matter what she did. And I won't!

John: I know what you mean, Bill. I just think fighting is wrong. If two people love each other, they aren't going to want to hurt one another that way.

Leader: I'm hearing a couple of things. One, I think, is a misunderstanding of the word *fight*. When I say fight, you're thinking of throwing things and hurting people. But that's not what I mean to be talking about. I was talking about talking out the differences between us. But there is something else that's beyond just my choice of words. I'm hearing from you that you think bringing up differences like irritation over faucets not quite turned off or your spouse leaving lights on all over the house aren't really worth discussing because they just cause hurt and more trouble.

John: Yeah. [*Others nod.*]

Leader: Well, now that's an important difference. Maybe we need to spend some time looking at what is and isn't worth talking about. Because I have some different ideas than you do and I want to hear more about your ideas and I *certainly* want to tell you more about mine! [*Group laughter and nods of assent.*]

Loss of Group Members

If a couple's problem pervades their relationship, they may find it too difficult to sustain involvement in the group's process without pulling the group's attention back to their problem continually. When such a pattern emerges, the leader and the couple need to consider together privately whether the couple should continue in the group. A couple may feel too uncomfortable to continue in the group, either because their involvement in the crisis precludes their focusing on anything else or because they find it difficult to face the group's knowledge of their difficulty. In either case, the leader may be unable to persuade them to continue in the group. If a couple decides to drop out, the leader needs to help them terminate with the group in such a way that both the group and the couple experience a sense of closure. The leader may ask the couple to attend a last session with the group to briefly explain their reasons for leaving and to express their appreciation to the group. The leader needs to protect the couple from any possible coerciveness from other group members trying to persuade them to continue in the group. One way to avert such coercion is focus the group's feedback on the couple's strengths and on the group's hope for them as they work on identified issues.

If this couple is unwilling to say good-bye to the group in person, the leader may ask them to write a brief note to the group, which the leader can read, explaining their reasons for leaving. Or the leader may ask the couple's permission to explain those reasons for them. Whatever strategy is used, it is important that the group have some understanding of why a couple has dropped out in order to cope with their feelings of loss and move on.

Not infrequently, a couple or several couples drop out of an enrichment group that is meeting over a period of time rather than in a retreat setting. Dropouts early in the group's history are often the result of contracts that did not genuinely reflect the couples' expectations for the group, the group failing to develop the resources to meet those expectations, or the identification of crisis or conflict requiring counseling services instead of marriage enrichment.

Enrichment group couples develop interest and involvement with one another with remarkable rapidity, so that couples who do not return after the first session or subsequent sessions are a subject of concern to the group. There are two important issues involved: the cohesion of the group is threatened and there is a feeling of loss. Early in the group's history, cohesion is most relevant, whereas later, feelings of loss gain more salience.

The issues of cohesion involve questions about the reasons a couple leaves the group. Participants may ask themselves, usually covertly, "Weren't we good enough for them?" "Did I say something wrong?" "What's wrong with the group?" If it is known that the couple is leaving because of problems they want to explore in another context, participants may be saying to themselves, "They aren't that different from us. Maybe we're in worse trouble than I thought we were!" The more developed the group, the more likely that there are established roles and patterns of interaction which will be interrupted by a couple leaving. All these issues raise participants' anxiety and make it difficult to pursue the group's tasks without dealing with the anxiety first. Feelings of loss also disrupt the group, particularly if a couple drops out after several sessions, when the group has developed its patterns of relating and is settling down to work. The loss is greater in groups that are structured so that the members take on leadership roles.

To the extent that the group is disrupted, the leader needs to take time to help participants deal with the loss. It is important, at the very least, that the leader acknowledge that the couple will not be returning. If at all possible, the group needs to understand the reasons for the couple's decision to leave; the ramifications of their decision can then be discussed. For example, the couple moving away and the couple stating that the group hasn't been what they expected will generate quite different responses. Discussion of the loss can be an occasion for examining what the group means to each of the participants, ways of enhancing its effectiveness in reaching the couple's objectives, and how the participants cope with the mobile society in which people move in and out of their lives, as well as anticipating the termination of the group.

Conclusions

This has been a cursory examination of some of the problems leaders of marriage enrichment groups encounter. The

strategies that have been presented are offered by way of expla-
nation rather than prescription—choosing methods is a complex
process that requires professional expertise. Each situation is
unique and requires a unique response, based on the nature of
the group, its structure and leadership patterns, the stage of its
development, and the purpose of the group.

The discussion of each problem identifies, however, the
two levels on which leaders must work. As they provide direction for the group, help the group accomplish its tasks, and nurture interpersonal relationships, they also provide an example of
how to accomplish these same functions within participants'
marital relationships. As the leaders attempt to deal with problems in the group's functioning, whether they be ambivalence,
crises, anger, conflict, or feelings of loss, they are also modeling
ways of handling parallel problems in the interpersonal relationships between spouses. If leaders can keep their modeling function in mind, it may help them remain focused on the processes
of coping with a problem rather than be distracted by the content
of the problem. The goal, after all, is not just to enhance the
functioning of a particular group, but to provide couples with
models of skills and attitudes that will enhance their marital
relationships.

7

Evaluating
Marriage Enrichment
Services

One of the major objectives of this book is to encourage those who conduct marriage enrichment programs to consider and to implement evaluation of their services. Theorists are needed to conceptualize the purposes of enrichment, and educators must conceptualize ways to accomplish those purposes. Moreover, practitioners must test the whys and hows that have been developed already. Without establishing strong roots in research and program evaluation, the growth in marriage enrichment services cannot continue. Those providing services must find out whether they are meeting the objectives that have been established for a given group and whether these objectives indeed further the goals of the marriage enrichment movement.

A serious stumbling block in the development of research for marriage enrichment services is the false assumption held by many practitioners that unless they can conduct systematic research which is rigorous in its control of change factors and complex in its evaluation procedures—research that takes considerable time, resources, and clients—evaluation research is not possible. However, even the simplest of evaluation studies can provide useful information for understanding the effects of enrichment services. In fact, the most pressing need for research in the marriage enrichment field is the examination of the factors affecting the numerous settings, leadership capabilities and styles, and populations receiving marriage enrichment services. Chapter Three stresses the similarity of the processes used by both the researcher and the practitioner to develop a marriage enrichment group. The major difference between the two lies only in how they initiate the program: the practitioner begins with specific client need and the researcher begins with hypotheses to test. It is crucial that practitioners take seriously their responsibility and understand their capability to conduct practical research. Researchers in academic settings cannot possibly keep pace with the need for answers to the crucial questions of which services are effective and how they can become more effective. Only practitioners have the resources provided by a variety of clients, settings, programs—and practical questions—to conduct the necessary research.

Conducting practical research does not alter the service being evaluated though it does require valuing the service enough to examine it. Certainly, this practical evaluation is not as rigorous in its design or as well executed as that conducted in a controlled setting. However, research that controls all the factors involved in marriage enrichment services is impossible and practically sterile. Gurman and Kniskern (1981, p. 753), in a summary and commentary on family therapy research, have suggested the need for uncontrolled research, a suggestion that applies equally to marriage enrichment: "The field is still sufficiently in flux that empirical research oriented toward *discovery* rather than verification is also in order. This kind of discovery process is not especially well served by tightly controlled investigation. On the contrary, thoughtful study of family therapy [and marriage enrichment] in uncontrolled designs can be enormously profitable for this end." Even in verification research, patterns of results imply the consistency and power of intervention phenomenon that override issues of design quality and faults of individual studies (Gurman and Kniskern, 1981). In other words, it is not the precision of any particular research study that is most relevant but rather the persistent examination of the effects of services in group after group after group.

It would be exciting to have small evaluation studies being done in community agencies, private practices, churches, and other settings, on a variety of target groups in communities around the world. The practical information that could be accumulated would be unequaled by the finest of research projects. The need for gathering practical information is heightened by the fact that projects designed for research purposes do not often answer the questions that must be answered to develop effective services (Olson, 1976a). These studies often focus on whether a particular program accomplished its objectives rather than determining factors that increase and detract from program effectiveness.

Beyond the value of research for the development of the theory and practice of marriage enrichment services, other important advantages of research conducted by service providers exist. For instance, the evaluation methods, such as tests to measure use of communication skills, attitudes about the marital relationship, and other relevant information, can be used to assess the needs of specific couples. Using information from these instruments, program developers can gear services to meet these specific needs; they will not have to rely on leaders to more or less correctly intuit needs. Evaluation research has the ability to make services more relevant to client needs and thus more effective.

Evaluation methods can also provide direct feedback to couples. Many times self-awareness that results from completing a marital assessment instrument or relationship inventory is a powerful intervention in itself, and many couples experience this input about themselves as a revelation (Garland, 1981). The feedback generates motivation to learn and to change problematic aspects of the relationship, and to develop new skills and attitudes.

Finally, if the same instruments are administered both at the beginning and the end of a marriage enrichment program, they can provide practitioners with useful information about the effectiveness of their leadership style and their selected intervention model. Leaders must continually refine both leadership and intervention techniques.

What Is Program Evaluation?

Weiss (1972, p. 4) defines the purposes of program evaluation as the measuring of the "effects of a program against the goals it set out to accomplish as a means of contributing to subsequent decision making about the program and improving future programming. Within that definition are four key features:'To measure the effects' refers to the *research methodology* that is used. 'The effects' emphasizes the *outcomes* of the program rather than its efficiency, honesty, morale, or adherence to rules or standards. The comparison of effects with goals stresses the use of explicit *criteria* for judging how well the program is doing. The contribution to subsequent decision making and the improvement of future programming denote the *social purpose* of evaluation."

For example, if the goal of the program is to increase marital satisfaction, the program effects may be measured by administering a marital satisfaction inventory both before and after clients have participated in the marriage enrichment group. If group leaders find that satisfaction is not increased by participation in the program, they begin to evaluate why the goal was not achieved. They determine whether changes in the services should be made and whether their expectations are valid. This kind of research does not negate the importance of intuitive insight and professional interpretation of program results. It provides additional valuable information by which to assess and improve services.

Establishing Program Goals

For program evaluation to be meaningful, the program must have clearly established goals. These goals provide a basis from which evaluation criteria are developed. Also, as discussed in Chapter Three, program goals are a necessary basis for the development of program objectives and learning activities.

Program goals are a statement of the intended consequences of the program. They should be stated in terms that are
clear, specific, and measurable (Weiss, 1972). *Clear* implies that
the practitioner knows what the participant will do when it is
achieved. "Better communication" is not a clear goal; "individuals will use active listening skills with their spouse" more clearly defines *better communication*. For a goal to be specific, it
must refer to a change in knowledge, behavior, or attitude that
can be operationalized. The goal that "individuals will use active listening skills with their spouse" is specific in its reference
to a particular observable behavior. Knowledge and attitudes
can also be operationalized into observable behaviors such as responses on tests and opinion surveys, and nonverbal behaviors
such as using eye contact, smiling, and establishing physical distance. Finally, a goal should be measurable by some method of
research, which can include anything from questionnaires to
coding systems for observing actual behaviors.

Of course, a program probably has a number of goals;
evaluation of the program effects may be based on one or more
of these, depending on the needs and resources of the practitioner. Hof, Epstein, and Miller (1980, p. 242) suggest that a
marriage enrichment program should be evaluated on two criteria: "(a) whether it lives up to its proponents' claims (that is,
it produces valid, intended change) and (b) if effective as intended, whether it is appropriate for the specific needs of a particular couple."

The Focus of Evaluation

The purpose of evaluation research is to provide information about program effects that enables the practitioner to determine whether the program is accomplishing its goals. Research
can also provide information about how marriage enrichment
services can be improved and thus be more effective. These purposes seem to be relatively straightforward. However, marriage
enrichment programs are not uniform interventions. As was discussed in Chapter Two, they vary according to theoretical bases,
objectives, structures, content, and participants. Furthermore,

the outcomes in two groups exposed to the same program may be different because of each group's unique composition, needs, and developmental process. Hof and Miller (1980, p. 13) have stated that "the programs are interactionally oriented, and any control over the process, including provisions for research on outcome, is often not valued or sought."

If a marriage enrichment program whose goals are increasing marital happiness and skill in communication is provided to a group, and the participants' resultant scores on measures of marital happiness and communication skills are significantly higher than those of couples who are on a waiting list for marriage enrichment, the program presumably had the intended effects. However, the program's effectiveness is determined by a number of factors, some of which need to be explored. They are (1) the theoretical approach of the program, (2) the use of particular learning activities, (3) the use of weekly sessions rather than a weekend retreat, (4) the use of two leaders instead of one, (5) the use of contact and discussion with other couples rather than single couple learning or the learning structured by the leader, and (6) the specific population of the group. Any one or combination of these factors may contribute to a program's success. Of course, knowing which factors contribute to or detract from the effectiveness of the intervention is important in designing and implementing future programs.

Hof, Epstein, and Miller (1980) suggest that evaluation research needs to distinguish three kinds of effects. First, valid specific effects are those that can be attributed to intervention based on a particular theoretical approach. For example, increases in understanding of spouses' thoughts and feelings can be attributed to training spouses in active listening skills, as predicted by the Rogerian approach. Second, valid nonspecific effects are those that cannot be explained by the theoretical approach but are significant, and for which theoretical explanations can or should be developed. An example is the increase in marital happiness in a control group which met for unguided group discussion. If increases in happiness are not significantly higher in the experimental group, the theory on which the experimental intervention is based cannot be assumed to be responsible for the changes. This does not mean that the group has not been effective in reaching its objectives. But, presumably, the group has been effective because of couples' sharing with one another rather than because of the leaders' specific interventions—thus a valid effect not attributable to the intervention itself. Finally, the truly illusory (invalid) effects are those that do not produce substantive change although they seem to. An example is participants' reporting that they can communicate better and are happier with one another only to please the program leaders. Hof, Epstein, and Miller (1980, p. 243) conclude: "Only the illusory effects will be of no positive utility, and any limitations (e.g., duration, generalizability) of valid specific and nonspecific treatment effects can be addressed by either modifying the enrichment experiences or supplementing them with other treatments."

The accepted process used to determine which aspects of the enrichment program are contributing to its effectiveness is first to select the particular factor or factors to be assessed and next control for as many of the other factors as possible. This control is achieved by conducting two or more programs that are as alike as possible *except* for the one factor being evaluated. For instance, to determine whether a program is more effective when led by a married couple than by one person, a researcher studies two groups that are identical except for the leadership component—one group is led by a couple, the other by an individual. To add more weight to the results, the study can be repeated several times, using different leaders each time to eliminate the possibility that any observable differences could be attributed to leaders' personalities or to the groups' composition.

In reality, few practitioners are willing to conduct identical groups for the purpose of controlling variables. Programs are designed to respond to each group's unique development, not to force a group into a particular program design. Consequently, continuous evaluation of many different groups becomes important. That a particular program has consistently effective results in group after group despite observable differences in group composition, development, and structures is a more practical conclusion than that a program is effective given a particular set of controlled variables. In many respects, however, the examination of a variety of groups is more demanding because it requires continual evaluation of one's work and continual definition of the factors that influence each group's goal achievement.

The effects of four factors of marriage enrichment programs can be evaluated. They are (1) the theoretical approach, (2) specific interventions based on the theoretical approach, (3) structural variables, and (4) population variables.

Theoretical Approaches. Most marriage enrichment program evaluation has attempted to determine the effectiveness of the theoretical approaches summarized in Chapter Two. Usually, this kind of evaluation is conducted by comparing the results on specified outcome measures of a group participating in a program based on the targeted theory with those of a group that has not participated in any program (a waiting list control group). A group participating in a program based on a theoretical approach different from the targeted one (an alternate intervention control group) may be compared instead of or in addition to the waiting list control group. For example, leaders may decide to determine the effects of a weekend retreat model. They therefore form two groups of couples; the groups meet on consecutive weekends. The leaders can then measure marital satisfaction by comparing the postretreat scores of the group that already met with the preretreat scores of the group that has not yet met. If the program is effective, the scores of the group that completed the program should be significantly higher.

One major consideration in this kind of evaluation is the criteria for determining effectiveness. Different theoretical approaches emphasize different desired outcomes, and it is essential to keep these outcomes in mind when comparing approaches. For instance, some approaches of the marriage enrichment movement aim to increase intimacy and eliminate interpersonal differences whereas other approaches attempt to highlight differences and to teach participants to accept them. More often, however, goals are not contradictory. They simply focus on different levels of change, such as relationship satisfaction (attitudes) and skill learning (behavior).

In their commentary on family therapy outcome research, Gurman and Kniskern (1981) suggest that researchers include among their outcome measures *other* variables that are central to theoretical orientations than those reflected in the treatment methods being evaluated. This suggestion also applies to marriage enrichment research. For example, it would be most interesting to determine whether a Marriage Encounter program, with its emphasis on marital satisfaction and intimacy, has any effect on the communication behavior of spouses. An applicable hypothesis might be that spouses already have appropriate communication skills in their behavioral repertoires but are inhibited in their use because of relationship distance and hostility.

A second consideration in evaluation research on theoretical approaches includes both mediating goals and ultimate treatment goals. For example, in a communication skills training approach like the Minnesota Couples Communication Program, mediating goals such as completion of homework and use of the skills in practice sessions could be examined as well as ultimate goals of increased intimacy and marital satisfaction, increased self-esteem, and perhaps even change in parent-child communication patterns. On this issue Gurman and Kniskern (1981, p. 763) have suggested that it is "essential to . . . outcome research, on both logical and clinical grounds, (a) that the distinction between mediating and ultimate treatment goals be kept in clear focus, and (b) that studies of treatment outcome include measures of both categories of goal achievement. Furthermore, we see no reason to assume that when mediating goals have been achieved, the achievement of ultimate goals must follow closely in time. Rather, the latter outcomes may be temporally quite distant 'sleeper effects' (Rosman, 1977, p. 7). The need for multiple follow-ups in outcome studies is thus essential, for this reason, in addition to its more common purpose of determining the durability of changes manifest at the end of treatment."

A third consideration in the evaluation of theoretical approaches is efficiency of the program. Gurman and Kniskern (1981) suggest evaluation criteria from which the following list has been developed: (1) the degree of client compliance, or drop-out rates; (2) disseminative quality of treatment method, or the number of couples to whom services can be administered; (3) length of time clients need to be receive the services; (4) client costs, both financial and psychological; and (5) costs of leader training, for example, cost of hiring paraprofessionals and volunteers compared to professionals.

Most marriage enrichment program evaluators choose classical experimental design to conduct research on theoretical approaches. In this design couples are randomly assigned to a specific program and to a waiting list control group. Appropriate evaluation instruments are administered to both groups before the program begins (pretest), after the program has been completed (posttest), and after a follow-up period of a number of weeks (follow-up test). (For examples of this classical evaluation, see Miller, Nunnally, and Wackman, 1976; Nunnally, 1971; Ely, 1970; Harrell and Guerney, 1976; Guerney, 1977; Schlein, 1972.)

One disadvantage of this classical design is that determining whether program results are due to the intervention itself or to other unspecified factors is difficult. Factors relating to participation that may affect results include use of a structured time each week for couples to talk with one another, providing a night away from the children, and the development of a couple support system. For this reason some evaluators have used the alternate intervention control group in which these unspecified factors can also operate (for example, Pierce, 1973; Fisher, 1973). Therefore, instead of having two groups meet on consecutive weekends and comparing the scores of the first group after its weekend with the scores of the second group before its weekend, the evaluator compares one group in a Marriage Encounter program with one in a communication skill training program. In this case, the two groups' posttest scores would be compared.

A more rigorous design incorporates both kinds of control groups. With this three-group design, evaluators can determine whether the intervention program is significantly more effective in achieving program objectives than all the nonspecified factors, and also whether the nonspecified factors themselves provide significant results, which can then be further explored and evaluated. Wieman (1973) and Garland (1981) have conducted this kind of research. This design uses two groups in marriage enrichment programs (for example, an Encounter group and a communication skills training group) and one waiting list group. By comparing the scores of all three, the researchers can determine the effects of each intervention method as well as the effect of no intervention.

Finally, evaluation can be conducted without any control groups. Administering evaluation instruments before and after intervention to determine any significant changes is the simplest research design. It is most useful when exploring whether a new program is effective enough to warrant further use and evaluation. It is ideal for many practitioners who are not as concerned with clean research as they are with assuring that marriages are being enriched, whatever the factors. This design is also useful when used as part of ongoing evaluation of groups whose differences are explored and defined. Of course, because the design is used in a single group, evaluators cannot determine whether effects are really due to the program or to other factors. However, if no significant effects are found, a leader can, with some justification, find other services to meet the program objectives, without having expended resources unnecessarily on a pilot project. This research design can be refined by having participants wait some time (however brief) to begin the program and administering the criteria measures when participants are put on the waiting list. This procedure can be easily accomplished if the practitioner uses a screening interview. The practitioner can ask couples to complete a questionnaire during the interview and administer it again during both the first and last session of the program. By establishing the baseline (from the waiting list testing to the program pretesting), the leader can assume, with some assurance, that changes occurring during the program in contrast to changes occurring during the waiting period are attributable to the intervention. (For examples of this design, see Rappaport, 1971, 1976; Rose, 1977; Weiss, Hops, and Patterson, 1973; Frederiksen and others, 1976; Larsen, 1974; Liberman, 1970; Stuart, 1970.)

A very different kind of evaluation is required for the open-ended, self-help groups promoted by the marriage enrichment movement, groups that frequently follow a more traditional, time limited, professionally led group. Obviously, pretest and posttest measures are not as easily used in an ongoing group whose members may enter and terminate the program at different times, and may continue for extended periods. Evaluation of this group requires quasi-experimental methodology (Lieberman and Bond, 1979). It is extremely difficult to use control groups because evaluators have no control over who participates. However, there are some useful strategies that do not require that kind of control. "Members may . . . differ in their *kinds* of involvement, and we may indirectly determine the active ingredients of help giving for a group by distinguishing among member status" (Lieberman and Bond, 1979, p. 338). For example, some couples may attend all meetings and be active in planning group activities whereas others may attend on occasion. Within-group comparisons can thus provide an indirect strategy for evaluating program effects.

Lieberman and Bond (1979) suggest using a large normative sample as the standard against which to evaluate the marriages of participants in ongoing enrichment groups. "The normative sample is not a true control group, nor a statistical standard that the members of a self-help group must achieve in order to say that the group is effective. It may, however, give us some perspective on what effects the group is having" (Lieberman and Bond, 1979, p. 340). In this design couples in the group and others who have not experienced such a group can be compared, perhaps several times. This kind of comparison carries even more weight when the criterion measures are also administered to couples in the group before the program begins. Thus their initial differences from the nonparticipating couples can be evaluated.

Specific Interventions. Once a theoretical approach to marriage enrichment has proved effective as expressed in a particular program, the specific interventions of the program must be evaluated. This evaluation should focus on determining which aspects make the program effective, and which, if any, are extraneous or even deleterious to the program's objectives. Evaluation research focusing on specific interventions is currently the type most needed: "The components which are primarily responsible for change in marital enrichment programs are yet to be identified. If enrichment programs are to be improved, the specific effects of programmatic elements need to be delineated" (Gurman and Kniskern, 1977).

The most typical design used to research interventions involves conducting two or more enrichment groups that are as alike as possible except for the presence, absence, or alteration of a specific intervention component. For instance, a particular group of skills may be presented, discussed, and practiced in one group, but the skills may be only presented and discussed in a second group. The leader can then determine either that practicing the skills contributes to the changes in couples' communication or that merely talking about the skills is sufficient for creating changes. (See Garland, 1981, and Turner, 1972, for examples of this research design.)

Groups will always exhibit differences in addition to those planned for by the leader. Such differences between groups as amount of competition among members, rate of group development, and goals need to be defined and examined for their contributions to a program's effects and for their interaction with the components being evaluated.

Structural Variables. Many variables in a program are not dictated by theoretical approach and are independent of the teaching components. These variables may include number of leaders, whether leaders are a married couple, directiveness of leaders, size and composition of group, length and frequency of sessions, time structure of sessions (weekly or retreat), amount of group discussion and the effects of intercouple interaction, use of smaller groups within the large group, degree of formality, type of setting, order in which the teaching components are presented, and use of a combination of approaches (for example, combining skill training and support groups). Judgments about the significance of these variables to program outcome may differ, but at some point they must be objectively verified.

Some of the research on variables has produced results

that are useful. For example, L'Abate (1978) has found that a group receiving written homework assignments has a higher percentage of improvement in marital adjustment, measured by participants rating their marriages on inventories, than a group without such assignments and a waiting list control group. Spouses in an enrichment group who listened to each other's self-disclosures on audiotape showed significant improvement over couples in another enrichment group and waiting list control group who did not listen to self-disclosures (L'Abate, 1978). In examining the issue of time structure of sessions, Davis and others (1982) have found that participants in a group meeting weekly for five sessions showed more indications of improved marital adjustment than those in a weekend retreat group, even though both groups showed gains.

Zarle and Boyd (1977) have found that individuals in a communication skills training program aimed at teaching self-disclosure through skills practice and members of a group aimed at teaching self-disclosure through observation and discussion of modeled skills both showed significant increases on measures of self-disclosure in contrast to a no-treatment control group.

In their research Kilmann, Julian, and Moreault (1978) randomly assigned couples to two experimental groups and to a no-treatment control group. The experimental groups both received "fair fight" training and a sexual enhancement program, but in differing orders. The researchers have found that the sequence of the interventions did not differentially affect the outcomes of the two groups, but couples reported more successful marital functioning in these groups than in the control group.

Rowland and Haynes (1978) administered questionnaires to elderly couples in a sexual enhancement program. The program consisted of an initial waiting period, an educational phase in which they received information, and a communication exercises-sexual techniques phase. Significant increases in sexual satisfaction and reports of positive attitudes occurred indiscriminately across the phases, indicating that the testing itself, rather than any specific intervention, may have been responsible for the program's effectiveness.

These findings indicate the importance of determining the effects of structural variables on the achievement of program goals. The designs for this kind of research are usually identical to those used for exploring the effects of specific teaching components.

Population Variables. The influence of population variables on the effectiveness of theoretical approaches, interventions, and structures must be evaluated. A behavioral approach may be quite effective for a group of young married couples in an inner-city church, but not nearly as effective for retired couples in a suburban community center group. Lecture presentations may be more effective in presenting content to college educated couples. Experiential exercises may be more effective for couples having prior experience in educational services or counseling. Individual couple activities may be more effective for couples who are receiving professional services for the first time. None of these hypotheses have been tested. Differences between the effects of programs and structures must be tested empirically as well as predicted intuitively, and whether these differences are important must also be determined. Of course, this kind of evaluation can be done by presenting comparable programs to different population groups and exploring the outcomes. It is probable that different combinations of enrichment experiences are needed for diverse populations (Hof, Epstein, and Miller, 1980). No one has yet conducted this kind of research, vital to enrichment programs.

Group Process Variables. Group processes interfere frequently with ensuring that the programs being compared are controlled in all aspects except the one under examination. Groups develop their own history, culture, norms, role expectations, and objectives, and they develop these in processes that are always unique to each group. Trying to control the development of groups so that they are comparable in their structure and cohesion is unprofessional; it defeats one of the major purposes of marriage enrichment—to develop a support group in which couples can learn from one another's experiences. To be truly effective as a support group, the group must be responsive to its members' unique needs, skills, and levels of involvement.

This factor suggests that leaders cannot merely compare two groups and state decisively that any differences between them are due to the leaders' manipulations or structuring; differences may in fact exist in couples' experiences of group cohesiveness, group development, members' place in the group's role structure, and so on. Nevertheless, as an information base is formed gradually from many groups, each with its unique developmental history, a pattern of outcomes will develop. With this information, outcomes can be attributed with more assurance to the program factors (for example, whether it is an Encounter group or a skills training group) than differences between groups' composition and development. This highlights the need for ongoing evaluation as an integral part of enrichment with all kinds of groups more than the need for a few highly controlled studies that do not mirror the realities of groups with all of their variability.

Objectives of Intervention and Criteria of Evaluation

The term *effectiveness* has been used in research as though a single continuum existed on which to measure marriage enrichment programs. However, *effectiveness* is a relative term, applying to one of several possible objectives of a program. This qualification is important because so many possible objectives for marriage enrichment programs exist, and these objectives frequently conflict with one another. For instance, a program goal may be to "increase the accuracy of spouses' understanding of each other." The program's effectiveness, then, would be measured on the ability of spouses to predict their partner's responses on measures of attitudes, feelings, and behaviors. A program that is effective in reaching this goal will produce couples who gain accuracy in these predictions. As a result of spouses' increased awareness of each other, they may discover aspects about one another that they find abrasive, disquieting, and difficult to accept. Therefore, the "happiness" in the relationship may or may not be increased and, in fact, may be temporarily lessened. This "effective" program thus produces results that may be different from the outcome of another program whose goal is to increase happiness and satisfaction in marital relationships.

Criteria of Program Effectiveness. One criterion of program effectiveness that has received much attention has been marital adjustment. Jessie Bernard (1964) defines *adjustment* as a process of functional change. Therefore, using adjustment as the criterion for determining program effectiveness requires some method of examining this ongoing process. As Buckley (1968) has stated, the state of a system (in this case the degree of adjustment of a marital relationship) is really the interaction of process with time and space (in this case at the time of program completion or at a specified follow-up date).

One of the problems with using "to increase marital adjustment" as a program goal is that without being further defined, it is neither specific nor measurable. Therefore, the goal has been refined into a number of different, and at times conflictual, definitions of adjustment. One of the first of these has been stability, or the permanence of a relationship—measured by the number of couples who remain married over a specified period. This is not a popular definition of adjustment in our society, which emphasizes the importance of individual fulfillment over marital stability. The second definition, then, has been identified as personal development, or the degree to which individuals are able to experience continuing development or growth, as measured by personality and attitudinal instruments. A third definition, which expands on personal development, has been functionality, or the degree to which the marriage meets the needs of society—for example, the degree to which children are socialized "appropriately" and the degree to which husband and wife can fulfill societal roles.

Integration has also been used as a definition of adjustment; it is usually measured by examining the amount of consensus in the relationship. Integration has, in fact, been one of the criteria used most often by marriage enrichment researchers interested in marital adjustment.

Individual reporting of satisfaction with the marriage, however, has been the most popular definition of effective marriage enrichment. Marital satisfaction can be defined as the spouse's report of the degree of happiness or satisfaction with the marital relationship; "satisfaction with any domain of life experience is produced by the difference between an individual's perceived reality of the current situation and his or her aspirations concerning the domain" (Rhyne, 1981, p. 942). Marital satisfaction is used so often that it has been mistaken for marital adjustment in the literature. Many of the marital adjustment scales or inventories, completed by individual spouses, are actually measuring marital satisfaction.

A number of issues must be considered when marital satisfaction measures are used. First, these measures often assume an absolute standard of satisfaction—that is, a couple's scores are compared with the norms of a given measure, not with their own relationship in the past. Second, many of the measures implicitly define marital satisfaction as spouses' agreement or consensus on key marital issues. Here the criterion of integration is misconceived as satisfaction. This definition of marital satisfaction implies that conflict and differences signify lack of marital adjustment, which may or may not be the case. It also suggests that agreement is a more important factor in satisfaction than the process used to reach that agreement, which is also a debatable issue.

A third issue that creates problems in using marital satisfaction measures is that satisfaction in a marriage tends to be significantly influenced by other aspects of the individual's life (Hicks and Platt, 1971). For example, job satisfaction, the stage of psychosocial development, health, and relationships with children often color a spouse's judgments of happiness or marital satisfaction. A fourth problem is that marital satisfaction measures indicate the individual's subjective sentiment about the relationship, which may not necessarily be related to the existence or nonexistence of adjustment problems in the relationship. The term *marital satisfaction* itself suggests an assessment of the marital relationship, whereas in reality a spouse's *perception* of the marriage is what is actually being assessed. Again, it is important that individual satisfaction not be equated with relationship adjustment, as it is in many measures. Finally, these measures must by definition rely on self-report information, which is affected by social desirability (Edmonds, Withers, and Dibatista, 1972; Murstein and Beck, 1972; Hawkins, Weisburg, and Ray, 1977). Persons frequently have difficulty reporting marital dissatisfaction in a society that tends to encourage either correcting marital difficulties or dissolving the marriage. Therefore, spouses' responses may be biased, particularly after participating in a marriage enrichment group that they assumed would make the relationship more satisfying.

Nevertheless, self-report measures of marital satisfaction are and will remain important indices of the effectiveness of marriage enrichment services. Although other people's objective observations of a couple's relationship provide important information, how the *spouses themselves* experience the relationship is the critical assessment for people in our culture. "It is not what happens in that marriage, but how the partners understand or define what has happened, that is critical. At the same time, this drama is amplified by a pervasive societal ideology whose themes of marital satisfaction, self-actualization in marriage, sexuality, or companionship within marriage and the rest, occur in all levels of society and which form a system of ready made typifications of marriage that continue to be held in common and which are taken for granted. It is in this way that marital satisfaction may be viewed as a socially constructed reality, created by the partners to the marriage" (Rhyne, 1981, p. 942). In using measures of marital satisfaction, therefore, evaluators must: (1) distinguish clearly between marital satisfaction and marital adjustment, including such factors as integration; (2) accept this criterion as individual rather than interpersonal in its focus, and, insofar as possible, determine what effects factors such as health, developmental growth and change, work situation, and such relationships as those with children and extended family may have on perceptions about the marriage; (3) assess measures and their resulting data carefully for social desirability biases; and (4) make assessments relative to the spouse's own experiences, not to some normative expectation.

In exploring this last point further, it should be emphasized that measures of marital satisfaction must deal with the spouses' own perceptions of their relationship and not be confused—or compared—with other couples' perceptions of their marriages. Bernard (1964) suggests the need for a relativistic point of view with two criteria for effectiveness: (1) the rewards to each of the participants in the relationship outweigh the costs and (2) the relationship is better than any other alternative. These criteria do not presume that the development of a happy relationship is the measure of treatment success. Instead, they suggest that, assuming the givens in a particular relationship, the current relationship has become the best possible, not necessarily the best imaginable. Such criteria presume that a particular marriage, with its assets and limitations, has been examined in terms of success or failure of intervention, not compared to an absolute standard or even to the relationship itself at a time in the past when its resources and limitations may have been different.

This approach to evaluation is appealing; evaluation of each couple's resources and strategies for coping with problems is an essential part of the enrichment service. It examines the particular services provided to each couple based on their unique situation and personal and relationship goals. This individualized evaluation does not readily lend itself to the standardized measures that evaluators have used to make comparisons in studies. The significant virtue of standardized measures is that they allow for at least partial comparability across studies that otherwise would occur largely by chance (Gurman and Kniskern, 1981). Therefore, standardized measures, which can consider the current resources available to a couple, instead of an absolute standard, should be used.

Measures of marital satisfaction, whether individualized or standardized, do not by themselves provide all the evaluative information needed. A multidimensional approach is necessary, including both individual measures of satisfaction (criteria that assess the past history and future possibilities of a relationship) and relationship and transactional criteria which are based on the observations of outsiders.

Levels of Program Effectiveness. In evaluating services, the practitioner must be concerned with a number of levels of program effectiveness—the personal level, the interactional level, and the marital system level as it relates to the environment. Olson (1972) has developed a comprehensive and sensitive multilevel approach to evaluation of intervention effectiveness. Whereas Bernard is more concerned with the sociological variables in her relativistic point of view, based on subjective judgments of rewards and costs to spouses, Olson strives to examine several layers of psychological and sociopsychological variables using both subjective and objective measures. He proposes five system levels that may be differentially affected by intervention and which are also the targets of different approaches. The first level is the intrapersonal level. It is concerned with personal development, which is measured by such personality measures as the Minnesota Multiphasic Personality Inventory (MMPI) and Rorschach. This level has been somewhat ignored but is nevertheless important in judging the effectiveness of marriage enrichment programs. The second level is the interpersonal level, which is concerned with spouses' subjective evaluations of their relationship (they report marital satisfaction). This level is determined through scales and inventories and is the most popular kind of evaluation. The third level is the quasi-interactional level, determined by self-reporting of concrete behavior. For instance, spouses may be asked to report the use of specific communication skills or the amount of the time they spend with one another during a given week. The interactional level is the fourth level. It is determined by having observers code samples of interaction behavior using scales such as those developed by Thomas, Carter, and Gambrill (1971) and Patterson and Hops (1972). A person observes spouses talking with each other or listens to a tape of their interaction and records such behaviors as interrupting one another, expressing appreciation, and repeating one another's statements. Finally, the fifth level is the transactional level. At this level interaction behavior is coded as it occurs in the natural environment. As in the interactional level, an observer records behavior, but now the couple are interacting in their own home.

Patterson (1973), Wills, Weiss, and Patterson (1974), Weiss, Hops, and Patterson (1973), Epstein and Jackson (1978), and Olson and Ryder (1970) have conducted research at different system levels, and they have found that data gathered at the various levels is not necessarily correlated. This finding is significant because an intervention technique may effect change at one level and not another, and thus judgments of effectiveness must indicate at what level success can be reported. Moreover, these research studies have shown that interactional behavior changes more readily than spouses' perceptions of and satisfaction with the relationship (see also Gurman and Kniskern, 1977). For example, though couples may learn and actually use the Rogerian listening skills or they may learn to positively reinforce one another, their perceptions of the relationship do not necessarily change.

The most comprehensive approach to evaluation involves two or more levels, involving both subjective reports from the individuals within the relationship and an objective measure of their behavior. The conflicting data that result from this kind of evaluation should not be viewed as problematic, but rather as multidimensional—the evaluation is more sensitive to program outcomes. Sometimes, sleeper effects, those not immediately apparent, may be indicated by other effects. For example, couples who begin to increase their use of positive reinforcement techniques may not feel very differently about their relationship after a few weeks. However, if this behavior continues for six months to a year, significant changes in their evaluations of the relationship may occur. This hypothesis may be useful in exploring many of the behavioral skills taught in enrichment programs.

Marriage Enrichment Evaluation—A Model

There are two major methods of marriage enrichment evaluation: self-report and observation. Self-report methods refer to "formal testing procedures where clients are asked to fill out inventories or verbally answer standardized questions. Self-report methods may reflect information about family behavior in general or the behavior of a particular individual within the family. The individual is the major source of information from self-report methods. . . . Self-report assessment devices do not measure actual interaction" (Cromwell, Olson, and Fournier, 1976, p. 527).

Most self-report methods of marriage enrichment evaluation are aimed at determining the individual's assessment of marital happiness, adjustment, and problems, or the individual's attitudes toward specific aspects of marriage, such as conflict, sexuality, or sex roles. This is usually the primary focus of marriage enrichment evaluation because the goal of most programs is to increase satisfaction with the marriage. Self-report methods address Olson's intrapersonal, interpersonal, and quasi-interactional levels.

Self-report methods may also allow participants to specify aspects of the group that enhanced or detracted from their achievement of goals. Examples might be "it was friendly" or "the leader really listened to us." Such reports help clarify what group members think they benefited from in a group and whether they feel they did so "in spite of" specific aspects of the group's composition, development, or leadership. Similarly, group members may think that the group was supportive, the leader dynamic, and the content useful, even though they did not experience significant changes in their marital relationships.

Observational methods differ from self-report methods in that "actual behavior is the subject of investigation rather than individual perceptions of behavior. The 'outsiders' (observers) may be a part of the interaction or observing via one-way mirrors, audiotape recordings, or videotape. Interaction may be generated from self-report methods such as the *Inventory of Marital Conflicts* or other revealed differences techniques. The overriding purpose of observation techniques is to elicit specific sequences of interaction characteristic of typical behaviors" (Cromwell, Olson, and Fournier, 1976, p. 537).

Observational methods usually focus on three kinds of change: cognitive (what people know), affective (what people value) and behavioral (what people are doing). These methods include a variety of tests and rating scales to determine, for example, whether cognitive content was learned, the extent to which spouses actually use the communication skills that have been presented, and to discover how individuals perceive their own values. Many of these methods can be used either in the group or in the couple's home. Olson's interactional and transactional levels of evaluation, for example, use behavioral rating scales, which are observational measures.

Both self-report and observational methods can be used to assess not only how participants' individual behaviors affect their marriages but also how they affect the group. Evaluation is here concerned with the development of leadership and other roles in the group, how friendships and antipathies form among couples, and what styles of leadership are used by the designated leader. Observational systems such as Bales Interaction Process Analysis (Bales, 1950) can be used for this kind of evaluation.

A group's goals and objectives are the best indicators of what evaluation methods will be most relevant. For example, a weekend retreat, the goals of which are building hope in the future of the marital relationship, increasing relationship satisfaction, and establishing a continuing program to learn specific communication and conflict management skills, requires several kinds of evaluation. Self-assessment would be useful to determine the attitudes of participants toward the future of their own marriages. For example, participants might be asked to predict the probability of remaining married to their spouses for five years or for ten years. Participants also might be asked to predict their marital happiness now, in five years, and in ten years. This goal might also be evaluated by observational means. For example, couples might be asked to discuss what they want to see happen in the next five years and how they might achieve this. Their discussion could be recorded and ranked on a scale of the degree of hope for the future or analyzed, using a behavioral coding system, for factors such as positive reinforcement, withdrawal, sarcasm, and anger.

The second goal of the group, to increase relationship satisfaction, is most easily evaluated at the self-report level. A scale of marital satisfaction could be administered, such as the Marital Satisfaction Scale (Roach, Frazier, and Bowden, 1981). This could be combined with questions about future marital happiness into one instrument.

Finally, the goal of establishing a program for learning skills indicates self-report evaluation most directly. The participants could be asked to indicate the probability that they will enroll in the continuing program ("not probable," "possible," "most likely"). This goal could also be evaluated quite easily by observational means; the number of participants who go on to participate in another group can merely be counted.

Depending on the leader's interests and resources, he or she may choose to use one, two, or all of the above suggested evaluation methods. For leaders whose resources are somewhat limited, the use of the Marital Satisfaction Scale, including questions about future marital happiness, would be quite easy to administer when couples are screened for the group and at the beginning and end of the weekend. It takes only a few moments and provides some good baseline information with which to compare scale data at the end of the program. It could be further strengthened by conducting a follow-up session with the couples after a given period of time to assess whether changes are maintained or enhanced over time. This simple evaluation method provides good indications of how participants assess changes in their marital relationship both for evaluation purposes and as a basis of the leader's and each couple's assessment of their relationship.

Choosing or Developing Appropriate
Evaluation Instruments

A number of instruments and methods for marriage enrichment group evaluation are listed in detail in Resource B. They are listed according to the characteristics they would most commonly be used to evaluate. Methods that are widely used or that are particularly applicable to the objectives of the "average" marriage enrichment service are indicated by an asterisk; brief descriptions of these instruments appear in Resource B. Other methods in the list are followed by citations of their main sources in the literature; complete bibliographic information is given in the References. Methods so listed serve specialized functions or need to be adapted to marriage enrichment evaluation. In reviewing Resource B, the reader should keep in mind the possibility of multiple uses of instruments. Any given instrument for evaluating a marriage enrichment program may have a variety of uses, depending on the program's goals and objectives. For example, an instrument that asks spouses to assess specific aspects of their relationship is an appropriate self-report instrument. However, if spouses are also asked to predict their partners' responses on the instrument, those responses can be used as indicators of spouses' understanding of one another's feelings, and the instrument thus provides appropriate observational information on cognitive changes. Or, if the spouses are asked to share their responses and to discuss those that are different, their resulting interaction can be recorded on audio- or videotape. In this way the original self-report instrument melds with observational methods for evaluating affective or behavioral changes.

In deciding upon particular evaluation tools, it is necessary to distinguish among program objectives; for example, individual change, relationship satisfaction, spouses understanding each other better, changes in verbal behavior, and group development. These indicate the evaluation categories that will provide the most relevant information. In assessing the available instruments or methods, or in developing a new or improved method, the following criteria (adapted from Cromwell, Olson, and Fournier, 1976, pp. 544-545) can be applied:

1. The method should relate collected data to the operational definitions of relevant theoretical concepts. This provides some linkage among theory, research, and practice. Relevant concepts may include assertiveness, authority, control, role expectations, role performance, supportiveness, empathy, feeling expression, and so on. (A listing of evaluation methods that tap these concepts can be found in Resource B.)

2. The method should involve issues and data that are specific to the couple or group being evaluated. This specificity will ensure the involvement of the participants and thus will minimize the error variance. For example, in assessing the degree to which couples have learned conflict manage-

ment skills it would be more useful to have spouses discuss a real issue in their relationship than to role play using a standard situation. Although both methods would provide data for observation, in a discussion of real issues, the couple would probably be more receptive to feedback, whereas in role playing they may be concerned to a degree with performing well and may see feedback as less directly relevant to their relationship.

3. Look for procedures that include multimethod approaches because they provide more than one perspective on the same dimension. For example, an instrument which combines both self-report and behavioral-observation approaches enables the leader to obtain and compare these two rich sources of data.

4. The instruments should be evaluated for both reliability and validity. Self-report methods need to be assessed in terms of some measure of internal consistency reliability, such as split-half or test-retest. Observational instruments require the same assessment, in addition to inter-rater reliability.

5. The procedure should be designed so the clients do not feel tricked or deceived during its administration. If deception is involved, participants will tend not to trust the group experience that follows or future marriage enrichment leaders, and such mistrust might distort their responses.

6. The equipment, facilities, cost, and time required to administer and score instruments should be well within the program's resources. For example, a leader would probably not choose a two-hour battery of evaluation testing for a weekend retreat.

7. The instruments should be appropriate for a wide variety of age groups and social classes. If an instrument is too narrowly focused or demands sophisticated verbal skills, it will be appropriate only for a limited range of potential participants. Tests with sexual biases should also be carefully avoided.

Choosing a coding system for analyzing observed behaviors requires some additional considerations. Pinsof (1981, pp.

726–727) has listed the following criteria, which are useful in deciding on a coding system:

1. Reconstructivity, or the ability of the coding system to permit meaningful reconstruction of the actual behaviors or experiences from which the data was abstracted.
2. Modality-system fit, or the degree to which the coding system describes the factors that are relevant to a specific program.
3. Orientation-system fit, or the degree to which the coding system is applicable to the theory underlying the program.
4. Exhaustiveness, or the ability of the coding system to record all intelligible behaviors meaningfully rather than as "other" behaviors.

It is advisable to use instruments which have already been proven workable. Developing reliable instruments involves a great deal of trial and error and is demanding, sometimes disappointing, work. Existing instruments not only save this work but also make it possible to compare results with other research derived using the same instruments. This facilitates larger assessments of the relative effectiveness of different programs, techniques, and program structures and comparison of services to different populations across groups and research studies.

Finally, in choosing evaluation instruments, the leader may need to search persistently for ones that discriminate finely between levels of functioning. Many marital adjustment measures are designed to focus on symptoms of problematic interaction rather than on improvement from "a satisfactory to a more-than-satisfactory level" (Hof and Miller, 1981, p. 52). If couples who are already functioning adequately are evaluated on measures that were originally developed for clinical couples, they may score so high that there is little room for improvement. In fact, it seems probable that this is one of the reasons research has shown marriage enrichment programs to be more effective in changing behavior than in changing marital satisfaction. The traditional measures of satisfaction have been used, and because they are not designed to do so, they have not measured change from "good" to "better."

Evaluation Designs

This book is not intended to provide a comprehensive overview of the research methodology and experimental designs useful in evaluative research; there are a number of such overviews available (Campbell and Stanley, 1963; Weiss, 1972; Jayaratne and Levy, 1979). Campbell and Stanley's (1963) classic presentation of designs for research is a common place to begin in determining the appropriate design for accomplishing the purposes of program evaluation. Several of the designs they describe have already been mentioned as being particularly useful for enrichment group evaluations. Those that require little in the way of additional time and resources, and that are ideal for continuing program evaluation, are described in the sections that follow in terms common to evaluation methodology. For the more energetic practitioner who would like to pursue more rigorous methods, experimental designs that are particularly applicable to marriage enrichment services are discussed briefly at the end of this section.

Designs for the Practitioner. Three of the most common designs used in evaluation have been defined by Campbell and Stanley (1963) as the one-shot case study, the one-group pretest-posttest, and the static-group comparison.

In the one-shot case study, an evaluative measure is administered at the end of the group; there is no data available to compare the group to itself prior to the marriage enrichment program or to other groups. Such comparisons are based on assumptions that the group is comparable to other groups in its composition and development and that the evaluator had an accurate perception of relevant dimensions of the group at its inception. For example, a leader may conduct a marriage enrichment retreat and administer Spanier's Dyadic Adjustment Scale (Spanier, 1976) during the last session. The leader may then compare participants' scores to the norms for this measure, presuming that any differences are due to the retreat. However, a number of other factors may be responsible for the variances, including initial difference in the group from the normative sample.

In the one-group pretest-posttest design, the group is

measured before and after the marriage enrichment program and the two measures are compared. The assumption is that any changes are due to the marriage enrichment program. This assumption can be considered well-founded, thus this is the most commonly used design. It has the advantage of providing assessment information that may be useful to the leader, the couple, and the group at the beginning, as well as feedback at the end regarding the extent of change. When combined with a long-term follow-up, this is a useful approach to evaluation. Nevertheless, conclusions about the effectiveness of the intervention should be made cautiously because the influence of other factors cannot be ruled out. Such factors might include a natural maturing process within the marriages and in the group relationships and insight derived by participants through being exposed to the evaluation instrument (for example, many couples report that they understand their relationship better after having completed one of the marriage inventories).

In the static-group comparison the group is measured after the marriage enrichment program and compared with a group that has not experienced a marriage enrichment program. The assumption that the two groups are comparable is a subjective judgment; significant differences between the two groups may well be innate rather than due to one group's marriage enrichment experience. Consequently, this design is less reliable than the one-group pretest-posttest design.

Problems with drawing scientifically sound conclusions from evaluations notwithstanding, the pretest-posttest design can be quite useful for preliminary studies of new programs or techniques, as has already been discussed, and in the ongoing evaluation of services. (In evaluating continuing programs, confounding factors are not as relevant as in evaluation of a single group.) Unless the measure itself requires a great deal of time and resources, this design requires very little prior planning by the group leader. It does allow judgment to be made about whether a particular program or technique appears to be effective enough to warrant further study and use.

Experimental Designs. For the professional who chooses, somewhat more rigorous evaluation designs can be used to determine whether a specified program or technique, or some other structure or population characteristic, is responsible for the effectiveness of marriage enrichment services.

The essential requirement for classical experimental designs is that participants be assigned randomly to experimental and control groups. This is not difficult to do; the only significant problem involved is ensuring that in the process of random assignment, one group is not by chance made larger than the other. Equally sized groups can be achieved prior to recruiting couples by randomly assigning slots in each group in the following manner. First, consult the table of random numbers for consecutive pairs of numbers—one and two, three and four, and so on. The number that appears first becomes the first slot in working group and the number that appears second is assigned to the waiting group. That is, if number one appears first, assign the first slot to the working group and the second slot to the waiting group. Then, moving to the next pair of numbers, if number four appears before three, assign the fourth slot to the working group and the third slot to the waiting group. (Continue this procedure until all slots have been assigned to one of the groups.) As couples are recruited, they are assigned consecutive numbers; the numbers correspond to the slots already designated as being either in the working or the waiting group. In the example just described, the first and fourth couples to sign up for the program would be assigned to the working group and the second and third couples would be assigned to the waiting group. This procedure can be expanded to randomly form any number of groups of equal size.

The major difficulty with random assignment is that it does not allow leaders to control composition factors in forming groups. However, if an experimental design is desirable for research purposes, this problem can be addressed by deciding first on a single set of composition criteria to be used in both groups and then using the screening interview to ensure that all applicants fall within these boundaries.

When working with ready-formed groups such as church groups and clubs, it is impossible to assign couples randomly to groups. However, the ready-made groups themselves can be assigned a research status—for example, waiting or working, as in the previous example—so that over a period of time data accrue for a number of groups in varying settings.

Groups assigned a waiting status would complete the evaluation processes prior to the marriage enrichment experience. In comparing evaluation results, participants' scores in each group are averaged to provide a group score and the number of groups in each category becomes the experimental N. For example, if there are three working groups and four waiting groups, $N = 3$ and 4. The N thus represents the number of groups rather than the number of participants.

The most useful experimental designs for enrichment evaluation are the pretest-posttest control group and the posttest-only control group designs. In each of these, participants (or groups) are randomly assigned to experimental and control conditions. In the pretest-posttest control design, criteria measures are made both before and after marriage enrichment and the amounts of change in each of the two groups can be compared. Usually, the experimental group is expected to show significantly more improvement than a group that has not experienced the program or one that has experienced a program based on another theoretical approach.

In the posttest-only design, there is no measure prior to intervention, and comparisons are made only between the outcome scores of the two groups. Although the lack of a pretest makes it impossible to measure changes made by a particular couple, one advantage of this design is that it allows the leader to rule out the possibility that the pretest itself may be responsible for the change in scores. For example, couples who in a pretesting session are asked to complete and discuss one of the standard marital adjustment scales will learn a great deal about each other's thoughts and feelings and initiate relationship changes as a consequence. They may be aided in doing so by learning communication skills, which is the content of the experimental group, whereas couples in the control group are not able to create such change. Of course, in practice, what is a problem in evaluation design is actually an advantage in achieving the group's goals. Misunderstanding can occur when it is assumed that significant changes in adjustment scores at posttesting are *due to skill training,* when in fact, the changes may be the result of *interaction between the measurement itself and the skill training.* It is not readily apparent, however, when the testing process is a stimulus to change rather than a passive record of behavior (Campbell and Stanley, 1963). The possibility of interaction such as this between evaluative procedures and the intervention itself is, of course, controlled by the posttest-only design. However, if group leaders want to stimulate this kind of change deliberately through the evaluation procedures, they can use the pretest-posttest design and label the evaluation methods as part of the experience being evaluated.

When assigning participants or groups randomly to research statuses is impossible or not desirable because of group composition issues, there are still other research designs which can be used, although there is a greater chance that factors other than the marriage enrichment program may be responsible for evaluation findings. The nonequivalent control group design may be most useful for evaluating outcomes in, for example, already existing groups. In this design two existing groups, such as two church groups, are given a pretest and a posttest. It is important that the groups not be defined as experimental or control group based on their pretest scores, which makes possible seemingly significant outcomes as a result of regression to the mean. (Regression to the mean occurs when some individuals score high and others low because of chance factors. This is more likely to occur, for example, if the group with the lowest scores is assigned working status and the group with highest scores is assigned waiting status. Without any intervention at all, it is probable that the low scores will improve and the high scores will decline on a second testing. For further discussion of this factor, see Weiss, 1972, pp. 70–72.)

Another problem in drawing conclusions from this kind of design is that characteristics of the experimental group, which are different from characteristics of the control group, in some way interact with the experimental variable. For instance, if the experimental group consists of couples who have sought counseling for marital difficulties from an agency, and the control group consists of couples in a university class, greater gains on a marital adjustment inventory by the experimental group may be due to fluctuations in hope and despair in such a group being much greater than in the other group.

Other designs are available which are quite useful for certain evaluative objectives (such as the ongoing self-help groups), although they are not widely applicable to the most common kinds of marriage enrichment group evaluation. Among these are the time series, separate-sample pretest-posttest control group, multiple time-series, and institutional cycle designs (Campbell and Stanley, 1963).

In summary, there are a variety of approaches to evaluating a marriage enrichment service. Perhaps the most useful to the practitioner is the pretest-posttest design with planned follow-up evaluation, conducted in each group with which the practitioner works. Conclusions about effectiveness can then be drawn from the pattern of outcomes that become apparent over time. These conclusions can be supported by more rigorous experimental studies, although such studies can never take the place of ongoing evaluation.

8

Marriage Enrichment: Current Status and Future Prospects

The purpose of marriage enrichment is to teach couples attitudes, communication behaviors, and knowledge about family and marital relationships. This education is designed to help them develop relationships that meet personal needs and enhance individual development. This is education in the very best sense of the term—experiencing new ideas and new approaches to relating, not just learning about them. It is education that enables spouses to change the way they think, what they feel, and how they care for each other. Marriage enrichment did not begin by determining what an optimal marriage relationship is through behavioral science investigation and then informing the public about services needed to obtain this norm. Rather, marriage enrichment developed as individuals, couples, and religious leaders identified unmet needs for learning about living and explored ways to satisfy those needs. Meanwhile, other helping professionals were becoming disillusioned with remedial approaches to helping and were experimenting successfully with preventive approaches. Some went even further to suggest enhancing personal and interpersonal functioning through a focus

217

on growth and development; this new approach was as radical a change from prevention as prevention had been from remediation. For helping professionals working with marital couples, the new focus was bolstered by the growing church-related marriage enrichment movement.

The energetic development of the grass-roots marriage enrichment movement and the helping professions' emerging focus on educational approaches have parallel purposes and thus the two groups have begun to build on one another's resources and discoveries. Both have turned from borrowing to merging goals and strategies, which has resulted in the burgeoning of marriage enrichment services in the past fifteen years. Fifteen years suggests that this movement is only in its adolescence. The marriage enrichment movement is characterized by grand schemes to help the marital relationship become a source of personal security and continuing growth. Examining the literature is almost like brainstorming all the possible approaches to strengthening marital relationships. Methods and strategies for enrichment services seem to be developing much faster than the ability to understand and integrate them. The theoretical and methodological bases include General Systems theory, Rogerian theory, behavioral theories, Gestalt approaches, transactional analysis, Maslow's self-actualization theory, Rankian philosophy, rational emotive theory, choice awareness, and assertion training. The philosophy of the church-related marriage enrichment movement provides an additional dimension to many of the approaches to enrichment services.

The church-related marriage enrichment movement is more than just another approach to helping couples; it began with a focus different from that of professional services and has maintained that focus despite the borrowing and blending of objectives and methods with the human service professions. The focus of religious groups in marriage enrichment programs is not just to strengthen couples' marriages, but through these couples, to strengthen the institution of marriage at a time when the validity of traditional marriage is being questioned and attacked on several fronts. The institutions of marriage and family are basic resources in the work of the church.

The human service professions and religious groups have benefited from sharing mostly because human service professionals who work in both movements have carefully interpreted context, philosophy, and programs. These social workers, psychologists, and pastoral counselors make it possible for the groups to have access to each other's knowledge and methodology.

It is in the spirit of sharing between religious groups and the human service professions that this book has been written. Many of the marriage enrichment materials currently available follow a basic structure: a summary of the field, a presentation of a particular theoretical model, and a step-by-step description of how to conduct a marriage enrichment group based on that model. Certainly the models are valuable, but at times numerous approaches can be confusing. Many models of marriage enrichment do not include an assessment of their particular strengths and weaknesses in meeting the needs of a specific group within a particular context. In addition, such models seldom suggest how they might be combined with other approaches to provide a service that can meet the unique needs of a group. "Most mental health theorists and practitioners have concentrated too much on developing theories and methods limited to a single perspective, failing even to try to combine elements from different philosophical and theoretical perspectives into one program, even when such an effect might create a more realistic and powerful program than any single perspective could provide. . . . No major theoretical position and no psychological technology has a claim on the full truth, yet . . . all probably have something valuable to contribute to the overall struggle toward reducing intrapsychic and interpersonal conflict and increasing personal satisfaction and social harmony" (Guerney, 1977, pp. 320–321).

Although I have described particular programs and many activities for marriage enrichment groups, they are not rigid models that should be applied to every group, irrespective of its needs. Although this book is a "how to" approach, it tells how to use the available programs and materials rather than constituting such an approach in itself. I have examined the basic processes used in composing a group, deciding on group leadership styles, developing a program to meet the group's goals, maintaining changes that are made, and evaluating the effects of the marriage enrichment services. I have suggested that rather than forming a group to experience a particular program, providers of marriage enrichment services should determine the needs of a particular group of couples and then select or design a program that focuses on the group's unique composition and goals. This latter process requires much more expertise from the leaders: they must not only know the theory and methodology of a number of approaches but also how to create and blend methodologies to meet the needs of particular groups. They must understand groups—the dynamics of composition, structure, norms, development, leadership, decision making, group learning, goal achievement, and termination. Finally, they must be able to evaluate whether the services provided meet the established goals and determine the program's short- and long-term effects, both intended and unintended. These are high expectations for any leader to fulfill. This book is an initial effort to help leaders meet the needs and enhance the growth of couples in marriage enrichment groups.

In one respect, marriage enrichment services and the church-related marriage enrichment movement are only part of a larger movement working toward the enhancement of the growth and development of individuals, families, and communities through education. The knowledge and methodologies of the human service professions and the behavioral sciences can enrich lives as well as remedy suffering. Marriage enrichment is, in this respect, part of the larger movement to institutionalize through education the resources of the helping professions— now serving only the casualties of society through prevention and remediation—so that everyone can benefit throughout the life cycle. Guerney (1977, p. 337) has dreamed of a School for Living, "the pure institutional form to which the educational model could give birth. Such an institution would be an educational resource for those who wanted to be more successful in shaping their personalities and behaviors to accord with their ideals for themselves. Such an institution would develop unhampered by built-in restraints of the politics and tradition of already existing institutions."

This new model of service for the helping professions is indeed an exciting one. It implies that the wealth of educational theories and methodologies will provide useful perspectives on the practice of human service professionals, perspectives which have previously been ignored.

Because this book covers the processes of marriage enrichment rather than specific content for a particular group, the material can be applied to many different educational groups. For example, the suggestions for the determination of group composition, the development of group structures and norms, and the model of group leadership apply to groups with such focuses as parenting and family enrichment, breaking undesirable habits (smoking, overeating, and abusing alcohol and drugs), reducing fears, developing interpersonal skills (assertiveness, anger and aggression management, developing intimacy, and male-female relationships), and coping with stages of life development (grief, retirement, adolescence, and career changes).

An educational approach to helping services has many advantages over therapeutic approaches, and it becomes particularly useful when combined with them to provide a comprehensive approach to practice. From an educational perspective, therapy can be seen as remedial education, designed to correct skill deficits in communication, self-awareness, problem solving, conflict management, sexual expression, and other areas. Thus the therapist is a tutor. When the tutored couple also belongs to a group in which couples can share common struggles, develop hope and realistic expectations about what the marital relationship can become, and work toward their established goals, then personal and relational enrichment that exemplifies the vision of the marriage enrichment movement can occur. The categorization of marital relationships as healthy or dysfunctional is replaced with behavioral objectives and goals that do not label interpersonal conflicts as deviations from normalcy.

The vision of the marriage enrichment movement is that by teaching the knowledge, attitudes, and skills that enhance marital relationships, spouses will learn not only to better their own relationship but also to improve their relationships with parents, children, colleagues, and friends. Understanding sexuality, intimacy, and expressions of feeling, and acquiring skills in communication, conflict management, problem solving, and values clarification help improve interaction in all these relationships.

Therapy and education together can offer more than either can alone. Guerney (1977, p. 315) notes that their marriage enrichment approach is neither preventive, enriching, nor therapeutic alone, but rather is all three: "Which of these functions an RE [relationship enhancement] program is serving is a matter of when it is undertaken, how long it lasts, and, most of all, what perspective guides it—the perspective of the agency offering it and the person participating in it." To truly understand the marriage enrichment movement and the movement toward educational services is to recognize that both of these services, at their best, perform all three functions. The best therapy is designed to prevent future difficulties by providing individuals enrichment and education that will enable them to resolve their own difficulties and find their own resources. The best education is geared to meet the individual's needs, not to push the individual through a preestablished program that may or may not suit strengths and weaknesses. This education is remedial because learning deficits are systematically determined and addressed. It is preventive because it focuses on the knowledge, attitudes, and skills that will help individuals cope with normal developmental processes. Furthermore, it is enriching because it develops and builds on personal strengths.

These enrichment services are based on the interaction of leader with group members, and through this interaction, on the mutually agreed upon group goals. This model of service delivery suggests that a program developed through theory rather than through interaction with participants is inadequate. In essence, a marriage enrichment program must always be based on the objectives of the group; it must create a unique program for a unique group. Once the goals of a particular marriage enrichment group have been defined, leaders decide on relevant theoretical approaches and select or create appropriate learning activities while considering the sequential steps to cognitive, affective, and skills learning.

This book includes descriptions of structured activities and a list of resources for such activities. Used in conjunction with brief lectures, readings, and structured and unstructured discussions, these activities can be powerful learning contexts. Leaders can use them as described or adapt them in infinite ways to fit the needs of a particular couple or marriage enrichment group; the activities may even be adapted for a different kind of group. For example, the listening exercises and conflict management exercises would work well in a parent-teen communication group. The Brainstorming About Sex exercise could easily be adapted to initiate discussion about sex in an adolescent group. Several of the group formation activities would be useful in a variety of group settings, such as assertiveness training groups, parenting groups, and anxiety management groups. These activities should be only a beginning point. Depending upon their modification, they can be used in various ways—with a troubled couple in counseling or as homework for students in a university classroom. The needs of the particular group or individuals and the competence of the professional in presenting activities as the basis for learning through experience and discussion determine their usefulness.

Helping professionals, however, must always try to understand how their interventions are affecting their clients. In marriage enrichment services provided by helping professionals and by the church-related marriage enrichment movement, research has lagged behind the development of program models and structured activities because, unfortunately, evaluation is not often as exciting as designing programs to address crucial issues. Research and evaluation have not been a priority of the movement because couples report that their marriage enrichment experiences are valuable and professionals believe in what they are doing.

Although research has not been a priority (prioritizing it in the idea development stage could not be expected), in the last eight years or so helping professionals have begun to assess the effects of services, both those provided by the church-related marriage enrichment movement and those conducted under the auspices of the helping professions. This research is rapidly becoming a concentrated effort to examine what marriage enrichment is accomplishing, the methods it is using, and how it can be more effective. Perhaps one reason for this increase in research is that initial findings have been positive. Studies on all of the major approaches to marriage enrichment—General Systems theory approaches, Rogerian approaches, and the behavioral approaches, as well as approaches that integrate two or more of these theories—indicate that enrichment has had significant positive effects on the marital relationship. Results have been confusing, however, because different approaches emphasize different outcomes, and various studies have reported different and at times conflicting results. These studies indicate the diverse effects of marriage enrichment programs, which can be expected. However, they also indicate a need to rethink the function of evaluation and the issues related to that function. Therefore, a need exists to nurture a spirit of excitement and creativity in conceptualizing evaluation approaches that will strengthen marriage enrichment.

Research needs to become a part of *every* marriage enrichment service because, besides evaluating the effectiveness of service, it increases the service's effectiveness by being an integral part of the intervention. Evaluation procedures enable services to be designed to meet the participants' unique needs as they are defined through the evaluation process. The evaluation process itself has the potential of providing important knowledge and powerful feedback to participants; this potential is an advantage of many evaluation procedures and is being increasingly recognized. Guided discussion focused on the outcomes of inventories, scales, or behavior recorded by an observer can help couples learn more about one another, identify strengths, determine areas for improvement, gauge the success of their attempts to initiate change, and establish relevant relational, personal, or group objectives.

Before evaluation can become an integral part of all enrichment services, and, for that matter, of educational services, a number of pressing tasks must be accomplished: (1) the development of appropriate research models, (2) the definition of evaluative criteria, and (3) the development of evaluation methods and tools.

First, research models are needed that fit the needs of practitioners and that are built on the belief that services are unique because they are designed to accomplish a unique group's goals, goals that are defined in interaction with that group. The models must also be based on the premise that participants share in the evaluation process as part of the service provided. However, to control for any differences caused by the intervention variables themselves, research designs often demand that a specified program be rigidly imposed on the group regardless of its needs or its composition. The models demand that groups be as homogeneous as possible rather than encouraging the formation of groups that meet participants' needs—perhaps by being heterogeneous. Finally, they often demand that participants be ignorant of the research procedures so that their awareness of the evaluation does not contaminate the results—participants often learn about themselves from evaluation procedures and change as a result of the evaluation. This increases service effectiveness, while having a negative effect on research that tries to control any interaction between evaluation and intervention.

Consequently, services have been developed to conform to the demands of research methodology rather than methodologies to meet the needs of the services. Yet, the purpose of evaluation is to increase the effectiveness of services, not limit their effectiveness by stifling creative practice with the claim that it cannot be evaluated unless it is replicable. This problem has grown as practitioners take seriously the need to evaluate their practices and yet can work only with the procedures that have served well in the laboratory. Instead, models of research and evaluation designed not only to tolerate but to accentuate and encourage individualized, creative services are needed. Such a model would include descriptions of the group's context, composition, development, norms, leadership, and goals. It would focus on examining patterns of outcomes over time, patterns resulting from a number of groups with different composition, development, and goals. The model would assume that evaluation is an integral part of the group's experience; it is not to be disguised or minimized. The classic research designs that use random sampling may provide a base for development of these new models of research. In the next decade, I hope to see the proliferation of research models for practice in marriage enrichment, as in the past decade the number of practice models has increased. Research is much like good marriage enrichment leadership—it goes beyond a cookbook approach of applying the defined models to any group regardless of its needs and instead develops creative evaluation approaches based on the participants' objectives and the group context. This approach to research will include the established methods when they work and develop new methods when they do not. It will require a belief in the power of evaluation as a potent intervention tool and the desire to conduct research with creativity rather than with the resignation and boredom that seem to pervade enrichment evaluation. It will be difficult to establish this approach; it is easier to adapt services to the current models of research than to take the leap into creativity and develop models that enhance the effectiveness of services by emphasizing the uniqueness of each individual and each group.

The second pressing task, to define more adequately the criteria of effectiveness, cannot be accomplished without first determining what marriage enrichment programs and services are trying to achieve. A primary focus of evaluation has been the amount of satisfaction spouses report in their marital relationship. This criterion is important although it has often been confused with marital adjustment, made up of a complex of variables including stability, integration, degree of conflict, personal development, and functionality. These variables are evaluated through spouse reports and perceptions as well as through observations and evaluations of others.

There are many techniques, instruments, and methods that are potentially useful in marriage enrichment evaluation. The tools listed in Resource B are to evaluation what the structured activities in Resource A are to program planning—they are structured methods to adapt to specific purposes. Unfortunately, most enrichment research has used instruments that were not designed to evaluate educational programs. Most of the instruments, particularly those used to measure marital satisfaction, were designed for troubled couples in therapy. In pretesting, many couples in enrichment score so high on these instruments that they can show no improvement—change that indicates program effectiveness cannot be measured. Also, the instruments measure such variables as marital stability and the degree of conflict, which have not been clearly distinguished from marital satisfaction (some of the most satisfying marriages are also conflictual). Thus there is a pressing need for creative work in developing reliable and valid instruments and methodologies, applicable to the needs of marriage enrichment services.

These methods must satisfy five requirements. First, they must measure relevant variables such as marital satisfaction and other attitudes and perceptions, skills such as communication and conflict management, and knowledge that enhances the marital relationship. Second, the methods must evaluate the current status of the relationship, not its development over the years. Questions that focus on the past, such as Have you ever wished that you had never married? do not allow for change. Third, evaluative methods must measure changes in a particular relationship rather than comparing a particular couple to some unobtainable ideal. Fourth, the method must allow for a range of responses from the most unhappy couples to the most blissful couples; couples who are already happy must be able to measure growth in their relationship. There must also be adequate calibration of the evaluative tool so that even small increments of change, either positive or negative, are measurable. It is unrealistic to expect that a troubled couple can develop into a blissful couple in one marriage enrichment weekend retreat. Finally, these methods need to provide information that leaders and couples can use to evaluate needs, establish marriage enrichment group goals, and assess progress toward these goals.

Clearly, the development of such methodologies is no small task. The summaries of available instruments and strategies in Resource B are just a small beginning. However, the future of marriage enrichment services very much depends on the ability to use the resource of evaluation methodologies and to rethink the importance of evaluation research as an integral part of marriage enrichment services and of educational services as a whole.

The importance of evaluation has been recognized in part because findings have implied that the effects of marriage enrichment processes and programs go beyond the "making good marriages better," the slogan of early advocates of the movement. The emphasis on education and mutual support for couples in time-limited, professionally directed groups and in ongoing supportive networks is a powerful alternative to traditional helping services for troubled couples. Further, this new emphasis in professional services brings with it the potential for reaching a large segment of society. This capability has developed as professional services have merged with the grass-roots and church-related movement. Therefore, the combination of a new approach in human services and a network of support and involvement, with much greater potential for reaching a variety of people than traditional human service delivery systems, has created a marriage enrichment movement that is growing rapidly.

Some professional groups have dreamed of the more or less universal acknowledgment of the need for and benefits of human services, and marriage enrichment services have made this dream a reality. Currently, training programs all across the country are preparing couples to provide marriage enrichment services. Major church denominations are sending literature and program guides on how to provide marriage enrichment to their churches—small rural congregations, large urban churches, and their social service agencies. Thus couples who would never seek marriage counseling are using enrichment services as an opportunity to learn alternative ways to interact, to share thoughts and feelings with one another, and to form relationships with other couples with whom they can share common concerns.

Professionals are finding that groups of people can strengthen the interventions made in troubled marriages and that learning new ways of relating and managing conflict in a group of couples is a useful adjunct to, or even substitute for, traditional conjoint counseling. Therefore, counselors who have translated theories of group dynamics to understanding family relationships use these same theories to understand groups of families. One of the most pressing needs in enrichment services is to apply what is known about groups to marriage enrichment groups. Group development, leadership, task accomplishment, and norms have not really been systematically examined in the context of marriage enrichment groups. Although I have made some suggestions in this book for examining and using these group dynamics, they must be tested to determine how successfully a professional can translate knowledge about groups to a group of couples. These issues are vital in exploiting the group experience to enrich marriages.

Therefore, some aspects of marriage enrichment services are yet to be explored—development and integration of theoretical approaches, conceptualization and testing of appropriate leadership styles and models of group development, and evaluation. In addition to the need for growth in these areas, the need exists to emphasize and build upon the integration of professional services with natural support and education networks. Perhaps no other aspect of the marriage enrichment movement is as essential as the integration of professional knowledge and services into the natural systems of concern, support, and socialization. Professional services do not function as an alternative to natural support services—they complement the work done by churches, friends, and schools to build strong, flexible marital relationships. This integration of human services into the support networks of "average" couples is the hope and the future strength of the marriage enrichment movement.

Resource A:
Structured Activities

Research on the use of structured activities in groups consistently reveals that such activities have a number of advantages. In summarizing this literature, Hof and Miller (1981) report that the activities lead to greater group cohesiveness, greater participant involvement in group activities, and greater participant learning as a result of the group experience. This Resource presents structured activities organized in five sections based on their content focus. The five sections are A: Group Formation; B: Communication; C: Problem Solving and Conflict Management; D: Values and Priorities; and E: Intimacy and Sexuality. At the beginning of each section is a list of the activities that appear within it. For easy reference, each activity is identified with the letter for the section and a numeral, in addition to its title. Thus the first activity in section A, Group Formation, is number A-1; its title is Getting Acquainted.

Of course, the content of an activity does not always reflect the objectives that can be achieved with it. For example, two of the activities with intimacy and sexuality content (E-1, Inside and Outside Circles, and E-4, Brainstorming About Sex) have been designed with the objective of building group cohesion in mind. In other cases, the content of the activity and its objectives may mirror one another. To aid the reader in finding an activity that addresses specific goals and objectives, I prepared the following list, which effectively sorts the activities according to goals that are common in marriage enrichment groups, primarily in the areas of group development and developing knowledge, attitudes, and behaviors. Because activities are usually designed to accomplish several objectives, any given activity may be listed under several different goal headings.

The leader may also devise uses in addition to those that have been identified here for many of these activities. Indeed, the listings and activities offered here are meant as suggestions; they can and should be altered to fit the purposes of the group. However, group objectives should not be altered just to include an "interesting-looking" activity.

Although I have created several of these activities, many belong to the oral tradition of the marriage enrichment movement and have defied my attempt to identify authors. Leaders often use activities they have read about or observed others using, and adapt them to their own needs; these activities are passed on to others in conversation, in handwritten notes, and in unsigned, undated program outlines. Consequently, the origins of activities are often impossible to determine. Nonetheless, I have given credit to sources whenever I could identify them.

A brief listing of additional sources of structured activities is included at the end of this Resource. Some of these sources were not designed for marriage enrichment groups per se but can be adapted for them.

These activities are to be used as resources; practitioners should feel free to reproduce and modify these materials for use in groups as long as appropriate credit is given.

Activities in Resource A Listed
According to Goals and Objectives

Group Development

Group Cohesion

A-1. Getting Acquainted
A-2. Naming
A-3. Anonymous Statements
A-4. Listing Our Strengths
A-5. Show and Tell
E-1. Inside and Outside Circles
E-4. Brainstorming About Sex

Defining Norms

A-2. Naming
A-3. Anonymous Statements
A-4. Listing Our Strengths
A-5. Show and Tell

Defining Group Goals

A-3. Anonymous Statements
A-4. Listing Our Strengths

Developing Knowledge, Attitudes, and Behaviors

Learning Systems Theory

A-1. Getting Acquainted

Communication Skills

B-1. Attending
B-2. Active Listening
B-3. Understanding One Another
B-4. How You Tell Me You Love Me
B-5. Nonverbal Communication
D-4. Special Times
E-3. Assessing Our Sexual Relationship

Understanding Differences and Conflict Management

B-3.   Understanding One Another
C-1.   Win/Win Conflict Negotiation
C-3.   Fighting for Optimal Distance
C-4.   Problem-Solving Areas
C-5.   Why We Fight
D-3.   Fill in the Blank

Expression of Feelings

B-3.   Understanding One Another
B-4.   How You Tell Me You Love Me
B-5.   Nonverbal Communication
C-1.   Win/Win Conflict Negotiation
E-2.   Sharing My Feelings With You
E-3.   Assessing Our Sexual Relationship
E-5.   Love Letters

Decision Making

A-5.   Show and Tell
C-1.   Win/Win Conflict Negotiation
C-2.   Decision Making
D-1.   Home Responsibilities
D-4.   Special Times

Roles and Power Distribution

C-2.   Decision Making
D-1.   Home Responsibilities

Use of Time

D-2.   Couple Time

Values and Values Clarification

C-4.   Problem-Solving Areas
D-2.   Couple Time
D-3.   Fill in the Blank
D-5.   Priorities

Sexuality and Intimacy

    B-1.   Attending
    B-5.   Nonverbal Communication
    C-3.   Fighting for Optimal Distance
    D-3.   Fill in the Blank
    D-5.   Priorities
    E-1.   Inside and Outside Circles
    E-2.   Sharing My Feelings With You
    E-3.   Assessing Our Sexual Relationship
    E-4.   Brainstorming About Sex

Generalizing Learning to the Home Environment

    D-4.   Special Times
    E-5.   Love Letters

Building Hope and Commitment

    D-4.   Special Times
    D-5.   Priorities
    E-2.   Sharing My Feelings With You
    E-5.   Love Letters

A: GROUP FORMATION

    A-1.   Getting Acquainted
    A-2.   Naming
    A-3.   Anonymous Statements
    A-4.   Listing Our Strengths
    A-5.   Show and Tell

A-1: Getting Acquainted

Individuals are asked to list five distinctive characteristics of themselves, combine their lists with their spouse's to describe their relationship, and then share their descriptions with the group (adapted from Zinker and Leon, 1976).

Major Focus: To introduce couples to one another, focusing on the marital relationship.

Goals: (1) To meet other couples in the group. (2) To define and introduce one's own self in terms of the marital relationship. *Other possible outcomes:* An initial appreciation of the appropriateness of systems theory in understanding marital relationships.

Type of Learning: Cognitive.

Size and Configuration: No more than eleven couples. Couples work alone and then share in the group.

Time: Thirty to forty minutes (additional time for groups of more than eight couples).

Materials: Pencils and paper.

Process:
1. Ask participants to describe five distinctive characteristics of themselves. Give examples: "very neat—everything has a place and is in it"; "love sports and like to both play and observe"; "can't stand to have money in my pocket—want to spend it all"; "work and play best in the mornings, and go to bed early"; and so on.
2. Ask couples to try to combine their lists so that they provide some understanding of what their married life is like. Give examples: "I'm very neat and she is very messy so I am always after her to clean up after herself, and I'm the one that does the housework"; "We both love sports and play tennis together"; "He likes to spend money and I like to have a nest egg, so we decided that I would handle the money"; "We are both 'morning people' so we get up and have a big breakfast together, spend time together before work, and go to bed by 10 P.M." (This should help couples begin to identify how they interact as an integrated system.)

3. Ask couples to share their marital descriptions with the larger group, so that they will know something about one another's marriages. Others may want to ask questions.
4. The exercise may be concluded by summarizing how individual differences may either be complementary or be the source of conflictual issues, and by leading the group in a discussion of these differences.

A-2: Naming

Each person is asked to call every other group member by name.

Major Focus: To learn the names of all the group participants.

Goals: Each member will learn others in the group by name; a sense of group cohesion will begin to develop. *Other possible outcomes:* Develop the norm that each person will be expected to participate in the group.

Type of Learning: Cognitive.

Size and Configuration: No more than eleven couples.

Time: Fifteen minutes.

Materials: None.

Process: Ask each person to go around the circle and name every person in the group. After each person has taken a turn, or after every few persons, ask the group to "fruit basket upset," to change seats. In this way individuals are forced to connect faces with names rather than learning a particular order of names.

A-3. Anonymous Statements

Participants anonymously complete three unfinished sentences about their expectations for the group, and leaders read them and lead the group in a discussion of the group's goals and norms.

Major Focus: To elicit the group's hopes, goals, and fears about the group experience in a nonthreatening way.

Goals: (1) By making anonymous statements about their goals, hopes, and fears, participants will more freely express their feelings so that the group's experiences can be structured to meet their needs. (2) The group will become more cohesive as participants hear that others have similar expectations and as common goals are identified. (3) Norms are established by the group to meet the group's needs for participant sharing and privacy. *Other possible outcomes:* Leaders may be able to foresee the need for particular emphases and to recognize the potential difficulties in meeting individual expectations in the group.

Type of Learning: Cognitive, affective.

Size and Configuration: No more than eleven couples.

Time: Thirty minutes.

Materials: White slip of paper for each participant with the statement: "I would be happier in our marriage if _____." Blue slip of paper for each participant with the statement: "I think our marriage could be improved if I learn to _____." Pink slip of paper for each participant with the statement: "The one thing I would hope *won't* happen in this group is _____." Pencils, small box to hold slips of paper, newsprint, and marker.

Process:
1. Discuss all participants having come with their own hopes, goals, and fears regarding the marriage enrichment group and its effects on their own lives. Say: "It is helpful if we all know what we would like to get out of this experience, as well as the areas in which some of us hope that the group will be sensitive to personal discomfort. However, sometimes it is hard to say out loud what our hopes and fears are, particularly when we do not know one another well yet. Therefore, we would like for you to do this anonymously. Each of you is being given three slips of paper and a pencil." (Hand out materials.) "On the white slip is the statement, 'I would be happier in our marriage if _____.' On the blue slip is

the statement, 'I think our marriage could be improved if I learn to _____.' On the pink slip is the statement, 'The one thing I hope *won't* happen in this group is _____.' Write your response to each of these and when you have finished place the slips in the box in the corner. Do not put your name on them."

2. After all the statements have been turned in, sort them by color and read them aloud or write the answers on newsprint. (They may be read immediately after being turned in or later in the session.) Lead the group in a discussion of group goals, content members want to be sure to cover, and possible norms for the group that will make everyone more comfortable.

A-4: Listing Our Strengths

Couples list their marital strengths and share their lists with the group. (This activity may be particularly useful in a group in which couples have experienced some marital discord; it sets the tone for focusing on strengths rather than problems.)

Major Focus: In identifying the strengths in their relationship, couples develop a sense of optimism, which will make possible the redefinition of problems as areas of growth.

Goals: (1) To establish that marriage enrichment focuses on enhancing strengths. (2) To introduce participants to one another's marriages. (3) To establish the norm of sharing information about one's marriage with the group in a relatively nonthreatening way. (4) To identify resources within the group. *Other possible outcomes:* Couples may identify others as "learning partners"—couples from whom they would like to learn, and to whom they can contribute their own strengths.

Type of Learning: Affective.

Size and Configuration: A maximum of twelve couples. Couples work privately and then have a group discussion.

Time: Forty minutes (additional time with a group of more than five couples).

Materials: Newsprint or poster paper, and markers for each couple.

Process:

1. Say: "There is a piece of newsprint and two felt-tip markers for each couple. We would like spouses to brainstorm with each other to list all the strengths that you have as a couple—all the aspects of your marriage that are good. For example, some of you might list mutual commitment, shared faith, we have fun together, are good friends, enjoy one another's company, want the same things in life, and so on. Do not censor one another's thoughts—if one of you thinks it is a strength, then count it as a strength."

2. When couples have finished working, attach their posters to the walls. Ask couples to introduce themselves using their posters. Talk about the emphasis in marriage enrichment on building on the strengths couples bring to the group. Also stress that one primary source of learning will be other couples; comment on the variety of resources available in the group.

A-5: Show and Tell

Couples are asked to share objects or pictures they have brought which depict their marital relationship.

Major Focus: Getting to know one another.

Goals: (1) Participants will learn about each other's marriages and begin to build group cohesiveness. (2) The expectation of sharing information about one's marital relationship with the group will be established. *Other possible outcomes:* Spouses will examine how they determine who makes decisions in their relationship.

Type of Learning: Cognitive.

Size and Configuration: No more than eleven couples.

Time: Forty-five minutes (more time for more than eight couples).

Materials: Show-and-tell items brought by the participants.

Process:
1. At the end of a session or before couples begin the program, ask them to decide on one object or picture that will best describe their marriage for the group. Emphasize that they are to decide together what to bring—one partner should not decide alone.
2. Ask each couple to tell the group about their item and why it describes their marriage. Encourage the group to ask questions.
3. When all couples have participated, ask them to describe how they decided what to bring. Ask: "Do you usually make these kinds of decisions together? If not, who usually does? What kinds of things did you think about bringing but decide against? Why?"

Variation: Ask couples to bring their wedding pictures. Place the pictures on a table so that couples can look at them during breaks.

B: COMMUNICATION

B-1.   Attending
B-2.   Active Listening
B-3.   Understanding One Another
B-4.   How You Tell Me You Love Me
B-5.   Nonverbal Communication

B-1: Attending

By assuming different body positions, participants will experience the difference between communication in which attending skills are used and communication in which they are not (adapted from Pfeiffer and Jones, 1975, pp. 13-15).

Major Focus: To experience the importance of attending and to learn how to use the skill.

Goals: (1) Participants will, through experiencing the presence and absence of attending behaviors in their partners, learn the value of attending in communicating understanding and concern for the other. (2) They will also be able to enact the skill. *Other possible outcomes:* Couples may be able to identify other aspects of their communication style which are problematic to a caring, empathic relationship.

Type of Learning: Cognitive, affective, behavioral.

Size and Configuration: Any size group. Couples work alone.

Time: Thirty minutes.

Materials: Moveable chairs.

Process:
1. Present material on the verbal and nonverbal aspects of communication, emphasizing that although individuals seem to rely primarily on verbal cues, nonverbal cues (gestures, posture, tone of voice, and so on) are also important. Conclude by demonstrating through a role play with the coleader or with a participant how nonverbal cues can either contradict or confirm a verbal message. For example, shout "I'm not either mad!" while scowling and pounding fists.
2. Announce that the activity will consist of exploring the nonverbal messages that use time and space. Tell couples that they are to discuss ways they think their communication breaks down. Ask them to begin this discussion with their chairs back to back (couples should scatter throughout the room but stay within hearing distance of the leader).
3. In two to three minutes, ask couples (while they continue to discuss the topic) to place their chairs side by side.
4. In two to three minutes, ask couples (while they continue to discuss the topic) to place their chairs facing each other, and to slouch in their seats and look away from one another.
5. In two to three minutes, ask couples (while they continue to discuss the topic) to lean forward and look into each other's eyes. In this position have them summarize how this activity relates to ways they may communicate with one

another—for example, sitting back to back is similar to trying to converse when two people are in different rooms of the house; side by side is like trying to converse while watching TV together; slouched and looking away from each other is like trying to converse while reading the newspaper.
6. Summarize by asking for participants' reactions to this exercise and by presenting material on attending from Middleman and Goldberg (1974) and/or other resources.

B-2: Active Listening

Leaders will define the skills of active listening and model them in a role play. Participants will then practice the skills in small groups.

Major Focus: Listening skills.

Goals: (1) Couples will define the skills of active listening. (2) Participants will demonstrate skills in a practice session. *Other possible outcomes:* To value the use of listening skills.

Type of Learning: Behavioral.

Size and Configuration: Small groups of two to three couples each.

Time: Thirty minutes.

Materials: Handout B-2a; Handout B-2b.

Process:
1. Give each participant a copy of Handout B-2a. Discuss the importance of listening in understanding one another, in communicating care, and in working through conflict.
2. Demonstrate the skills in a role play of a marital discussion.
3. Divide couples into small groups of two to three couples. Couples then take turns using the skills to discuss one or more of the following topics: (a) "What characteristics did we find attractive in one another that led us to marry?" (b) "In what areas of our relationship do we communicate most effectively?" (c) "What do we want for ourselves and our family in the next five years?" Other couples in the group are to listen quietly while the practicing couple inter-

acts. They may interrupt to assist if the practicing couple is having difficulty using the skills. After five minutes of interaction, the process is stopped. Observing couples then give feedback to the practicing couple on the ways they effectively used the skills and ways they could be more effective.

4. One of the observing couples then becomes the practicing couple, and the process is repeated until all couples have had a chance to practice the skills.

5. Leaders should circulate among groups during the practice sessions to coach couples as they practice the skills.

6. Call the small groups back together in a large group to discuss their reactions to the use of the skills. Point out that learning new skills always creates a sense of awkwardness and artificiality, just as learning to ride a bicycle or drive a car. Couples will need to continue to practice the skills in order to master them and to develop an individual style with which they are comfortable.

7. In order to help spouses practice the skills at home, copies of Handout B-2b, for rating spouses' communication, can be distributed to each participant. Spouses should use this form to rank each other's application of listening skills as a way of providing feedback. Advise participants that if they wish to discuss the rating sheets at home, they should be sure to remark on each other's good use of the skills, not just concentrate on lapses.

   If leaders sense that spouses would resent feedback from each other or would couch such feedback as criticism instead of as reinforcement, the forms can be used as *self-assessment* devices. Either way, they serve the purposes of reminding participants to practice the skills and providing leaders with indicators of skill usage.

Handout B-2a. Active Listening Skills.

Attending: Listener orients body position toward speaker and maintains eye contact.

Paraphrasing: Listener paraphrases the content and emotional tone of what the speaker has communicated.

Confirmation: Speaker affirms that the listener's restatement is accurate, or if not, clarifies the original message without adding to it.

Listening skills are the foundation for effective communication. When giving feedback to another couple, tell them how effectively you saw them using the skills listed above and give examples. Point to specific instances when they could have used the skills but did not. Also be sure to point out those skills they are using effectively.

(Adapted from Garland, 1978; Ivey, 1971; Middleman and Goldberg, 1974.)

Handout B-2b. Daily Rating of Spouse's Communication.

Date ———————

Put a check next to the sentence that best describes the way your spouse communicated with you during the day. Please check *only one* description.

Today my partner:

——— Communicated understanding of my deepest feelings and let me know by what he or she said that my thoughts and feelings were acceptable.

——— Communicated understanding of some but not all of my feelings and let me know that my thoughts and feelings were acceptable.

——— Paid attention to what I had to say, and most of the time checked with me to make sure he or she was understanding me correctly but did not communicate understanding of my feelings.

——— Tended to switch around what I said to get his or her message across.

——— Listened to me and responded with "yes" and "uhm, uhm."

——— Interrupted me to say what he or she wanted to say.

——— Contradicted what I had to say and rejected my thoughts and feelings.

Bring the six completed ratings with you to our next session.

(Adapted from Wieman, 1973.)

B-3: Understanding One Another

Each couple chooses an issue that has elicited conflict between them and attempts to learn each other's thoughts and feelings about the issue by using active listening skills and receiving feedback from other couples about their skill usage.

Major Focus: Practicing the skills of active listening in a conflict situation.

Goals: (1) Spouses use active listening skills to understand more clearly each other's position on a conflictual issue. (2) Once positions are more clearly understood, spouses more readily see solutions to the conflict. (3) Spouses recognize that use of active listening skills in conflictual situations limits the amount of anger generated because each person takes more responsibility for his or her own thoughts and feelings. *Other possible outcomes:* Observation of the kinds of conflicts that other couples experience makes one's own conflicts seem more normal.

Type of Learning: Cognitive, behavioral, affective.

Size and Configuration: Small groups of two to three couples each. Convene the large group for discussion of the experience.

Time: Forty-five minutes to one hour.

Materials: None.

Process:
1. Discuss the use of active listening skills and the importance of suspending judgment in conflict. These skills are useful for "setting the stage" for effective conflict resolution. Couples should have had opportunity to practice using skills before attempting this activity. Groups that have performed activity B-2a, in which the skills were initially introduced, will have had this practice.
2. Ask spouses to work together (five to ten minutes) to list three issues over which they have disagreed in the past month and which they would be willing to discuss in front of others. Ask them to pick the issue which they feel most

comfortable discussing and which will probably not generate more conflict than they are willing to deal with in front of a small group.

3. Divide the group into groups of two or three couples each. Tell each couple to take a turn discussing their issue in front of the other couples. Using active listening skills, spouses are to try to become aware of their partner's thoughts and feelings about the issue. Emphasize that couples are *not* to attempt to resolve the issue. Instruct listening couples to make sure that the couple having their discussion do not work toward a resolution and that they use the skills appropriately.

4. Process the experience in the large group. Ask: "How was this discussion different from the first discussion on the issue? Were the skills useful? Not useful?"

B-4: How You Tell Me You Love Me

Participants write down ways they think their spouses express love, and ways they would like their spouses to express love. Spouses then discuss their responses with each other and the experience is processed in the large group.

Major Focus: Communication of feelings.

Goals: (1) Spouses will identify behavior that clearly communicates each one's love for the other and behavior that does not communicate love clearly. (2) Participants will identify ways they want their spouses to express affection. *Other possible outcomes:* Spouses will contract for desired behaviors from each other.

Type of Learning: Cognitive, affective.

Size and Configuration: Couples work individually and then reconvene for large-group discussion.

Time: Forty minutes.

Materials: Paper and pencils.

Process:

1. Say: "An area of communication that is *very* important in intimate relationships is our ability to share our feelings with one another. However, sometimes this is one of the hardest kinds of communication because we can be easily misunderstood and because we are not always sure how to say just what we mean. However, as we continue to relate to one another, we as couples develop our own language so that we understand one another easily. This is what has happened when couples reach the point that they can say, 'We understand one another without ever saying a word.' "

2. Say: "What are some of the ways you communicate your feelings with one another? On a sheet of paper, list seven ways that you think your spouse tells you that he or she loves you." (Wait for all or most to finish.) "Now draw a line below your list and write down three ways that you would like your spouse to express his or her love for you—how would you like to be loved?"

3. Say: "As a couple, share your responses with each other. Do you agree about how you currently express your feelings? Can you give each other the kind of loving that you would really like?"

4. Discuss the experience in the large group. Ask: "How did it feel to talk about how you want to communicate with your spouse? What did you learn about how your spouse understands you and how you understand your spouse? In what ways can you better communicate your feelings?"

B-5: Nonverbal Communication

Participants will experience expressing and receiving the communication of various emotions using their eyes and hands, and will communicate by making a gift for one another.

Major Focus: To experience the importance of nonverbal communication and learn in what ways participants are comfortable and uncomfortable with it.

Goals: (1) Participants will experiment with different modes of nonverbal communication and will learn ways they use nonverbal communication in their own relationships. (2) Participants will explore their feelings about expressing both positive and negative emotions to their partners. *Other possible outcomes:* Participants may find themselves communicating in ways they have not for a long while, or have never done, such as looking into one another's eyes lovingly.

Type of Learning: Cognitive, affective.

Size and Configuration: Couples work together. Individuals work alone and then rejoin their partner.

Time: Thirty to forty-five minutes.

Materials: Clay for each participant.

Process:

1. Give a brief presentation on nonverbal communication and the use of nonverbal communication in the communication of feelings. Tell participants that they are going to experiment with communicating feelings nonverbally to one another.

2. Ask spouses to turn their chairs facing each other. They are to use their eyes to communicate the feelings they are asked to communicate—they are to try not to use any other part of their face or body. Have spouses begin by communicating sadness (pause for sixty seconds while they do this.) Then ask them to communicate joy, anger, and love.
    Variation: spouses may alternate being the communicator and the recipient of the communication.

3. Ask spouses to join hands and have the partner who is to begin communicate sadness by using only their joined hands (pause for thirty to forty seconds while they do this). Now have the other partner communicate the same feeling in the same way. Then ask them to communicate joy, anger and love.
    Variation: one spouse may be the recipient of all the emotions, then switch to communicator.

4. Give each participant a lump of clay. Have spouses move to different parts of the room to make something to give their partner. After fifteen minutes have them exchange gifts and interpret them.

5. Discuss the experience in the large group. Ask the following discussion questions (or make up similar ones): "How did you feel as you tried to communicate your feelings? What was hard? Easy? Which part did you enjoy? How do you usually use nonverbal channels to communicate with one another? What nonverbal communications most frequently need verbal interpretation or clarification?"

C: PROBLEM SOLVING AND CONFLICT MANAGEMENT

C-1. Win/Win Conflict Negotiation
C-2. Decision Making
C-3. Fighting for Optimal Distance
C-4. Problem-Solving Areas
C-5. Why We Fight

C-1: Win/Win Conflict Negotiation

Leaders will present and model the use of the Win/Win Model of Conflict Negotiation. In small groups couples will practice using the model on a minor issue of their own while other participants coach and observe (adapted from Gordon, 1975).

Major Focus: Presentation of a model of conflict negotiation and practice in using it.

Goals: (1) Participants will be able to list and define the steps in a conflict negotiation procedure. (2) Participants will practice using the procedure by working through a minor disagreement

which is currently an issue for them. *Other possible outcomes:*
Participants will learn the value of expressing feelings, exploring
alternatives, and deciding together on viable options for conflictual issues.

Type of Learning: Cognitive, behavioral.

Size and Configuration: Large group presentation; small groups
of two to three couples.

Time: One to two hours.

Materials: Handout C-1, blackboard and chalk or newsprint and
marker for each group.

Process:
1. Explain the various reasons for arguing: because we are an-
    gry at someone or something and the spouse becomes the
    focus of that anger; because we disagree about the facts of
    an issue; or because behaviors based on our attitudes and
    values conflict. Only when behaviors based on attitudes and
    values conflict is there a need to argue and negotiate. Mis-
    directed anger can be redirected, and disagreements about
    the facts of an issue can be resolved by seeking the facts.
    When negotiation is necessary, the win/win method can be
    helpful.
2. Distribute Handout C-1 and discuss it with the group.
3. Role play a conflict using the win/win steps.
4. Ask couples to confer with one another and decide upon a
    relatively minor issue which they would be willing to nego-
    tiate in front of a small group. Emphasize that the purpose
    is to become familiar with the steps, and for that reason
    "relationship-shaking" issues should be avoided.
5. Divide the group into groups of two to three couples each.
    Couples are to take turns working through the steps with
    one another. The couples observing are asked to help the
    working couple to use the steps appropriately and to brain-
    storm alternatives with the couple during the second step,
    generating alternatives. During the practice period, move
    from group to group, providing assistance and direction
    when needed.

Handout C-1. Six Steps of the Win/Win Method.

1. Identifying and defining the conflict and the feelings associated with it.
2. Generating alternative solutions without evaluating them.
3. Evaluating the alternative solutions.
4. Deciding on the best solution: one that is satisfactory to all.
5. Implementing the decision.
6. Evaluating whether the solution was effective.

C-2: Decision Making

Spouses fill out Handout C-2 and discuss it with one another privately or in small groups.

Major Focus: To define who makes decisions in the family.

Goals: (1) Couples evaluate how decisions are made in the family and whether these responsibilities are mutually agreed upon. (2) Couples determine if change is needed. *Other possible outcomes:* (1) Identification of perceptual differences of how power is distributed in the marriage; identification of sex-role expectations. (2) Exposure to different ways other couples in the group structure marital responsibilities.

Type of Learning: Cognitive, affective.

Size and Configuration: Individual couples or small groups for discussion; one large group for processing the experience.

Time: Forty-five minutes.

Materials: Handout C-2 and pencils.

Process:
1. Discuss how the roles assumed in marriage affect decision making. Say: "Clear role expectations define who is supposed to do what and thus make for a more efficient decision-making process than exists when no one is sure what the roles and responsibilities are. There are times when it can be useful to examine the ways we make decisions in

our marriage and family to make sure that we are being efficient, and also that we are both satisfied with the way we have allocated responsibility."

2. Distribute the Handout C-2 and ask participants to complete it. They are then to share and discuss their responses with their partners. Depending upon the needs of the group, spouses may work with each other, or several couples may work together in a small group.

3. Process the activity in the large group. Ask discussion questions such as: "Were you able to identify any differences in expectations that may be the source of recurring conflict?" "Who makes most of the decisions in your family?" "What areas could have been listed that might have changed the picture?" "Would you like to reallocate any responsibilities for decision-making?"

Handout C-2. Decision Making.

In every marriage and family decisions are made about how we are going to decide. It is useful to understand clearly our agreement about who is going to decide what. For each of the items listed put a check mark under the alternative that identifies who is usually responsible for that decision.

	Usually the wife	Usually the husband	We make this decision together
1. What to have for supper.			
2. When to buy a new car.			
3. What city to live in.			
4. When we can afford to make large purchases.			
5. Where to go on vacation.			
6. How many children we will have/have had.			
7. When to invite friends for supper.			
8. How to discipline the children.			
9. How much time we will spend together.			
10. How to decorate the house.			
11. When to have sex.			
12. When to go out for the evening.			
13. What gifts to purchase relatives, children, friends for special occasions.			
14. What TV shows to watch.			
15. When children are sick enough to need the doctor.			

Now circle those check marks which you would like to be able to put in a different column.

Compare your responses with your spouse's. Did you both see your responsibilities in the same way? On which items did your perceptions of who makes the decisions differ? Discuss the items one or both of you circled.

C-3: Fighting for Optimal Distance

By physically moving toward and away from one another, spouses establish at what distance from one another each is most comfortable. They discuss these optimal distances as a possible indication of differences in their need for distance and closeness emotionally as well as physically (adapted from Bach and Wyden, 1968).

Major Focus: Learning how much closeness and distance are comfortable for each spouse.

Goals: (1) Couples will identify through the exercise which partner prefers more closeness and which more privacy. (2) Couples will identify some of the ways these differences are expressed in their relationship. (3) In discussion with other couples, participants will identify ways of handling these differences. *Other possible outcomes:* Couples will learn that others share similar issues as sources of chronic conflict and that such conflict is "normal."

Type of Learning: Cognitive, affective.

Size and Configuration: Couples scatter through a large room or in several rooms and then reconvene for group discussion.

Time: Thirty minutes.

Materials: Tape measures for each couple.

Process:
1. Say: "One of the basic issues with which couples have to deal in some manner is how close—both physically and emotionally—to be to one another. For instance, some of us prefer a great deal of time alone, whereas others like a great deal of togetherness. Rarely are spouses evenly matched in their needs for closeness and distance. This issue of how close to be sometimes lies behind many other issues about which we fight." (For more discussion material, see Bach and Wyden, 1968.)
2. Say: "To get a better understanding of your needs for privacy and closeness, each couple find a place in the room. Stand facing each other, about ten feet apart. We would like for you to talk about how you think the issues of pri-

vacy and closeness are apparent in your own relationship. As you talk, wife, walk toward your husband until you touch him, and then very slowly back away until you reach a distance that is comfortable for conversation. Measure the distance with the tape measure we give you. Then do the same thing again—but the husband tests distance and the wife stands still. When you have finished, find a place to finish your conversation."

3. Process the experience. Use discussion questions such as "What did you find?" "Did this exercise suggest your own tolerance for closeness?" "Who usually starts the arguments for more privacy or more togetherness in your relationship?" "How do the two of you resolve this difference?"

C-4: Problem-Solving Areas

Couples list areas in their relationship that cause relatively few difficulties, those that create difficulty, and those they avoid. They then discuss the factors that make some issues easy to discuss and others difficult or almost impossible to discuss.

Major Focus: Identifying areas in which couples have difficulty and ease in problem solving.

Goals: (1) Through discussion of the areas in their relationship that cause little problem-solving difficulty, those that cause difficulty, and those that cannot be discussed at all, couples will identify the factors that make problem solving difficult. (2) Through identification of these factors, couples will approach the issues with a greater awareness of the underlying difficulties in their communication. (3) In the discussion with other couples, individual couples will gain assurance that others share similar difficulties. *Other possible outcomes:* In the recognition of different value bases which create problem-solving difficulties, couples will develop greater tolerance for and acceptance of one another's differences.

Type of Learning: Cognitive, affective.

Size and Configuration: Individuals work alone, then with partners, and then in discussion groups of three to four couples (the entire group can work together if it consists of no more than six couples).

Time: Forty-five minutes to one hour.

Materials: Handout C-4, pencils, and paper.

Process:

1. Discuss briefly that couples are not able to solve problems equally well in all areas of their relationship. Say: "Sometimes we are able to discuss, argue, and come to some agreement about certain issues, for example, how to discipline the children, but other times we reach a stalemate or are not even able to discuss some issues—our in-laws, for example, or dissatisfaction in some aspect of our intimate relationship. It is helpful to identify those areas of difficulty and those areas in which we are skilled in problem solving, in order to begin to identify what helps us to solve problems, and what makes some issues particularly difficult."

2. Say: "The handout you will receive lists topics that couples usually have to face and make decisions about. This is merely a list to help you think; you will need to add to it from your own experience. From this list and from your own experience, we would like each of you to make three lists: (a) Issues we can discuss and make decisions on easily. (b) Issues causing some difficulty that we need to learn to discuss more effectively and decide about. (c) Issues we try to avoid because we have quite a bit of difficulty discussing them and reaching decisions on them."

3. Say: "When you have finished, share your list with your partner and compare the issues on which you have agreed and those on which you have disagreed." (fifteen minutes)

4. Move the group into small discussion groups of three to four couples, or into the large group for discussion if it consists of no more than six couples. Say: "As you look at your lists of issues that you can discuss relatively easily, what kinds of patterns do you see? What makes issues easy for you to deal with as a couple? What makes issues difficult or impossible for you to deal with? What are some things you could do as couples to make these difficult areas easier to talk about and easier to deal with when problems arise?"

Handout C-4. Problem Solving Issues.

1. Relationship to in-laws.
2. How to discipline children.
3. How much time to spend with children.
4. How much time to spend with friends.
5. How to spend our money.
6. Whether to spend money or save it.
7. Where to go on vacation.
8. How to decorate the house.
9. Who should do what chores.
10. How many children to have.
11. What kind of birth control to use.
12. When to have sex.
13. How to spend your leisure time.
14. Whether or not to have a pet.
15. How much to tell others about our personal life and one another.
16. Expectations for the other to be involved in one's career and attend business functions.
17. How to express our feelings.
18. How to fight.
19. How to show our love for one another.
20. Expectations for fidelity.
21. Expectations for children's achievement.
22. How to have sex.
23. Where to go to church.
24. When to go to church.
25. What kind of car to buy.
26. How much money to spend on personal things (clothes, books, hobbies).
27. What kind of care or education to give children (baby-sitting, nursery school, public or private school, college).
28. How much we will be involved in outside organizations.
29. Whether or not to move (because of husband's or wife's job, to live in a certain area).
30. How open our home is to others.
31. Politics.
32. How much time and money we will use to support causes—political, religious, charitable.
33. Individual relationships to other men and women at work and socially.
34. How to invest our money.

C-5: Why We Fight

Couples will work together to complete Handout C-5 and then form a large group for discussion.

Major Focus: Identification of the issues about which couples fight and their styles of fighting.

Goals: (1) Couples will identify conflictual issues in their relationships. (2) Spouses will discuss with each other the ways they fight, identify strengths in their fighting styles, and discuss ways of eliminating aspects of their styles that make one or both of them particularly uncomfortable. *Other possible outcomes:* Couples will contract for a change in behavior during conflict.

Type of Learning: Cognitive, affective.

Size and Configuration: Spouses work together, then group reconvenes for discussion.

Time: One hour.

Materials: Handout C-5 and pencils.

Process:
1. Give a short presentation on the necessity of dealing with conflict or fighting in a marital relationship. Lead the group in discussing this sessions aim to develop productive conflict management patterns rather than to eliminate conflict.
2. Give each participant a copy of Handout C-5. Ask spouses to discuss the material on the handout and determine responses together.
3. Lead the group in a discussion of the handout. Use discussion questions such as: "What are some of the good things you have accomplished from your fighting?" "What kinds of fights do you need to have?" "What kinds of fights would you like to eliminate?" "How can you do that?" "What aspects of your fighting make you uncomfortable?" "Do you need to change your ways of fighting with one another or do you need to develop more comfort with the ways you do fight?" Encourage the group to discuss which aspects listed in part two of the handout are sometimes useful in conflict management, and which need to be eliminated and how they have tried to do so.

Handout C-5. Why We Fight.

1. Couples fight for many reasons. Some of these reasons are listed below. Put a check in the column that most accurately describes the degree to which each item fits your own marriage.

	Never	Sometimes	Often
A. We can't agree.			
B. To get you to listen to me.			
C. It's fun to make up.			
D. One of us is upset about something outside the marriage and brings it home.			
E. We feel pressure on us.			
F. We are very different in how we see things.			
G. One of us lets little things build up until we explode.			
H. It is a good way to get problems worked out.			
I. I want something very much and it is the only way to convince you.			
J. To clear the air.			
K. To feel close.			

2. All couples need to fight, but some aspects of fighting may make one or both of the partners uncomfortable. Put a check in the column that most accurately describes how you feel about each tactic in the list.

	We never use this tactic.	It is okay.	It makes me a little uncomfortable.	It makes me very uncomfortable.
A. Name calling.				
B. Raising our voices.				
C. Leaving a fight unfinished.				
D. Bringing up other issues.				
E. Bringing up the past.				

(continued on next page)

Handout C-5. Why We Fight, Cont'd.

	We never use this tactic.	It is okay.	It makes me a little uncomfortable.	It makes me very uncomfortable.
F. Crying.				
G. Physically striking one another.				
H. One of us leaves the scene.				
I. Allowing the children to hear us.				
J. Fighting in front of friends/relatives.				
K. Keeping up the fight for a long time.				
L. Getting into fights often; not letting things go.				
M. One of us won't apologize.				
N. One of us has to apologize.				
O. Saying things to hurt one another.				

3. If there were one thing you could change about the way you fight as a couple, what would it be? (Write your answer in the space below.)

D: VALUES/PRIORITIES

D-1. Home Responsibilities
D-2. Couple Time
D-3. Fill in the Blank
D-4. Special Times
D-5. Priorities

D-1: Home Responsibilities

Participants individually list their own roles/responsibilities in managing the home. Couples then share their lists and discuss how equitable their arrangement is, whether they change roles when needed, and whether change is currently needed.

Major Focus: Defining each spouse's role in the home and discovering how such definitions are made and changed; examining role responsibilities.

Goals: (1) Couples determine each spouse's role in the home, how the roles are determined, and how they are changed. (2) Couples evaluate whether role definitions are satisfying and functional, and if change is needed, determine how it will occur. *Other possible outcomes:* Examination of sex-role stereotypes.

Type of Learning: Cognitive, affective.

Size and Configuration: Individuals and then individual couples or small groups for discussion.

Time: Forty-five minutes.

Materials: Pencils and paper.

Process:
1. Give a brief presentation on defining roles and applying the concept of roles in marriage.
2. For ten minutes have participants list all of their own roles and responsibilities in the home—everything they can think of. Give examples such as taking out the garbage, paying the bills, handling correspondence, mopping the kitchen

floor, doing the laundry, buying gifts, and so on. Point out
that each individual is to list those things he or she is *responsible* for even though the spouse may help out. If responsibility is shared, how it is divided can be noted. During this activity each person works only on his or her own
list; participants should not contribute to each other's lists.

3. The group can then be divided into groups of two to three
    couples or couples can work alone. (Couples in groups
    should take turns sharing their lists.) They should discuss
    the following questions: (a) Do we agree with one anoth-
    er's lists—are they accurate? (b) Which assignments have
    caused problems? How do we handle these? (c) Is our ar-
    rangement equitable? Can we make it more so? (d) How
    were assignments made? How fixed are they? Do we change
    roles when it is useful to do so? (e) How do we make
    changes? (f) What changes do we need to make? During
    this phase, leaders may circulate among the couples or
    groups to assist participants and to determine what issues
    should be discussed in the large group.

4. Reassemble the group and discuss what participants learned
    from this activity and how they feel about it. Leaders
    should focus on issues they noted during the discussion
    that are relevant to the whole group.

D-2: Couple Time

Couples will chart how their time is spent during a typical
week and identify periods for individual solitude, family interaction, household management, and intimacy.

Major Focus: Becoming aware of how time is spent.

Goals: (1) Participants will become aware of how they spend
their time. (2) Participants will evaluate whether quality couple
time is available in their daily schedule, and whether adjustments need to be made to give their relationship more priority.
Other possible outcomes: Evaluation of the time allocated to
family activities. Reevaluation of the use of leisure time.

Type of Learning: Cognitive, affective.

Size and Configuration: Individual couples.

Time: Forty-five minutes to one hour.

Materials: Large sheets of paper (poster size), pencils, and boxes of crayons or colored markers for each couple.

Process:

1. Give each couple a large sheet of paper, two pencils, and a box of crayons or markers. Ask them to draw seven columns on the paper and label them the days of the week. Mark the columns into sections indicating morning, afternoon, and evening hours. Only waking hours need be represented. Each day's column should then be divided in half lengthwise, and each partner should use half of each column to write in his or her activities for each day of a *typical* week, giving as much detail as possible. The schedules of spouses will then parallel each other.

2. Ask couples to use a blue marker to circle the periods they are with each other but do not necessarily interact, for instance, both are home but are engaged in separate activities, either in the same room or in different rooms. Then have them circle in green their interaction time—time when they share activities, jointly interact with children, and make decisions about child management, household management, or other family issues. Finally, have couples circle in red the time reserved for couple intimacy—time when they talk without negotiating conflict, resolving problems, or making decisions. This includes time for physical closeness, expressions of sexuality, and other sharing.

3. Ask couples to discuss the following questions: (a) What activities have you routinely scheduled? (b) Is time with your spouse one of them? (Couples experience problems when their time together is not defined—issues needing decisions are allowed to come up whenever spouses interact so that problems seem to engulf the relationship.) (c) What do you like/not like about your schedules? (d) What changes can/will you make?

4. Reassemble the group and discuss thoughts and feelings about this activity.

D-3: Fill in the Blank

   Spouses complete a questionnaire about their similarities and differences and discuss their responses.

Major Focus: Assessing how spouses' preferences and values are similar and how they are different.

Goals: In discussing their responses to a short questionnaire, spouses will identify personality characteristics and values that are different and assess which of these are sources of intimacy and which are sources of growth and conflict. *Other possible outcomes:* (1) Spouses may identify chronic conflictual issues that they previously had not realized were based in value and personality differences. (2) Spouses will develop appreciation for their differences as well as their similarities.

Type of Learning: Cognitive, affective.

Size and Configuration: Spouses work together, then convene in small groups or in the large group for discussion.

Time: One hour.

Materials: Handout D-3 and pencils.

Process:
1. Introduce the concept that similarities and differences affect a relationship. Say: "Many times we are attracted to another because that person is like us in ways that make for compatibility and because he or she is different in ways that tend to balance us. For instance, we may find ourselves attracted to someone with whom we share the same interests. However, that person may be even more attractive if he or she is emotional and expressive and we see ourselves as quiet and unable to let others know how we feel. When we marry, areas of alikeness provide a basis of comfort and security. The differences continue to point out and make possible change and growth, which sometimes also involve conflict. This exercise is to help us begin to identify some of those similarities and differences."
2. Distribute Handout D-3. Ask participants to complete it

individually and then share their responses with their spouses. Discussion of the handout may take place just between spouses or among couples forming small groups, depending upon the goals of the activity.

3. Process the activity in the large group. Use discussion questions such as: "In what ways are we alike? Different?" "Which make us feel close to one another?" "Which are sources of personal and relational growth?" "How do we handle the conflict that sometimes results?"

Handout D-3. Fill in the Blank.

Complete the following sentences by filling in the blanks. When you are finished, compare your answers with your spouse's. In what ways are your answers alike? Different? In what ways do these similarities and differences reflect ways you complement one another, and ways that promote conflict?

1. When I have the choice of spending a quiet evening at home or going to a party, I tend to choose to _____
    _____ .

2. My favorite way to spend a summer Saturday is _____
    _____ .

3. My favorite way to spend a winter Saturday is _____
    _____ .

4. The time of day I have the most energy and motivation is _____
    _____ .

5. When we get a little extra money, I would prefer to _____
    _____ .

6. My favorite meal of the day is _____ .

7. When I have had a hard day, I like to unwind by _____
    _____ .

8. Ten years from now I would like to _____
    _____ .

9. When I am upset about something that has happened, I wish my spouse would _____ .

10. When I am angry at my spouse, I usually _____ .
    I would like to be able to _____ .

11. I feel most loved when my spouse _____ .

12. I think the most effective way to keep a marriage growing is to
    _____ .

D-4: Special Times

Couples individually list fond memories about their relationship, try to identify common themes in them, and plan to engage in an enjoyable activity during the following week.

Major Focus: To identify activities that bring a couple particular enjoyment.

Goals: (1) To identify the activities that bring particular enjoyment to the marriage by analyzing fond memories. (2) To determine how to structure these activities into the relationship. (3) To plan a specific activity together. *Other possible outcomes:* (1) Through group discussion of activities participants find enjoyable, a couple may become aware of new possibilities for activities they may enjoy together. (2) Participants practice communication skills.

Type of Learning: Cognitive, affective, behavioral.

Size and Configuration: Each individual works alone and then either with his or her spouse or with other couples in a small discussion group; then the whole group discusses the experience.

Time: Forty-five minutes.

Materials: Paper and pencils.

Process:
1. Say: "There are certain times in our marriages that stand out in our minds as special because we felt close or had a lot of fun together. Take ten minutes or so by yourself and think back about the times that have been most special to you. List as many as you can, both the 'big times' and the special little times."
2. Say: "Share your lists." (Sharing may be done in small groups.) "Discuss the following: (a) In what ways are our lists similar? Different? (b) Are there any common themes; are there activities that are alike? (c) Which are the most enjoyable? Are these things we structure into our lives? If not, can we? (d) What is something we can do this week that will be special? Will we agree to do it?"

3. Process the experience in the large group. Ask couples to share what they have learned, and if they have made a special contract, to discuss their agreement if they so choose.

D-5: Priorities

Participants will imagine that they have six months to live, and will plan how to spend this time. In discussing this experience with their spouses and with the group, they will identify values they would like to develop more fully in their lives.

Major Focus: To identify values that individuals and couples would like to develop more fully.

Goals: (1) Through a fantasy, individuals will identify values that they would like to emphasize in their lives. (2) In sharing these values with one another, spouses will feel close to one another. *Other possible outcomes:* Couples will make plans to implement some of these values.

Type of Learning: Affective.

Size and Configuration: Individual contemplation, discussions between spouses, then large-group discussion.

Time: One hour.

Materials: Paper and pencils.

Process:
1. Tell the group to close their eyes. Then say: "You are sitting in your doctor's office. He has just told you that you have developed a rare heart dysfunction for which there is no cure. Although it will not cause you any particular disability, it will cause sudden heart failure some time in the future, probably six months to a year from now. Think over what you have been told. Say good-bye to the doctor and get in your car. You drive to the place you would go to be alone awhile to think. You are going to make some plans. What are you going to do in the next six months?"
2. Give participants a few minutes to think. Then say: "Now open your eyes and write down what your plans are for the time you have left to live." (fifteen minutes)

3. Say: "Find a quiet place and discuss this experience with your spouse." (twenty minutes)
4. Leaders reconvene the group and lead a discussion of the experience: "Would you live differently from the way you are living now? Are there any aspects of your plans that you would like to implement now?" (Leaders may choose to give couples some time to discuss these plans.)

E. INTIMACY AND SEXUALITY

E-1.   Inside and Outside Circles
E-2.   Sharing My Feelings with You
E-3.   Assessing Our Sexual Relationship
E-4.   Brainstorming About Sex
E-5.   Love Letters

E-1: Inside and Outside Circles

Men seated in a circle, with wives directly behind them, are led in a discussion of their sexual development. Men and women then switch places.

Major Focus: Understanding one's own and one's spouse's sexual development.

Goals: In sharing experiences in sexual development with other group members, participants will become comfortable discussing sexuality and will develop an awareness of similarities in sexual development with their spouses and other group members. *Other possible outcomes:* Increased understanding of "normal" sexual development.

Type of Learning: Affective, cognitive.

Size and Configuration: Three to ten couples; men sit in a circle with their wives directly behind them; then men and women switch places.

Time: Forty-five minutes.

Materials: Moveable chairs.

Process:

1. Place chairs in two concentric circles; place each chair in the outside circle directly behind a chair in the inside circle. Ask husbands to take seats in the inside circle; and ask wives to sit directly behind their husbands. Thus husbands cannot see their own wives. Instruct wives to listen and to be as quiet as possible.

2. Referring to his own experiences if helpful, the male leader discusses the following kinds of questions with the men: "How did my parents express affection, sexuality? How did my parents tell me about sex? In what other ways did I learn about sexuality? When I got married, what did I expect our sexual relationship to be like?"

3. Have husbands and wives switch places. Husbands are now seated directly behind their wives. Instruct husbands to listen and to be as quiet as possible.

4. The female leader discusses with the wives the questions listed in step two.

5. Reassemble the group in one large circle and discuss couples' observations and feelings about this experience.

E-2: Sharing My Feelings with You

Individuals complete Handout E-2 and share responses with spouses.

Major Focus: How intimacy is expressed in the marital relationship.

Goals: Couples identify ways needs for intimacy are being met in the relationship. *Other possible outcomes:* To engender a feeling of warmth and closeness between spouses.

Type of Learning: Cognitive, affective.

Size and Configuration: Individual couples in any size group.

Time: Twenty to thirty minutes.

Materials: Handout E-2 and pencils.

Process:

1. Give each participant a copy of Handout E-2. Ask them to fill in the blanks; inform them that they will share their answers only with their spouses.
2. Ask spouses to sit together and discuss their answers. Ask them to look particularly for ways they are meeting each other's needs for intimacy and closeness.

Handout E-2. Sharing My Feelings with You.

1. I am happiest with you when ――――――――――――――――――― .

2. One of the most relaxing times with you is when ―――――――― ――――――――――――― .

3. If I could go back and relive one period in time with you that is a special memory for me it would be ――――――――――――――― because ――――――――――――――――― .

4. The time I felt closest to you was ――――――――――――― .

5. When I think about the future with you, I look forward most to ――――――――――――――――――――――― .

E-3: Assessing Our Sexual Relationship

Couples are taught to use a specific procedure to discuss their own sexual relationship. They then discuss their relationship privately (adapted from Association of Couples for Marriage Enrichment, 1977).

Major Focus: To identify feelings, both positive and negative, about particular aspects of the sexual relationship, and to discuss specific changes that are possible.

Goals: (1) Participants will tell their spouses specific aspects of their sexual relationship they find enjoyable, those which make them uncomfortable, and changes they would like to see in their relationship. (2) Participants will identify particular aspects of their sexual relationship that they find difficult to discuss, which may or may not relate to their comfort or discomfort in nonverbal sexual expressions. (3) Participants will plan for specific behavior changes. *Other possible outcomes:* (1) Increased comfort with verbal communication about sexuality. (2) Definition of previously unclear nonverbal messages.

Type of Learning: Cognitive, affective.

Size and Configuration: Couples work alone with as much privacy as possible.

Time: Thirty to forty-five minutes.

Materials: Handout E-3.

Process:
1. Discuss briefly the value of couple's communicating their feelings about their sexual relationship, communication which may be necessary not only during a sexual encounter but at other times as well. Also discuss the need for clear communication, both verbal and nonverbal, during sexual activity.
2. Give each couple a copy of Handout E-3 and discuss the procedures for its use. Stress that spouses are to attempt to find out as much as possible about each other's feelings about their sexual relationship without becoming defensive

or judgmental. The goal of the activity is to open channels of communication. Also tell couples that the leaders will be available for brief consultation.

3. Ask couples to find a private place to complete the handout and to discuss it. Tell them when to reconvene.

4. When the group reconvenes, lead the group in a discussion of the ways the process in this activity helps and hinders communication.

Handout E-3. Assessing Our Sexual Relationship.

Each couple should find a private place where they can talk comfortably and freely. They should decide who will be partner A and who will be partner B. In the first stage of the exercise, there should be only one-way communication (both verbal and nonverbal). The partner who is speaking is responsible for keeping time. The partner who is listening should simply listen carefully, refraining from responding verbally. Couples should sit facing each other, maintain eye contact, and maintain some physical contact (such as holding hands).

Stage I (twenty minutes)

The topic for one-way communication is "regarding our lovemaking." Partners take turns completing each of the following sentences, allowing three minutes for each partner's responses to each sentence. Whoever is speaking should complete the sentence as many times as possible with as many specific feelings, attitudes, actions, and experiences as come to mind in three minutes. If you run out of things to say, sit quietly until the time elapses. Communication should cover all aspects of lovemaking including environment, foreplay, intercourse, and behavior after intercourse.

1. "I really like/enjoy/appreciate _____."
2. "I'm uncomfortable with/about/when _____."
3. "I'd like to/I wish _____."

Stage II (thirty minutes)

Spouses now discuss together the experience they have just had. Care should be taken to avoid blaming one another or becoming defensive. The following questions may help guide the discussion:

1. How did it feel to share your feelings verbally with each other?
2. What did you learn from each other?
3. Are there specific behaviors you would like to change or try? Plan for them.

E-4: Brainstorming About Sex

Participants are asked to brainstorm words that relate to sexuality and sexual anatomy.

Major Focus: Desensitizing the discussion of sex.

Goals: Group participants will become comfortable using sex-related words so that they can talk more easily with the group about their own sexuality and with their spouses about their sexual relationship. *Other possible outcomes:* Participants may learn the definitions of words they have heard but have been too embarrassed to ask about. By facing a difficult topic together with good humor and good will, the group may develop more cohesiveness.

Type of Learning: Affective.

Size and Configuration: No more than 12 couples.

Time: Twenty minutes.

Materials: Blackboard and chalk or newsprint and marker.

Process:
1. Explain: "In order to talk with others and with our spouses about our sexual relationships, we need to be comfortable using the vocabulary. Also, the words we use, both proper terminology and slang, influence how we think about what they name. In order for us to become more comfortable talking about sex and to begin to examine some of our culture's attitudes about sexuality, we are going to brainstorm words that relate to sex in any way, including parts of the body that are sexual. Just call words out as you think of them, and I will write them on the board (newsprint)." To get the group started, leaders may need to call out a few words or ask the group to name other words for sexual intercourse, breasts, vagina, and penis. When the leader hears a new term or observes that someone in the group does not know a particular term's meaning, the person who called it out should define it briefly.
2. Process the experience, using discussion questions such as:

"What words are real turn-offs? Why?" "What words do you like?" "What are the differences?" "Which words were harder to say?" "What do you think these words indicate about attitudes toward sexuality?"

E-5: Love Letters

Spouses are asked to write love letters to each other, which the leaders will mail.

Major Focus: To carry the feelings of closeness and affection engendered by the marriage enrichment experience into the home environment.

Goals: (1) By writing love letters to one another, spouses will practice expressing affection for one another. (2) Experiences of the group will be generalized to the home environment—the letters will remind the couples to use skills and attitudes that they have learned in the group. *Other possible outcomes:* Couples may experience a new excitement and anticipation about their relationship.

Type of Learning: Affective, behavioral.

Size and Configuration: Individuals work alone.

Time: Thirty-five minutes.

Materials: Letter paper, envelopes, and pens.

Process:
1. Say: "It is important on occasion to remove ourselves from all the day in, day out problems of running a household and family, and to reflect on how important our partners are in making our lives happy and meaningful. We all need to hear on occasion that despite the arguments and the problems and the day in, day out association with someone, we are very much valued, appreciated, and loved. Let's take some time to do that now. You have a piece of paper and an envelope. We want you to write a letter to your spouse. This will be private. After you have written it, address the envelope to your spouse at home or at work and

place the letter in it and seal it. We will mail the letters next week. In your letters, tell your spouses what they mean to you, why they are valuable to you, what in your life is different because they are there. In short, write a love letter. You will have thirty minutes to do this."

2. Collect the letters when they have been written and mail them several days later.

Other Sources of Structured Activities

Certo, S. C. *Sourcebook of Experiential Exercises: Interpersonal Skills.* Terre Haute: School of Business, Indiana State University, 1976.

Clinebell, H. J. *Growth Counseling for Marriage Enrichment.* Philadelphia: Fortress Press, 1975.

Communication Research Associates. *A Workbook of Interpersonal Communication.* (2nd ed.) Dubuque, Iowa: Kendall/ Hunt, 1978.

Drum, D. J., and Knott, J. E. *Structured Groups for Facilitating Development.* New York: Human Sciences Press, 1977.

Garland, D. R. *Couples Communication and Negotiation Skills.* New York: Family Service Association of America, 1978.

Hof, L., and Miller, W. R. *Marriage Enrichment: Philosophy, Process, and Program.* Bowie, Md.: Brady, 1981.

Krupar, K. R. *Communication Games.* New York: Free Press, 1973.

L'Abate, L., and others. *Manual: Enrichment Programs for the Family Life Cycle.* Atlanta, Ga.: Social Research Laboratories, 1975a.

L'Abate, L., and others. *Manual: Family Enrichment Programs.* Atlanta, Ga.: Social Research Laboratories, 1975b.

National Marriage Encounter. *Marriage Enrichment Resource Manual.* St. Paul, Minn.: National Marriage Encounter, 1978.

Otto, H. A. (Ed.). *Marriage and Family Enrichment: New Perspectives and Programs.* Nashville: Abingdon, 1976.

Pfeiffer, J. W., and Jones, J. E. *A Handbook of Structured Experiences for Human Relations Training, Vol. I-VII.* La Jolla, Calif.: University Associates, 1975.

Piercy, F. P., and Schultz, K. "Values Clarification Strategies for Couples' Enrichment." *The Family Coordinator,* 1978, *25,* 175-178.

Ruben, B. D., and Budd, R. W. *Human Communication Handbook.* Rochelle Park, N.J.: Hayden, 1975.

Smith, M. A. *A Practical Guide to Value Clarification.* La Jolla, Calif.: University Associates, 1977.

Resource B:
Evaluation Tools

Tools marriage enrichment leaders may find useful in evaluating programs are listed in this Resource. To help the user locate appropriate tools, they are listed here by subject—that is, by the content focus of the instrument or method. Instruments that are most commonly used are marked with an asterisk and are discussed in detail in the annotated sections following the list. The annotations include bibliographical references for published descriptions of each instrument, followed, where possible, by references for descriptions and critiques of applications. A summary of each tool's primary objective is also provided. Complete bibliographical information for instruments not marked with an asterisk appears in the References at the end of the book.

I have not attempted to evaluate the quality—the reliability, validity, or practicality—of these instruments and scales, and my including an instrument in this section does not indicate endorsement of it. Similarly, instruments may have been inadvertently omitted that are as useful as those that have been included. It is up to the user to determine the aptness, merits, and limitations of any instrument for a given purpose. For example, many of the standard marital adjustment measures have items that are not designed to measure relationship change, such as "Have you ever wished you had married someone else or not married at all?" Similarly, some predictors of marital adjustment, such as relationships to in-laws, are not the primary targets of change efforts in marriage enrichment. Such issues need to be considered when weighing the usefulness of a given tool. The following are additional sources of evaluation instruments and tools: Cromwell, Olson, and Fournier, 1976; and Pinsof, 1981.

Evaluation Tools Listed by Subject

Titles marked with an asterisk are described more fully in the sections following this list.

Adjustment (Marital)
　　Adjustment Inventory (Bell, 1961)
　　*Dyadic Adjustment Scale
　　Family Concept Q Sort (Novak and van der Veen, 1970)
　　Family Interest Scale (Kirkpatrick, 1937; and Stroup, 1956)
　　Family Strengths (Olson and others, 1982)
　　Locke Marital Adjustment Scale (Locke and Wallace, 1959; and Haynes and others, 1979)
　　*Marital Communication Inventory
　　*Marital Roles Inventory
　　*Marital Satisfaction Scale
　　Marriage Adjustment Form (Burgess, 1952)
　　*Sexual Interaction Inventory

Agreement
　　Ferreira-Winter Questionnaire (Ferreira and Winter, 1974)

Assertion/Confrontation
　　*FACES II
　　Family Attitude Measure (Delhees, Cattell, and Sweeney, 1970; and Barton and others, 1973)

Hill Interaction Matrix (Hill, 1965; Hardcastle, 1972; and
Zarle and Boyd, 1977)

Marriage Sentence Completion Test (Forer, 1950; and Karen, 1961)

Personal Orientation Inventory (Shostrom, 1966; and Travis and Travis, 1976b)

Rathus Assertiveness Scale (Rathus, 1973)

Ravich Interpersonal Game Test (Ravich, 1969)

Attitudes or Knowledge About the Spouse

Adjective Checklist (Gough and Heilbrun, 1980)

Family Interaction Apperception Test (Elbert and others,
1964)

Interpersonal Behavior Project Method (Knudson, Sommers, and Golding, 1980)

Interpersonal Checklist (LaForge and Suezek, 1955)

*Marital Attitudes Evaluation Empathy Ratio

Marriage Adjustment Sentence Completion Survey (Manson and Lerner, 1962; and Cookerly, 1974)

Marriage Analysis (Blazier and Goosman, 1966)

Marriage Personality Inventory (Buros, 1972)

Q Sort Technique (Ruesch, Block and Bennett, 1953; and
Corsini, 1956a)

Relationship Inventory (Wampler and Powell, 1982)

Semantic Differential Test (Osgood, Suci, and Tannenbaum, 1957; and Katz, 1965)

*Sexual Interaction Inventory

Willingness to Change Scale (Weiss and others, 1973; and
Tiggle and others, 1982)

Attitudes Toward the Relationship

*ENRICH

*FACES II

Family Attitude Measure (Delhees, Cattell, and Sweeney,
1970, and Barton and others, 1973)

*Marital Attitudes Evaluation Empathy Ratio

Marital Problem Story Completion Test (Komisar, 1949)

*Marital Satisfaction Scale

Marriage Adjustment Sentence Completion Survey (Manson and Lerner, 1962; and Cookerly, 1974)

Marriage Personality Inventory (Buros, 1972)

Marriage Sentence Completion Test (Forer, 1950; and Karen, 1961)

Semantic Differential Test (Osgood, Suci, and Tannenbaum, 1957; and Katz, 1965)

Caring/Loving
  *Caring Relationship Inventory
  Love Attitude Inventory (Knox, 1971)
  *Marriage Expectation Inventory
  Marriage Sentence Completion Test (Forer, 1950; and Karen, 1961)
  Yale Marital Interaction Battery (Buerkle and Badgley, 1959; and Levinger, 1965)

Cohesion/Closeness
  *FACES II
  Family Functioning Index (Pless and Satterwhite, 1973)
  Family Strengths (Olson and others, 1982)
  *Marriage Expectation Inventory

Compatibility
  Family Concept Q Sort (Novak and van der Veen, 1970)
  Marriage Personality Inventory (Buros, 1972)

Conventionalism
  Marital Conventionalism Scale (Edmonds, 1967; and Murstein and Beck, 1972)

Decision-Making
  *FACES II
  Family Functioning Index (Pless and Satterwhite, 1973)
  Marital Precounseling Inventory (Stuart, 1974; and Haynes and others, 1979)
  *Marriage Evaluation
  *Scale of Marriage Problems

Flexibility (Relationship)
  *FACES II

Family Agreement Measure (Bodin, 1969)
Spousal Adaptability Test (Kieren and Tallman, 1972)

Group—Individual's Response to or Participation In
Encounter Group Checklist (Egan, 1973; and L'Abate, 1978)
Q Sort Technique (Ruesch, Block and Bennett, 1953; and Corsini, 1956a)

Interaction/Communication
Acceptance of Other Scale (Guerney, 1977)
*Art Technique
Color Matching Test (Goodrich and Boomer, 1963)
Consensus Rorschach (Singer, 1968; and Wynne, 1968)
*ENRICH
Facilitative Self Disclosure Scale (Carkhuff, 1969; and Zarle and Boyd, 1977)
Family Agreement Measure (Bodin, 1969)
Family Dinner Time (Dreyer and Dreyer, 1973)
Family Environment Scale (Moos, Insel and Humphrey, 1974)
Family Functioning Index (Pless and Satterwhite, 1973)
*The Family Task
Henry Ittleson Center Family Interaction Scales (Behrens and others, 1969)
Hill Interaction Matrix (Hill, 1965; Hardcastle, 1972; and Zarle and Boyd, 1977)
Interpersonal Communication Inventory (Pfeiffer and Jones, 1974; and Bienvenu, 1971)
*Interpersonal Relationship Scale
*Marital Communication Inventory
Marital Communication Scale and Marital Communication Scale II (Kahn, 1970; and Gottman and Porterfield, 1981)
*Marital Interaction Coding System
Marital Precounseling Inventory (Stuart, 1974; and Haynes and others, 1979)
Marital Projection Series (Huntington, 1958)
*Marriage Evaluation

*Marriage Expectation Inventory

*Primary Communication Inventory

Relationship Change Scale (Guerney, 1977)

Relationship Inventory (Wampler and Powell, 1982)

Revealed Difference Technique (Strodtbeck, 1951; and Olson, 1969)

Rorschach (Rorschach and Oberholtzer, 1924; and Singer and Wynne, 1966)

*Scale of Marriage Problems

Self-Feeling Awareness Scale (Guerney, 1977)

*Sexual Communication Inventory

Sexual Compatibility Test (Foster, 1977)

Signal System for the Assessment and Modification of Behavior (Thomas and others, 1970; and Thomas, 1977)

Simulated Family Activity Measurement (Straus and Tallman, 1971; and Olson and Straus, 1972)

Stroking Scale (Rosenthal and Novey, 1976)

Thematic Apperception Test (Singer and Wynne, 1966; and Friedman and Friedman, 1970)

*Verbal Interaction Task

Verbal Problem Checklist (Carter and Thomas, 1973; and Thomas and others, 1974)

Wechsler Adult Intelligence Scale

Interaction—Conflict and Conflict Resolution

Color Matching Test (Goodrich and Boomer, 1963)

Day at Home (Herbst, 1952; and Brown, 1959)

*ENRICH

*FACES II

Family Agreement Measure (Bodin, 1969)

Interpersonal Behavior Project Method (Knudson, Sommers, and Golding, 1980)

*Inventory of Marital Conflict

*Marital Interaction Coding System

*Marriage Expectation Inventory

Prisoner's Dilemma Game (Santa-Barbara and Epstein, 1974; and Luce and Raiffa, 1957)

Ravich Interpersonal Game Test (Ravich, 1969)

Revealed Difference Technique (Strodtbeck, 1951; and Olson, 1969)

Simulated Family Activity Measurement (Straus and Tallman, 1971; and Olson and Straus, 1972)

Interaction—Decision Making
Day at Home (Herbst, 1952; and Brown, 1959)
Family Agreement Measure (Bodin, 1969)
*The Family Task
*Inventory of Marital Conflict
Kenkel Decision Making Test (Kenkel and Hoffman, 1956; and Kenkel, 1959)
*Marital Interaction Coding System
Ravich Interpersonal Game Test (Ravich, 1969)
Revealed Difference Technique (Strodtbeck, 1951; and Olson, 1969)
Rorschach (Rorschach and Oberholtzer, 1924; and Singer and Wynne, 1966)
Wechsler Adult Intelligence Scale (Sharan, 1966)

Interaction—Group
Encounter Group Checklist (Egan, 1973; and L'Abate, 1978)
*Flander's Interaction Analysis Categories
*Interaction Process Analysis
Q Sort Techniques (Ruesch, Block, and Bennett, 1953; and Corsini, 1956a)

Intimacy
*Interpersonal Relationship Scale
*Pair Inventory
Personal Orientation Inventory (Shostrom, 1966; and Travis and Travis, 1976b)
Relationship Change Scale (Guerney, 1977)

Needs (Relationship)
Family Interaction Apperception Test (Elbert and others, 1964)
*Marital Attitudes Evaluation Empathy Ratio
Marital Precounseling Inventory (Stuart, 1974; and Haynes and others, 1979)
Marital Projection Series (Huntington, 1958)

Personal Adjustment or Characteristics
> Adjective Checklist (Gough and Heilbrun, 1980)
> Adjustment Inventory (Bell, 1961)
> *Caring Relationship Inventory
> Edwards Personal Preference Schedule (Edwards, 1959; and Murstein, 1974)
> *ENRICH
> Family Interaction Apperception Test (Elbert and others, 1964)
> Interpersonal Checklist (LaForge and Suezek, 1955)
> Love Attitude Inventory (Knox, 1971)
> *Marital Attitudes Evaluation Empathy Ratio
> Marriage Inventory (Knox, 1971)
> Marriage Sentence Completion Test (Forer, 1950; and Karen, 1961)
> Orientation Inventory (Bass and others, 1963; and Bass, 1967)
> Personal Orientation Inventory (Shostrom, 1966; and Travis and Travis, 1976b)
> Q Sort Technique (Ruesch, Block and Bennett, 1953; and Corsini, 1956a)
> Thematic Apperception Test (Singer and Wynne, 1966; and Friedman and Friedman, 1970)

Personal Growth Emphasis
> Family Environment Scale (Moos, Insel and Humphrey, 1974)
> *Marriage Evaluation

Problems (Relationship) and Stress
> *ENRICH
> Family Strengths (Olson and others, 1982)
> Handling Problems Change Scale (Guerney, 1977)
> *Marital Problem Checklist
> *Marital Roles Inventory
> Marriage Adjustment Form (Burgess, 1952)
> Marriage Adjustment Sentence Completion Survey (Manson and Lerner, 1962; and Cookerly, 1974)
> *Marriage Evaluation

*Marriage Expectation Inventory
Marriage Inventory (Knox, 1971)
Rorschach (Rorschach and Oberholtzer, 1924; and Singer and Wynne, 1966)
*Scale of Marriage Problems
Willingness to Change Scale (Weiss and others, 1973; and Tiggle and others, 1982)

Roles (Task roles, leadership, power)
Day at Home (Herbst, 1952; and Brown, 1959)
*ENRICH
*FACES II
Henry Ittleson Center Family Interaction Scales (Behrens and others, 1969)
*Marital Roles Inventory
Marriage Analysis (Blazier and Goosman, 1966)
Revealed Difference Technique (Strodtbeck, 1951; and Olson, 1969)
Sex Role Survey (MacDonald, 1974)
Simulated Family Activity Measurement (Straus and Tallman, 1971; and Olson and Straus, 1972)
Thematic Apperception Test

Satisfaction and Happiness (Relationship)
*ENRICH
*FACES II
Family Concept Q Sort (Novak and Van der Veen, 1970)
Family Functioning Index (Pless and Satterwhite, 1973)
Family Interaction Apperception Test (Elbert and others, 1964)
Family Interest Scale (Kirkpatrick, 1937; and Stroup, 1956)
*Family Life Questionnaire
Locke Marital Adjustment Scale (Locke and Wallace, 1959; and Haynes and others, 1979)
*Marital Happiness Scale
Marital Precounseling Inventory (Stuart, 1974; and Haynes and others, 1979)
*Marital Problem Checklist
*Marital Satisfaction Scale

Marriage Adjustment Form (Burgess, 1952)
Marriage Analysis (Blazier and Goosman, 1966)
Relationship Change Scale (Guerney, 1977)
Satisfaction Change Scale (Guerney, 1977)
Sentence Completion Blank (Inselberg, 1961 and 1964)
*Sexual Interaction Inventory

Self Awareness
Marriage Inventory (Knox, 1971)
Self-Feeling Awareness Scale (Guerney, 1977)

Self-Disclosure
Facilitative Self Disclosure Scale (Carkhuff, 1969; and Zarle and Boyd, 1977)
Interpersonal Communication Inventory (Pfeiffer and Jones, 1974; and Bienvenu, 1971)
Relationship Change Scale (Guerney, 1977)
Relationship Inventory (Wampler and Powell, 1982)
Self Disclosure Questionnaire (Jourard, 1971; and Milholland and Avery, 1982)
*Verbal Interaction Task

Sexuality
*Caring Relationship Inventory
*ENRICH
Family Attitude Measure (Delhees, Cattell, and Sweeney, 1970, and Barton and others, 1973)
Family Interest Scale (Kirkpatrick, 1937; and Stroup, 1956)
Marital Precounseling Inventory (Stuart, 1974; and Haynes and others, 1979)
Marriage Analysis (Blazier and Goosman, 1966)
*Marriage Expectation Inventory
*Pair Inventory
Sex Attitude Survey and Profile (McHugh and McHugh, 1976)
Sex Knowledge and Attitude Test (Miller and Lief, 1979)
Sex Knowledge Inventory, Forms X and Y (McHugh, 1977 and 1979)
*Sexual Communication Inventory

Sexual Compatibility Test (Foster, 1977)
*Sexual Interaction Inventory

Structure of Relationship
Day at Home (Herbst, 1952; and Brown, 1959)
Family Dinner Time (Dreyer and Dreyer, 1973)
Family Environment Scale (Moos, Insel and Humphrey, 1974)
*The Family Task
Henry Ittleson Center Family Interaction Scales (Behrens and others, 1969)
Simulated Family Activity Measurement (Straus and Tallman, 1971; and Olson and Straus, 1972)
Wechsler Adult Intelligence Scale (Sharan, 1966)

Trust
*Interpersonal Relationship Scale

Understanding/Empathy
Acceptance of Other Scale (Guerney, 1977)
*Caring Relationship Inventory
Interpersonal Behavior Project Method (Knudson, Sommers and Golding, 1980)
Interpersonal Communication Inventory (Pfeiffer and Jones, 1974, and Bienvenu, 1971)
*Marital Attitudes Evaluation Empathy Ratio
Relationship Change Scale (Guerney, 1977)
Relationship Inventory (Wampler and Powell, 1982)
Spousal Adaptability Test (Kieren and Tallman, 1972)
Yale Marital Interaction Battery (Buerkle and Badgley, 1959; and Levinger, 1965)

Art Techniques

Author and Source: Wadeson, H. "Art Techniques Used in Conjoint Marital Therapy." *American Journal of Art Therapy,* 1973, *12,* 147–164.

Primary Objective: To elicit interactional processes in the marital relationship. (Art techniques are useful in combination with other instruments, such as interactional coding systems.)

Description: The technique involves three separate processes that can be used independently of each other: couples are instructed to develop one well-integrated picture together without verbal communication; simultaneously and without sharing ideas, spouses draw abstract pictures of their marital relationship; both spouses draw large self-portraits, then exchange them and do anything they would like to with the portraits.

Caring Relationship Inventory

Author and Source: Shostrom, E. L. *Manual: The Caring Relationship Inventory.* San Diego: Educational and Industrial Testing Service, 1966.

Primary Objective: To measure five aspects of caring or loving in human relationships: affection (helping, nurturing); friendship (common interest and respect for each other's equality); eros (inquisitiveness, jealousy, exclusiveness, and sexual desire); empathy (compassion, tolerance, and appreciation of another person as a unique human being); and self-love (the ability to accept one's own weaknesses and strengths). Two subscales are also available—"being love" (the ability to have and accept another as he or she is) and "deficiency love" (the love of another for his or her usefulness to the person).

Description: Male and female forms consist of eighty-three true or false statements such as "My feeling for him is characterized by patience" and "I am afraid to weep in front of her."
Respondents can be asked to answer each question a sec-

ond time, indicating how they would expect the "ideal" relationship to be, so that the discrepancy between the real and the ideal relationship can be assessed.

Supplementary Bibliography:
Lake D. G., Miles, M. B., and Earle, R. B., Jr. (Eds.). *Measuring Human Behavior.* New York: Teachers College Press, 1973.
Travis, R. P., and Travis, P. Y. "A Note on Changes in the Caring Relationship Following a Marriage Enrichment Program and Some Preliminary Findings." *Journal of Marriage Counseling,* 1976, *2,* 81-83.

Dyadic Adjustment Scale

Author and Source: Spanier, G. B. "Measuring Dyadic Adjustment: New Scales for Assessing the Quality of Marriage and Similar Dyads." *Journal of Marriage and the Family,* 1976, *38,* 15-28.

Primary Objective: To assess the quality of marriage.

Description: The thirty-two-item scale consists of such items as "How often do you or your mate leave the house after a fight? (all the time, most of the time, more often than not, occasionally, rarely, never)" and "Do you and your mate engage in outside interests together? (all of them, most of them, some of them, very few of them, none of them)."

Supplementary Bibliography:
Spanier, G. B. "The Measurement of Marital Quality." *Journal of Sex and Marital Therapy,* 1979, *5,* 288-300.

Enriching and Nurturing Relationship Issues, Communication, and Happiness (ENRICH)

Author and Source: Olson, D. H. *Family Inventories: Inventories Used in a National Survey of Families Across the Family Life Cycle.* St. Paul: University of Minnesota, 1982.

Primary Objective: To assess areas of strength and potential problem areas in a marriage.

Description: ENRICH uses eleven content categories—marital satisfaction, personality issues, communication, conflict resolution, financial management, leisure activities, sexual relationship, children and marriage, family and friends, equalitarian roles, and religious orientation. A control category of idealistic distortion determines the tendency of respondents to give socially desirable answers. The instrument consists of 125 items, with which the respondents rate their level of agreement on a scale of one to five. The items consist of statements such as "My partner and I seem to enjoy the same type of parties and social activities" and "It is very easy for me to express all my true feelings to my partner." *Prepare* is a variation of this instrument, used with premarital couples; *Prepare-MC* is a premarital instrument used for couples in which one or both partners have children.

Family Adaptability and Cohesion Evaluation Scales (FACES II)

Author and Source: Olson, D. H. *Family Inventories: Inventories Used in a National Survey of Families Across the Family Life Cycle.* St. Paul: University of Minnesota, 1982.

Primary Objective: To assess family satisfaction on the dimensions of cohesion and adaptability.

Description: The instrument measures the discrepancies between the perceived and ideal descriptions of the family system. It is based on the circumplex model of marital and family systems (Olson, Sprenkle, and Russell, 1979). There are thirty items such as "Family members are supportive of each other during difficult times." Subjects are asked to indicate how frequently each item occurs in their family: almost never, once in a while, sometimes, frequently, or almost always. They are then asked to respond again to all the items as they would *like* their family to be.

Family Life Questionnaire

Author and Source: Guerney, B. G. *Relationship Enhancement: Skill-Training Programs for Therapy, Problem Prevention, and Enrichment.* San Francisco: Jossey-Bass, 1977.

Primary Objective: To measure harmony and satisfaction in family life.

Description: The questionnaire consists of twenty-four items such as "It's easy to laugh and have fun when we are together." Subjects circle one of the following responses for each item: yes, strongly agree; yes, mildly agree or not so sure; no, mildly disagree or not so sure; no, strongly disagree. Forms are included for husband and wife, father and son, and mother and daughter.

Supplementary Bibliography:
Ely, A. L., Guerney, B. G., and Stover, L. "Efficacy of the Training Phase of Conjugal Therapy." *Psychotherapy: Theory, Research, and Practice,* 1973, *10,* 201-207.

The Family Task

Authors: Minuchin, S., Elbert, S., and Guerney, B. G.

Source: Family Research Unit, Wiltwyck School for Boys, Inc., 260 Park Ave. South, New York, N.Y. 10010.

Primary Objective: To permit observation of family members in interaction, and thus the examination of family structure.

Description: While the experimenter is out of the room, family members listen to six tape-recorded assignments and tape their responses. Nonverbal behavior is observed through a one-way screen. Tasks include planning a menu, deciding how to spend $10, assigning blame labels to the family members, describing what each individual likes and dislikes about the others, describing a family fight, and copying a constructed wooden model.

Supplementary Bibliography:
Elbert, S., and others. "A Method for the Clinical Study of

Family Interaction." *American Journal of Orthopsychiatry,* 1964, *34,* 885-894.

Flanders's Interaction Analysis Categories

Author and Source: Flanders, N. A. *Analyzing Teaching Behavior.* Reading, Mass.: Addison-Wesley, 1970.

Primary Objective: To analyze interaction in group settings, primarily in educational groups.

Description: Ten categories are used to study the balance between initiation and response on the part of teachers or group leaders and group members. The categories consist of three major sections: teacher talk; student talk; and silence, confusion, or anything other than teacher or student talk. There are two subdivisions of teacher behavior: direct influence, which includes lecturing, giving directions, and criticizing or justifying authority; and indirect influence, which includes accepting feeling, praising or encouraging, accepting ideas, and asking questions. There are only two categories for student talk: initiating talk and responding to teacher talk.

Supplementary Bibliography:
Amidon, E. J., and Flanders, N. A. *The Role of the Teacher in the Classroom.* (Rev. ed.) Minneapolis: Association for Productive Teaching, 1967.

Interaction Process Analysis

Author and Source: Bales, R. F. *Interaction Process Analysis: A Method for the Study of Small Groups.* Reading, Mass.: Addison-Wesley, 1950.

Primary Objective: To categorize interaction behavior in groups.

Description: Each overt act that occurs in a group is classified in one of twelve categories that include: (1) shows solidarity; (2) shows tension release; (3) agrees, showing passive acceptance; (4) gives suggestion and direction; (5) gives opinion, evaluation, and analysis; (6) gives orientation and information; (7) asks for orientation; (8) asks for opinion, evaluation, and analysis; (9) asks for suggestion, direction, and possible ways of action; (10) disagrees, showing passive rejection and formality; (11) shows tension and asks for help; and (12) shows antagonism. These twelve categories are grouped into the areas of task and socioemotional functions, and are further divided into positive and negative reactions.

Interpersonal Relationship Scale

Author: Schlein, S.

Source: Guerney, B. G. *Relationship Enhancement: Skill-Training Programs for Therapy, Problem Prevention, and Enrichment.* San Francisco: Jossey-Bass, 1977.

Primary Objective: To measure the quality of interpersonal relationships, particularly trust and intimacy.

Description: The questionnaire consists of fifty-two items such as "When serious disagreements arise between us, I respect my partner's position." For each item, subjects indicate whether they strongly agree, mildly agree, are neutral, mildly disagree, or strongly disagree.

Supplementary Bibliography:
Milholland, T. A., and Avery, A. W. "Effects of Marriage Encounter on Self-Disclosure, Trust, and Marital Satisfaction." *Journal of Marital and Family Therapy,* 1982, *8,* 87–89.

Inventory of Marital Conflict (IMC)

Authors: Olson, D. H. and Ryder, R. G.

Source: Family Social Science, University of Minnesota, 218 North Hall, St. Paul, Minn. 55108.

Primary Objective: To provide interaction data on decision-making processes and conflict resolution in couples.

Description: The IMC consists of eighteen vignettes that present various types of marital conflicts generally relevant to couples. Spouses individually decide who is primarily responsible for the problem in each vignette and then jointly resolve their differences. Two kinds of data are obtained: win scores (whose final decision was accepted when there was initial disagreement), and interaction data. A coding manual is available for the verbal interaction data.

Supplementary Bibliography:

Olson, D. H., and Ryder, R. G. "Inventory of Marital Conflicts (IMC): An Experimental Interaction Procedure." *Journal of Marriage and the Family,* 1970, *32,* 443-448.

Olson, D. H., and Ryder, R. G. *IMC Procedure Manual.* St. Paul: University of Minnesota, 1977.

Marital Attitudes Evaluation Empathy Ratio (MATE)

Author and Source: Schutz, W. *MATE: A FIRO Awareness Scale.* Palo Alto: Consulting Psychologists Press, Inc., 1976.

Primary Objective: To measure the following five dimensions of the individual's needs: (1) inclusion behavior, such as "I want my wife to spend more time with me and give me more attention"; (2) control behavior, such as "I want my wife to allow me more freedom, and to think more for myself"; (3) inclusion feelings, such as "I want my wife to be more interested in me and to feel more strongly that I am a significant person"; (4) control feelings, such as "I want my wife to have more respect for my ability to think and do things well"; and (5) affection behavior/feelings, such as "I want my wife to show and feel more love and affection for me." The questionnaire also measures the degree to which each spouse knows the needs of the other.

Description: Each spouse responds to forty-five items, each of which begins with "I want you to" (for example, "I want you to allow me more freedom"), by indicating the degree to which each item is true. The individual then responds similarly to the same forty-five items, this time prefaced with "You want me to. . . ." Partners' questionnaires can be compared to determine how accurately they know one another as well as to assess individual needs.

Supplementary Bibliography:
Pfeiffer, J. W., and Heslin, R. *Instrumentation in Human Relations Training.* Iowa City: University Associates, 1973.

Marital Communication Inventory

Author and Source: Bienvenu, M. J. *A Counselor's Guide to Accompany a Marital Communication Inventory.* Durham, N.C.: Family Life Publications, 1969.

Primary Objective: To measure the degree of success or failure in marital communication.

Description: Subjects respond to forty-six questions about communication with their spouses (for example, "Do you and your husband (wife) discuss the manner in which the family income should be spent?"). Subjects indicate whether each item occurs usually, often, seldom, or never.

Supplementary Bibliography:
Murphy, D. C., and Mendelson, L. A. "Communication and Adjustment in Marriage: Investigating the Relationship." *Family Process,* 1973, *12,* 317-326.

Marital Happiness Scale

Authors and Source: Azrin N. H., Naster, B. J., and Jones, R. "Reciprocity Counseling: A Rapid Learning-Based Procedure for Marital Counseling." *Behavior Research and Therapy,* 1973, *11,* 365-382.

Primary Objective: To measure reported marital happiness in nine specific categories (household responsibilities, rearing of children, social activities, money, communication, sex, academic or occupational progress, personal independence, and spouse independence) and in the category of general happiness.

Description: Spouses are asked to rate their degree of happiness in the ten categories on a scale from one to ten (completely happy to completely unhappy).

Supplementary Bibliography:
Dixon, D. N., and Sciara, A. D. "Effectiveness of Group Reciprocity Counseling with Married Couples." *Journal of Marriage and Family Counseling,* 1977, *3,* 77-83.

Marital Interaction Coding System

Authors and Source: Weiss, R. L., Hops, H., and Patterson, G. R. "A Framework for Conceptualizing Marital Conflict: A Technology for Altering It, Some Data for Evaluating It." In L. A. Hamerlynck, L. C. Handy, and E. J. Mash (Eds.), *Behavior Change: Methodology, Concepts and Practice.* Champaign: Research Press, 1973.

Primary Objective: To code interactional behavior using categories important within a social learning framework. The major kinds of categories are problem solving behaviors, problem description statements, and categories of verbal and nonverbal positive and negative exchanges.

Description: The categories are used to code videotaped interaction of spouses while they are negotiating a solution to a problem.

Supplementary Bibliography:
Haynes, S. N., Follingstad, D. R., and Sullivan, J. C. "Assessment of Marital Satisfaction and Interaction." *Journal of Consulting and Clinical Psychology,* 1979, *47,* 789-791.

Marital Problem Checklist

Authors and Source: Mathews, V. D., and Mihanovich, C. S. "New Orientations on Marital Maladjustment." *Marriage and Family Living,* 1963, *25,* 300-304.

Primary Objective: To identify the number and kinds of problems reported by couples, which strongly relate to the degree of marital happiness.

Description: A list of problems that occur in marriages is given to the respondents, who are instructed to underline the particular problems of concern to them in their married life. Problems include such items as "Don't think alike on many things" and "Say things that hurt each other."

Marital Roles Inventory

Author and Source: Hurvitz, N. "The Marital Roles Inventory and the Measurement of Marital Adjustment." *Journal of Clinical Psychology,* 1960, *16,* 377–380.

Primary Objective: To measure marital adjustment.

Description: Spouses individually rank the importance of items in a list of roles and functions that they perform in the family, and rank the order of preference they have for their spouse's role behavior. The difference between the rank order of the roles in the role-set, ranked as role performances by one and as role expectations by the other, produces an index of strain.

Supplementary Bibliography:
Hurvitz, N. "Marital Roles Inventory as a Counseling Instrument." *Journal of Marriage and the Family,* 1965, *27,* 492–501.

Marital Satisfaction Scale

Authors and Source: Roach, A. J., Frazier, L. P., and Bowden, S. R. "The Marital Satisfaction Scale: Development of a Measure for Intervention Research." *Journal of Marriage and the Family,* 1981, *43,* 537–546.

Primary Objective: To measure marital satisfaction, defined as the perception of one's marriage along a continuum of greater or lesser favorability at a given point in time. Satisfaction is by definition an attitude, which like any perception, is subject to change over time. This instrument was designed to measure changes in one's level of marital satisfaction that may occur in response to helping interventions.

Description: The instrument is in the form of a Likert-type attitudinal scale and consists of forty-eight items such as: "I know what my spouse expects of me in our marriage," "My spouse could make things easier for me if he or she cared to," and "Demonstrations of affection by me and my spouse are mutually acceptable."

Marriage Evaluation

Author and Source: Blount, H. C. *Counselor's Manual for A Marriage Evaluation.* Saluda, N.C.: Family Life Publications, Inc., 1977.

Primary Objective: To assess the couple's perception of problem areas in their marriage and to examine similarities and differences in those perceptions.

Description: In the decision-making section of this questionnaire, subjects indicate who makes certain kinds of decisions, such as when to discipline children, and whether decision-making is done equally, mostly by the husband, or mostly by the wife. In the communication section, subjects indicate the frequency with which they engage in ten communication behaviors by answering such questions as "Do you try to communicate understanding and empathy when your spouse is depressed?" In the values section, subjects mark "yes," "no," or "to a small degree" in response to ten questions such as "Do you value togetherness as a family?" Similarly structured questions are provided for assessing personal growth in marriage commitment and expectation.)

Marriage Expectation Inventory and the Marriage Climate Analysis

Authors and Source: McDonald, P. J., and McDonald, C. *Counselor's and Educator's Manual for the Marriage Expectation Inventories.* Saluda, N.C.: Family Life Publications, Inc., 1979.

Primary Objective: To help couples explore their relationships in depth.

Description: The questionnaire presents open-ended questions in nine key areas: love, communication, freedom, sex, money, selfishness, religious expectations, relatives, and children (for example, "Describe several things your partner does that make it difficult for you to share yourself with him or her."). These questions are used to begin discussion of pertinent issues in relationships. The answers to these questions can be used to evaluate marriages based on subjective criteria, or couples can discuss their responses and their interaction can then be evaluated based on subjective or objective criteria.

The Marriage Climate Analysis is a conceptual, contextual, content analysis of the Marriage Expectation Inventory, using computer technology. Each word in the response to the inventory is analyzed according to its frequency, content, and context. A profile is then developed based on four bonding forces: cohesion, friction, pressure, and stress. The user's manual is available from Family Life Publications.

Personal Assessment of Intimacy in Relationships (PAIR Inventory)

Authors: Schaefer, M. T., and Olson, D. H.

Source: D. H. Olson, professor of family social science, University of Minnesota, St. Paul, Minn. 55108.

Primary Objective: To provide systematic information on five types of intimacy: emotional, social, sexual, intellectual, and recreational. Partners describe their relationship in terms of how they currently perceive it and how they would like it to be.

Description: Partners independently respond to statements such as "My partner listens to me when I need someone to talk to" and "We enjoy spending time with other couples," using a five-point Likert Scale (agreement-disagreement). In the first step, partners respond to each item as it presently is in the relationship, and in the second step, as they would like it to be.

Supplementary Bibliography:
Schaefer, M. T., and Olson, D. H. "Assessing Intimacy: The Pair Inventory." *Journal of Marital and Family Therapy,* 1981, *7,* 47-60.

Primary Communication Inventory

Author: Locke, H. J.

Source: Navran, L. "Communication and Adjustment in Marriage." *Family Process,* 1967, *6,* 173-184.

Primary Objective: To measure the quality of husband and wife communication.

Description: Subjects respond to twenty-five questions regarding verbal and nonverbal communication with their spouses (for example, "How often do you and your spouse talk over pleasant things that happen during the day?"). Subjects indicate whether each communication occurs very frequently, frequently, occasionally, seldom, or never.

Supplementary Bibliography:
Ely, A. L., Guerney, B. G., and Stover, L. "Efficacy of the Training Phase of Conjugal Therapy." *Psychotherapy: Theory, Research, and Practice,* 1973, *10,* 201-207.

Scale of Marriage Problems

Authors and Source: Swensen, C. H., and Fiore, A. "Scale of Marriage Problems." In J. E. Jones and J. W. Pfeiffer (Eds.), *The 1975 Handbook for Group Facilitators.* La Jolla, Ca.: University Associates, 1975.

Primary Objective: To examine three dimensions underlying marriage interaction: dominance and submission, affection and hostility, and group facilitation and obstruction.

Description: This 100-item scale consists of the following six types of items: (1) problem solving, decision making, and goal setting; (2) child rearing and home labor; (3) relatives and in-laws; (4) personal care and appearance; (5) money management; and (6) expression of affection and outside friendships (for example, "One partner feels that he or she always has to 'give in' to his or her spouse.") Individuals choose one of the following responses: "This is never a problem," "This is somewhat of a problem or an occasional problem," or "This is a serious problem or a constant problem."

Sexual Communication Inventory

Author and Source: Bienvenu, M. J. *Counselor's and Teacher's Manual for the Sexual Communication Inventory.* Saluda, N.C.: Family Life Publications, Inc., 1980.

Primary Objective: To assess how couples communicate sexually.

Description: Each subject independently answers yes, no, or sometimes to thirty questions concerning communication with his or her partner about sex. The following is a sample item: "Do you let your partner know what turns you off sexually?" Additional descriptive information is elicited by asking subjects to complete seven open-ended sentences such as "Sexually, I'm. . . ."

Sexual Interaction Inventory

Authors: LoPiccolo, J., and Steger, J. C.

Source: J. LoPiccolo, Department of Psychiatry and Behavioral Science, State University of New York at Stony Brook, Stony Brook, N.Y. 11790.

Primary Objective: To assess sexual adjustment and satisfaction by obtaining information on seventeen specific sexual activities from each member of the couple, including how much each person enjoys them and each one's estimate of his or her partner's enjoyment.

Description: The instrument consists of a list of seventeen heterosexual behaviors. Spouses answer questions about the behaviors, which provides data about the degree of satisfaction with the frequency and range of sexual behaviors for each individually, self-acceptance of pleasure derived from sexual activities, pleasure derived from sexual activities, accuracy of knowledge of partner's preferred sexual activities, and degree of acceptance of partner.

Supplementary Bibliography:
LoPiccolo, J., and Steger, J. C. "The Sexual Interaction Inventory: A New Instrument for Assessment of Sexual Dysfunction." *Archives of Sexual Behavior,* 1974, *3,* 585–595.
Nowinski, J. K., and LoPiccolo, J. "Assessing Sexual Behavior in Couples." *Journal of Sex and Marital Therapy,* 1979, *5,* 225–243.

Verbal Interaction Task

Author and Source: Guerney, B. G. *Relationship Enhancement: Skill-Training Programs for Therapy, Problem Prevention, and Enrichment.* San Francisco: Jossey-Bass, 1977.

Primary Objective: To assess verbal interaction between partners.

Description: The measure consists of two tasks: discussing something subjects would like to see changed in themselves; and discussing something subjects would like to see changed in their partners. Further instructions are written on cards and handed to participants. Each couple is left alone for four minutes to discuss an issue and is informed that their dialogue is being tape recorded. The resulting dialogue may be scored according to any appropriate coding or rating system.

References

Association of Couples for Marriage Enrichment. "Assessing Our Sexual Relationship." Marriage Enrichment, *Association of Couples for Marriage Enrichment Newsletter.* January/February 1977, *IV,* 4.

Azrin, N. H., Naster, B. J., and Jones, R. "Reciprocity Counseling: A Rapid Learning-Based Procedure for Marital Counseling." *Behavior Research and Therapy,* 1973, *11,* 365–382.

Bach, G. R., and Wyden, P. *The Intimate Enemy.* New York: William Morrow, 1968.

Bach, T. R. "Adjustment Differences Related to Pattern of Rating of the Other." *Psychological Reports,* 1973, *32,* 19–22.

Baker, B. O., and Sarbin, T. R. "Differential Mediation of Social Perception as a Correlate of Social Adjustment." *Sociometry,* 1956, *19,* 69–83.

Baker, F. "General Systems Theory, Research, and Medical Care." In A. Sheldon, F. E. Baker, and C. McLaughlin (Eds.), *Systems and Medical Care.* Cambridge, Mass.: M.I.T. Press, 1970.

Bales, R. F. *Interaction Process Analysis.* Reading, Mass.: Addison-Wesley, 1950.

Ball, J. "Strengthening Families Through Marriage Enrichment." In N. Stinnett, B. Chesser, and J. DeFrain (Eds.), *Building Family Strengths: Blueprints for Action.* Lincoln: University of Nebraska Press, 1979.

Bandura, A. "Psychotherapy Based upon Modelling Principles." In A. Bergin and S. Garfield (Eds.), *Handbook of Psychotherapy and Behavior Change.* New York: Wiley, 1971.

"Baptist Marriage Enrichment System." Family Ministry Department, Southern Baptist Convention. Nashville, Tenn., 1981. (Mimeographed.)

Barton, K., Dielman, T. E., and Cattell, R. B. "An Item Factor Analysis of Intrafamilial Attitudes of Parents." *Journal of Social Psychology,* 1973, *90,* 67–72.

Bass, B. M. "Social Behavior and the Orientation Inventory: A Review." *Psychological Bulletin,* 1967, *68,* 260–292.

Bass, B. M., and others. "Self, Interaction, and Task Orientation Inventory Scores Associated with Overt Behavior and Personal Factors." *Educational and Psychological Measurement,* 1963, *23,* 101–116.

Bateson, G. *Steps to an Ecology of Mind.* New York: Ballantine, 1972.

Behrens, M. L., and others. "The Henry Ittleson Center Family Interaction Scales." *Genetic Psychology Monographs,* 1969, *80* (2), 203–295.

Bell, H. M. *Manual for the Adjustment Inventory.* Palo Alto: Consulting Psychologists Press, 1961.

Benne, K. "The Process of Re-Education: An Assessment of Kurt Lewin's Views." *Group and Organization Studies,* 1976, *1,* 26–42.

Benson, L., Berger, M., and Mease, W. "Family Communication Systems." In S. Miller (Ed.), *Marriages and Families: Enrichment Through Communication.* Beverly Hills, Calif.: Sage, 1975.

Bernard, J. "The Adjustments of Married Mates." In H. T. Christensen (Ed.), *Handbook of Marriage and the Family.* Chicago: Rand McNally, 1964.

Bertalanffy, L. "General System Theory—A Critical Review." In W. Buckley (Ed.), *Modern Systems Research for the Behavioral Scientist.* Hawthorne, N.Y.: Aldine, 1968.

Bertcher, H. J., and Maple, F. "Elements and Issues in Group Composition." In P. Glasser, R. Sarri, and R. Vinter (Eds.), *Individual Change Through Small Groups.* New York: Free Press, 1974.

Bienvenu, M. J. "An Interpersonal Communication Inventory." *The Journal of Communication,* 1971, *21,* 381-388.

Bienvenu, M. J. *A Counselor's Guide to Accompany a Marital Communication Inventory.* Saluda, N.C.: Family Life Publications, 1978.

Birchler, G. R. "Communication Skills in Married Couples." In A. S. Bellack and Hersen (Eds.), *Research and Practice in Social Skills Training.* New York: Plenum, 1979.

Birchler, G. R., Weiss, R. L., and Vincent, J. P. "Multimethod Analysis of Social Reinforcement Exchange Between Maritally Distressed and Nondistressed Spouse and Stranger Dyads." *Journal of Personality and Social Psychology,* 1975, *31,* 349-360.

Blazier, D. C., and Goosman, E. T. *A Marriage Counselor's Guide to Accompany a Marriage Analysis.* Saluda, N.C.: Family Life Publications, 1966.

Bodin, A. M. "Conjoint Family Assessment: An Evolving Field." In P. McReynolds (Ed.), *Advances in Psychological Assessment.* Vol. 1. Palo Alto, Calif.: Science and Behavior Books, 1968.

Bodin, A. M. "Family Interaction: A Social-Clinical Study of Synthetic, Normal, and Problem Family Triads." In W. D. Winter and A. J. Ferreira (Eds.), *Research in Family Interaction.* Palo Alto: Science and Behavior Books, 1969.

Boies, K. G. "Role Playing as a Behavior Change Technique: Review of the Empirical Literature." *Psychotherapy: Theory, Research and Practice,* 1972, *9,* 185-192.

Bormann, E. G. *Discussion and Group Methods.* (2nd ed.) New York: Harper & Row, 1975.

Bosco, A. *Marriage Encounter, A Rediscovery of Love.* St. Meinrad, Ind.: Abbey, 1973.

Bosco, A. "Marriage Encounter: An Ecumenical Enrichment Program." In H. A. Otto (Ed.), *Marriage and Family Enrichment: New Perspectives and Programs.* Nashville: Abingdon, 1976.

Bowen, M. "Principles and Techniques of Multiple Family Therapy." In J. O. Bradt and O. J. Moynihan (Eds.), *Systems Therapy—Selected Papers*. Washington, D.C.: Groome Child Guidance Center, 1975.

Boyd, E., and others. "Teaching Interpersonal Communication to Troubled Families." *Family Process*, 1974, *13*, 317–336.

Boyd, L. A., and Roach, A. J. "Interpersonal Communication Skills Differentiating More Satisfying From Less Satisfying Marital Relationships." *Journal of Counseling Psychology*, 1977, *24*, 540–542.

Bradford, L. P. (Ed.) *Group Development*. San Diego: University Associates, 1978.

Broderick, C. *Couples: How to Confront Problems and Maintain Relationships*. New York: Simon & Schuster, 1979.

Brown, L. B. "The 'Day at Home' in Wellington, New Zealand." *Journal of Social Psychology*, 1959, *50*, 189–206.

Buckley, W. "Society as a Complex Adaptive System." In W. Buckley (Ed.), *Modern Systems Research for the Behavioral Scientist*. Hawthorne, N.Y.: Aldine, 1968.

Buerkle, J. V., and Badgley, R. F. "Couple Role-Taking: The Yale Marital Interaction Battery." *Marriage and Family Living*, 1959, *21*, 53–58.

Burgess, E. W. *The Counselor's Guide: Administration, Scoring, and Interpretation of Scores for Use with a Marriage Prediction Schedule, A Marriage Adjustment Form*. Saluda, N.C.: Family Life Publications, 1952.

Buros, O. K. *The Seventh Mental Measurement Yearbook*. Highland Park, N.J.: Gryphon Press, 1972.

Burr, W. R. "Satisfaction with Various Aspects of Marriage over the Life Cycle: A Random Middle Class Sample." *Journal of Marriage and the Family*, 1970, *32*, 29–37.

Byrne, D., and Blaylock, B. "Similarity and Assumed Similarity of Attitudes Between Husbands and Wives." *Journal of Abnormal and Social Psychology*, 1963, *67*, 636–640.

Calden, G. *I Count—You Count: The "Do It Ourselves" Marriage Counseling and Enrichment Book*. Niles, Ill.: Argus Communications, 1976.

Campbell, D. T., and Stanley, J. C. *Experimental and Quasi-*

Experimental Designs for Research. Chicago: Rand McNally, 1963.

Capers, H., and Capers, B. "Transactional Analysis Tools for Use in Marriage Enrichment Programs." In H. A. Otto (Ed.), *Marriage and Family Enrichment: New Perspectives and Programs.* Nashville: Abingdon, 1976.

Carkhuff, R. R. *Helping and Human Relations: A Primer for Lay and Professional Helpers, Vol. 1.* New York: Holt, Rinehart and Winston, 1969.

Carkhuff, R. R., and Berenson, B. G. *Teaching as Treatment.* Amherst, Mass.: Human Resource Development Press, 1976.

Carkhuff, R. R., and Berenson, B. G. *Beyond Counseling and Therapy.* (2nd ed.) New York: Holt, Rinehart and Winston, 1977.

Carnes, P. J., and Laube, H. "Becoming Us: An Experiment in Family Learning and Teaching." In S. Miller (Ed.), *Marriages and Families: Enrichment Through Communication.* Beverly Hills, Calif.: Sage, 1975.

Carter, R. D., and Thomas, E. J. "Modification of Problematic Marital Communication Using Corrective Feedback and Instruction." *Behavior Therapy,* 1973, *4,* 100-109.

Cartwright, D., and Zander, A. *Group Dynamics.* (3rd ed.) New York: Harper & Row, 1968.

Certo, S. C. *Sourcebook of Experiential Exercises: Interpersonal Skills.* Terre Haute: School of Business, Indiana State University, 1976.

Cherry, C. *On Human Communication: A Review, a Survey, and a Criticism.* (2nd ed.) Cambridge, Mass.: M.I.T. Press, 1966.

Chesser, B. "Building Family Strengths in Dual-Career Marriages." In N. Stinnett, B. Chesser, and J. DeFrain (Eds.), *Building Family Strengths: Blueprints for Action.* Lincoln: University of Nebraska Press, 1979.

Christensen, L., and Wallace, L. "Perceptual Accuracy as a Variable in Marital Adjustment." *Journal of Sex and Marital Therapy,* 1976, *2,* 130-136.

Clarke, C. "Group Procedures for Increasing Positive Feedback Between Married Persons." *The Family Coordinator,* 1970, *20,* 324-328.

Clinebell, H. J. *Growth Counseling for Marriage Enrichment.* Philadelphia: Fortress Press, 1975.

Clinebell, H. J. "Cassette Programs for Training and Enrichment." In H. A. Otto (Ed.), *Marriage and Family Enrichment: New Perspectives and Programs.* Nashville: Abingdon, 1976.

Clinebell, H. J., and Clinebell, C. H. *The Intimate Marriage.* New York: Harper & Row, 1970.

Communication Research Associates. *A Workbook for Interpersonal Communication.* (2nd ed.) Dubuque, Iowa: Kendall/ Hunt, 1978.

Cookerly, J. R. "The Reduction of Psychopathology as Measured by the MMPI Clinical Scales in Three Forms of Marriage Counseling." *Journal of Marriage and the Family,* 1974, *36,* 332-335.

Corsini, R. J. "Multiple Predictors of Marital Happiness." *Marriage and Family Living,* 1956a, *18,* 240-242.

Corsini, R. J. "Understanding and Similarity in Marriage." *Journal of Abnormal and Social Psychology,* 1956b, *52,* 327-332.

Croake, J. W., and Lyon, R. S. "Research Design in Marital Adjustment Studies." *International Journal of Family Counseling,* 1978, *6,* 32-35.

Cromwell, R. E., Olson, D. H. L., and Fournier, D. G. "Diagnosis and Evaluation in Marital and Family Counseling." In D. H. Olson (Ed.), *Treating Relationships.* Lake Mills, Iowa: Graphic, 1976.

Curtis, J. H. "The Marriage and Family Counselor: Improved Image and Accessibility." In N. Stinnett, B. Chesser, and J. DeFrain (Eds.), *Building Family Strengths: Blueprints for Action.* Lincoln: University of Nebraska Press, 1979.

Davis, E. C., and others. "Effects of Weekend and Weekly Marriage Enrichment Program Formats." *Family Relations,* 1982, *31,* 85-90.

Dean, D. G., and Lucas, W. L. "Whose Marital Adjustment— Hers, His, or Theirs?" *Psychological Reports,* 1978, *43,* 978.

Dean, D. G., Lucas, W. L., and Cooper, G. L. "Perceptions of Color Preferences: A Clue to Marital Prediction?" *Journal of Psychology,* 1976, *93,* 243-244.

Deci, E. L. "Effects of Externally Mediated Rewards on Intrinsic Motivation." *Journal of Personality and Social Psychology*, 1971, *18*, 105-115.

Deci, E. L. "Work: Who Does Not Like It and Why." *Psychology Today*, 1972, *6*, 56-58.

Delhees, K. H., Cattell, R. B., and Sweeney, A. B. "The Structure of Parent's Intrafamilial Attitudes and Sentiments Measured by Objective Tests and a Vector Model." *Journal of Social Psychology*, 1970, *82*, 231-252.

Demarest, D., Sexton, J., and Sexton, M. *Marriage Encounter*. St. Paul: Carillon Books, 1977.

DeYoung, A. J. "Marriage Encounter: A Critical Examination." *Journal of Marital and Family Therapy*, 1979, *5*, 27-34.

Dixon, D. N., and Sciara, A. D. "Effectiveness of Group Reciprocity Counseling with Married Couples." *Journal of Marriage and Family Counseling*, 1977, *3*, 77-83.

Doherty, W. J., and Lester, M. E. "Casualties of Marriage Encounter Weekends." *Family Therapy News*, 1982, *13*, 4, 9.

Doherty, W. J., McCabe, P., and Ryder, R. G. "Marriage Encounter: A Critical Appraisal." *Journal of Marriage and Family Counseling*, 1978, *4*, 99-106.

Dreyer, C. A., and Dreyer, A. S. "Family Dinner Time as a Unique Behavior Habitat." *Family Process*, 1973, *12*, 291-301.

Drum, D. J., and Knott, J. E. *Structured Groups for Facilitating Development*. New York: Human Sciences Press, 1977.

Dyer, E. D. "Parenthood as Crisis: A Re-Study." *Marriage and Family Living*, 1963, *25*, 196-201.

Dymond, R. "Interpersonal Perception and Marital Happiness." *Canadian Journal of Psychology*, 1954, *8*, 164-171.

Edmonds, V. H. "Marital Conventionalization: Definition and Measurement." *Journal of Marriage and the Family*, 1967, *29*, 681-688.

Edmonds, V. H., Withers, G., and Dibatista, B. "Adjustment, Conservatism, and Marital Conventionalization." *Journal of Marriage and the Family*, 1972, *34*, 96-103.

Edwards, A. L. *Manual for the Edwards Personal Preference Schedule*. New York: Psychological Corporation, 1959.

Egan, G. *Face to Face: The Small Group Experience and Interpersonal Growth.* Monterey, Calif.: Brooks/Cole, 1973.

Egan, G. *The Skilled Helper: A Model for Systematic Helping and Interpersonal Relating.* Belmont, Calif.: Wadsworth, 1975.

Elbert, S., Rosman, B., Minuchin, S., and Guerney, B. "A Method for the Clinical Study of Family Interaction." *American Journal of Orthopsychiatry,* 1964, *34,* 885–894.

Elliott, S., and Saunders, B. "The Systems Marriage Enrichment Program: An Alternative Model Based on Systems Theory." *Family Relations,* 1982, *31,* 53–60.

Ely, A. L. "Efficacy of Training in Conjugal Therapy." Unpublished doctoral dissertation, Department of Clinical Psychology, Rutgers University, 1970.

Epstein, N., Degiovanni, I. S., and Jayne-Lazarus, C. "Assertion Training for Couples." *Journal of Behavior Therapy and Experimental Psychiatry,* 1978, *9,* 149–155.

Epstein, N., and Jackson, E. "An Outcome Study of Short-Term Communication Training with Married Couples." *Journal of Consulting and Clinical Psychology,* 1978, *46,* 207–212.

Faules, D. "The Relation of Communication Skill to the Ability to Elicit and Interpret Feedback Under Four Conditions." *Journal of Communication,* 1967, *17,* 362–371.

Feffer, M., and Suchotliff, L. "Decentering Implications of Social Interactions." *Journal of Personality and Social Psychology,* 1966, *4,* 415–422.

Ferreira, A. J. "Interpersonal Perceptivity Among Family Members." *American Journal of Orthopsychiatry,* 1964, *34,* 64–70.

Ferreira, A. J., and Winter, W. O. "On the Nature of Marital Relationships: Measurable Differences in Spontaneous Agreement." *Family Process,* 1974, *13,* 355–369.

Fiedler, F. E., Chemers, M. M., and Bons, P. M. "Implications of the Contingency Model for Improving Organizational Effectiveness." In P. Hersey and J. Stinson (Eds.), *Perspectives in Leader Effectiveness.* Ohio University: The Center for Leadership Studies, 1980.

Fisher, R. "The Effect of Two Group Counseling Methods on

Perceptual Congruence in Married Pairs." Unpublished doctoral dissertation, Department of Educational Psychology, University of Hawaii, 1973.

Flanders, N. A. *Analyzing Teaching Behavior.* Reading, Mass.: Addison-Wesley, 1970.

Forer, B. R. "A Structured Sentence Completion Test." *Journal of Projective Techniques,* 1950, *14,* 15-30.

Foster, A. L. "The Sexual Compatibility Test." *Journal of Consulting Clinical Psychology,* 1977, *45,* 332-333.

Frank, E., and Kupfer, D. "In Every Marriage There Are Two Marriages." *Journal of Sex and Marital Therapy,* 1976, *2,* 137-143.

Frederiksen, L. W., and others. "Social-Skills Training to Modify Abusive Verbal Outbursts in Adults." *Journal of Applied Behavior Analysis,* 1976, *9,* 117-125.

Fretz, B. R. "Postural Movements in a Counseling Dyad." *Journal of Counseling Psychology,* 1966, *13,* 335-343.

Friedman, C. J., and Friedman, A. S. "Characteristics of Schizogenic Families During a Joint Family Story-Telling Task." *Family Process,* 1970, *9,* 333-354.

Gant, R. L. "The Behavioral Approach to Building More Positive Marriage and Family Relationships." In N. Stinnett, B. Chesser, and J. DeFrain (Eds.), *Building Family Strengths: Blueprints for Action.* Lincoln: University of Nebraska Press, 1979.

Garland, D. R. *Couples Communication and Negotiation Skills.* New York: Family Service Association of America, 1978.

Garland, D. R. "Training Married Couples in Listening Skills: Effects on Behavior, Perceptual Accuracy, and Marital Adjustment." *Family Relations,* 1981, *30,* pp. 297-306.

Genovese, R. J. "Marriage Encounter." In S. Miller (Ed.), *Marriages and Families: Enrichment Through Communication.* Beverly Hills, Calif.: Sage, 1975.

Goldstein, A. "Behavior Therapy." In R. Corsini (Ed.), *Current Psychotherapies.* Itasca, Ill.: Peacock, 1973.

Goldstein, A. P., Heller, K., and Sechrest, L. B. *Psychotherapy and the Psychology of Behavior Change.* New York: Wiley, 1966.

Goodrich, D. W., and Boomer, D. S. "Experimental Assessment of Modes of Conflict Resolution." *Family Process,* 1963, *2,* 15–24.

Gordon, T. *P.E.T.: Parent Effectiveness Training.* New York: New American Library, 1975.

Gottman, J., and Porterfield, A. L. "Communicative Competence in the Nonverbal Behavior of Married Couples." *Journal of Marriage and the Family,* 1981, *43,* 817–824.

Gough, H. G., and Heilbrun, A. B., Jr. *The Adjective Checklist Manual.* Palo Alto: Consulting Psychologists, 1980.

Green, H. "A Christian Marriage Enrichment Retreat." In H. A. Otto (Ed.), *Marriage and Family Enrichment: New Perspectives and Programs.* Nashville: Abingdon, 1976.

Guerney, B. G., Jr. *Relationship Enhancement: Skill-Training Programs for Therapy, Problem Prevention, and Enrichment.* San Francisco: Jossey-Bass, 1977.

Gurman, A. S., and Kniskern, D. P. "Enriching Research on Marital Enrichment Programs." *Journal of Marriage and Family Counseling,* 1977, *3,* 3–9.

Gurman, A. S., and Kniskern, D. P. "Family Therapy Outcome Research: Knowns and Unknowns." In A. S. Gurman and D. P. Kniskern (Eds.), *Handbook of Family Therapy.* New York: Brunner/Mazel, 1981.

Haley, J. "Research on Family Patterns: An Instrument Measurement." *Family Process,* 1964, *3,* 41–65.

Haley, J. "A Review of the Family Therapy Field." In J. Haley (Ed.), *Changing Families.* New York: Grune & Stratton, 1971.

Haley, J. *Problem-Solving Therapy: New Strategies for Effective Family Therapy.* San Francisco: Jossey-Bass, 1976.

Hall, A. D., and Fagen, R. E. "Definition of System." In W. Buckley (Ed.), *Modern Systems Research for the Behavioral Scientist.* Hawthorne, N.Y.: Aldine, 1968.

Hardcastle, D. R. "Measuring Effectiveness in Group Marital Counseling." *The Family Coordinator,* 1972, p. 213–218.

Hardin, G. "The Cybernetics of Competition: A Biologist's View of Society." In W. Buckley (Ed.), *Modern Systems Research for the Behavioral Scientist.* Hawthorne, N.Y.: Aldine, 1968.

Hare, A. P. *Handbook of Small Group Research.* (2nd ed.) New York: Free Press, 1976.

Harrell, J., and Guerney, B. "Training Married Couples in Conflict Negotiation Skills." In D. H. Olson (Ed.), *Treating Relationships.* Lake Mills, Iowa: Graphic, 1976.

Harris, T. A. *I'm OK—You're OK.* New York: Harper & Row, 1967.

Hartford, M. *Groups in Social Work: Applications of Small Group Theory and Research to Social Work Practice.* New York: Columbia University Press, 1971.

Hawkins, J. L., Weisburg, C., and Ray, D. L. "Marital Communication Style and Social Class." *Journal of Marriage and the Family,* 1977, *39,* 479–490.

Haynes, S. N., Follingstad, D. R., and Sullivan, J. C. "Assessment of Marital Satisfaction and Interaction." *Journal of Consulting and Clinical Psychology,* 1979, *47,* 789–791.

Hayward, D. "A Marriage Enrichment Communication Course." In H. A. Otto (Ed.), *Marriage and Family Enrichment: New Perspectives and Programs.* Nashville: Abingdon, 1976.

Hekmat, H. "Some Personality Correlates of Empathy." *Journal of Consulting and Clinical Psychology,* 1975, *43,* 89.

Henry, S. *Group Skills in Social Work.* Itasca, Ill.: Peacock, 1981.

Herbst, P. G. "The Measurement of Family Relationships." *Human Relations,* 1952, *5,* 3–35.

Hersey, P., and Blanchard, K. H. *Management of Organizational Behavior.* (3rd ed.) Englewood Cliffs, N.J.: Prentice-Hall, 1977.

Hersey, P., Blanchard, K. H., and Hambleton, R. K. "Contracting for Leadership Style: A Process and Instrumentation for Building Effective Work Relationships." In P. Hersey and J. Stinson (Eds.), *Perspectives in Leader Effectiveness.* Ohio University: Center for Leadership Studies, 1980.

Hersey, P., and Stinson, T. *Perspectives in Leader Effectiveness.* Ohio University: Center for Leadership Studies, 1980.

Hicks, M., and Platt, M. "Marital Happiness and Stability: A Review of Research in the Sixties." In C. Broderick (Ed.), *A Decade of Family Research and Action: 1960–1966.* Minneapolis: National Council on Family Relations, 1971.

Hill, R. "Modern Systems Theory and the Family: A Confrontation." In M. B. Sussman (Ed.), *Sourcebook in Marriage and the Family*. Boston: Houghton Mifflin, 1974.

Hill, W. *Hill Interaction Matrix Monograph*. Los Angeles: University of Southern California, Youth Studies Center, 1965.

Hinkle, J. E., and Moore, M. "A Student Couples Program." *The Family Coordinator*, 1971, *20*, 153–158.

Hobart, C. W., and Fahlberg, N. "The Measurement of Empathy." *American Journal of Sociology*, 1965, *70*, 595–603.

Hobbs, D. E., Jr. "Parenthood as Crisis: A Third Study." *Journal of Marriage and the Family*, 1965, *27*, 367–372.

Hobbs, D. E., Jr. "Transition to Parenthood: A Replication and an Extension." *Journal of Marriage and the Family*, 1968, *30*, 413–417.

Hof, L., Epstein, N., and Miller, W. R. "Integrating Attitudinal and Behavioral Change in Marital Enrichment." *Family Relations*, 1980, *29*, 241–248.

Hof, L., and Miller, W. R. "Marriage Enrichment." *Marriage and Family Review*, 1980, *3*, 1–27.

Hof, L., and Miller, W. R. *Marriage Enrichment: Philosophy, Process, and Program*. Bowie, Md.: Brady, 1981.

Hoffman, L. "Deviation-Amplifying Processes in Natural Groups." In J. Haley (Ed.), *Changing Families*. New York: Grune & Stratton, 1971.

Hopkins, L., and others. *Toward Better Marriages: The Handbook of the Association of Couples for Marriage Enrichment (ACME)*. Winston-Salem, N.C.: Association of Couples for Marriage Enrichment, 1978.

Hopkins, P., and Hopkins, L. "The Marriage Communication Labs." In H. A. Otto (Ed.), *Marriage and Family Enrichment: New Perspectives and Programs*. Nashville: Abingdon, 1976.

Hunt, R. A. "The Effect of Item Weighting on the Locke-Wallace Marital Adjustment Scale." *Journal of Marriage and the Family*, 1978, *40*, 249–256.

Huntington, R. M. "The Personality-Interaction Approach to Study of the Marital Relationship." *Marriage and Family Living*, 1958, *20*, 43–46.

Inselberg, R. M. "Social and Psychological Factors Associated with High School Marriages." *Journal of Home Economics,* 1961, *53,* 766–772.

Inselberg, R. M. "The Sentence Completion Technique in the Measurement of Marital Satisfaction." *Journal of Marriage and the Family,* 1964, *26,* 339–341.

Ivey, A. E. *Microcounseling: Innovations in Interviewing Training.* Springfield, Ill.: Thomas, 1971.

Ivey, A. E., and others. "Microcounseling and Attending Behavior: An Approach to Prepracticum Counselor Training." *Journal of Counseling Psychology,* 1968, *15* (Part II), 1–12.

Jackson, D. D., and Weakland, J. H. "Conjoint Family Therapy. Some Considerations on Theory, Technique, and Results." *Psychiatry,* 1961, *24,* supplement to no. 2, 30–45.

Janis, I. L., and Mann, L. "Effectiveness of Emotional Role-Playing in Modifying Smoking Habits and Attitudes." *Journal of Experimental Research on Personality,* 1965, *1,* 84–90.

Jayaratne, S., and Levy, R. L. *Empirical Clinical Practice.* New York: Columbia University Press, 1979.

Joanning, H. "The Long-Term Effects of the Couple Communication Program." *Journal of Marital and Family Therapy,* 1982, *8,* 463–468.

Jones, S. E., Barnlund, D. C., and Haiman, F. S. *Dynamics of Discussion.* (2nd ed.) New York: Harper & Row, 1980.

Jourard, S. M. *The Transparent Self.* New York: Van Nostrand, 1971.

Kahn, M. "Non-Verbal Communication and Marital Satisfaction." *Family Process,* 1970, *9,* 449–456.

Karen, R. L. "A Method for Rating Sentence Completion Test Responses." *Journal of Projective Techniques,* 1961, *25,* 312–314.

Karlsson, G. *Adaptability and Communication in Marriage.* Totowa, N.J.: Bedminster Press, 1963.

Katz, D., and Kahn, R. L. *The Social Psychology of Organizations.* New York: Wiley, 1966.

Katz, M. "Agreement on Connotative Meaning in Marriage." *Family Process,* 1965, *4,* 64–74.

Kaufmann, R. F. *The Intimate Hours.* New York: William Morrow, 1978.

Kelly, G. A. *The Psychology of Personal Constructs.* New York: Norton, 1955.

Kelmann, P. R., Moreault, D., and Robinson, E. A. "Effects of a Marriage Enrichment Program: An Outcome Study." *Journal of Sex and Marital Therapy,* 1978, *4,* 54-57.

Kenkel, W. F. "Traditional Family Ideology and Spousal Roles in Decision Making." *Marriage and Family Living,* 1959, *21,* 334-339.

Kenkel, W. F., and Hoffman, D. K. "Real and Conceived Roles in Family Decision Making." *Marriage and Family Living,* 1956, *18,* 311-316.

Kersten, L. K. "An Exchange Approach to Building Better Interpersonal Relationships." In N. Stinnett, B. Chesser, and J. DeFrain (Eds.), *Building Family Strengths: Blueprints for Action.* Lincoln: University of Nebraska Press, 1979.

Kieren, D., and Tallman, I. "Spousal Adaptability: An Assessment of Marital Competence." *Journal of Marriage and the Family,* 1972, *34,* 247-256.

Kilmann, P. R., Julian, A., and Moreault, D. "The Impact of a Marriage Enrichment Program on Relationship Factors." *Journal of Sex and Marital Therapy,* 1978, *4,* 298-303.

Kirkpatrick, C. "Community of Interest and the Measurement of Marriage Adjustment." *The Family,* 1937, *18,* 133-137.

Kligfield, B. "The Jewish Marriage Encounter." In H. A. Otto (Ed.), *Marriage and Family Enrichment: New Perspectives and Programs.* Nashville: Abingdon, 1976.

Knox, D. *Discussion Guide to Accompany a Love Attitude Inventory.* Saluda, N.C.: Family Life Publications, 1971.

Knox, D. *Marriage Happiness: A Behavioral Approach to Counseling.* Champaign, Ill.: Research Press, 1971.

Knox, D. *Marriage Inventory.* Champaign, Ill.: Research Press, 1971.

Knox, D. *Dr. Knox's Marital Exercise Book.* New York: McKay, 1975.

Knox, D., and Patrick, J. A. "You Are What You Do: A New Approach in Preparation for Marriage." *The Family Coordinator,* 1971, *20,* 109-114.

Knudson, R. M., Sommers, A. A., and Golding, S. L. "Interpersonal Perception and Mode of Resolution in Marital Conflict." *Journal of Personality and Social Psychology,* 1980, *38,* 751-763.

Koch, T., and Koch, L. "Marriage Enrichment Courses: The Urgent Drive to Make Good Marriages Better." *Psychology Today,* 1976, *10,* 33-35, 83, 85, 95.

Komisar, D. D. "A Marriage Problem Story Completion Test." *Journal of Consulting Psychology,* 1949, *13,* 403-406.

Krupar, K. R. *Communication Games.* New York: Free Press, 1971.

L'Abate, L. "Family Enrichment Programs." *Journal of Family Counseling,* 1974, *2,* 32-38.

L'Abate, L. *Enrichment: Structured Interventions with Couples, Families, and Groups.* Washington, D.C.: University Press of America, 1978.

L'Abate, L. "Skill Training Programs for Couples and Families." In A. S. Gurman, and D. P. Kniskern (Eds.), *Handbook of Family Therapy.* New York: Brunner/Mazel, 1981.

L'Abate, L., and Allison, M. Q. "Planned Change Intervention: The Enrichment Model with Couples, Families, and Groups." *Transnational Mental Health Research Newsletter,* 1977, *19,* 11-15.

L'Abate, L., and O'Callaghan, J. B. "Implications of the Enrichment Model for Research and Training." *The Family Coordinator,* 1977, *26,* 61-64.

L'Abate, L., and others. *Manual: Enrichment Programs for the Family Life Cycle.* Atlanta, Ga.: Social Research Laboratories, 1975a.

L'Abate, L., and others. *Manual: Family Enrichment Programs.* Atlanta, Ga.: Social Research Laboratories, 1975b.

L'Abate, L., and Rupp, G. *Enrichment: Skills Training for Family Life.* Washington, D.C.: University Press of America, 1981.

LaForge, R., and Suezek, R. F. "The Interpersonal Dimension of Personality: III. An Interpersonal Checklist." *Journal of Personality,* 1955, *24,* 94-112.

Laing, R. D. *The Politics of the Family and Other Essays.* New York: Pantheon, 1971.

Laing, R. D., Phillipson, H., and Lee, A. R. *Interpersonal Perception.* London: Tavistock, 1966.

Laing, R. D., Phillipson, H., and Lee, A. R. *Interpersonal Perception: A Theory and Method of Research.* New York: Springer, 1966.

Larsen, G. R. "An Evaluation of the Minnesota Couple Communications Training Program's Influence on Marital Communication and Self and Mate Perceptions." Unpublished doctoral dissertation, Arizona State University, 1974.

Lazarus, A. A. "Behavior Therapy and Marriage Counseling." *Journal of the American Society of Psychosomatic Dentistry and Medicine,* 1968, *15,* 49-56.

Lazarus, A. A. "Modes of Treatment of Sexual Inadequacies." *Medical Aspects of Human Sexuality,* 1969, *3,* 53-58.

Lazarus, A. A. *Behavior Therapy and Beyond.* New York: McGraw-Hill, 1971.

Leavitt, H. J., and Mueller, R. A. H. "Some Effects of Feedback on Communication." *Human Relations,* 1951, *4,* 401-410.

LeBow, M. D. "Behavior Modification for the Family." In G. D. Erickson and I. P. Hogan (Eds.), *Family Therapy: An Introduction to Theory and Technique.* Monterey, Calif.: Brooks/ Cole, 1972.

LeMasters, E. E. "Parenthood as Crisis." *Marriage and Family Living,* 1957, *19,* 352-355.

Leslie, G. R. *The Family in Social Context.* (4th ed.) New York: Oxford University Press, 1979.

Levinger, G. "Altruism in Marriage: A Test of the Buerkle-Badgley Battery." *Journal of Marriage and the Family,* 1965, *27,* 32-33.

Levinger, G., and Breedlove, J. "Interpersonal Attraction and Agreement: A Study of Marriage Partners." *Journal of Personality and Social Psychology,* 1966, *3,* 367-372.

Lewis, J. M. *How's Your Family?* New York: Brunner/Mazel, 1979.

Lewis, J. M., and others. *No Single Thread: Psychological Health in Family Systems.* New York: Brunner/Mazel, 1976.

Liberman, R. "Behavioral Approaches to Family and Couple Therapy." *American Journal of Orthopsychiatry,* 1970, *40,* 106-117.

Lieberman, M. A., and Bond, G. R. "Problems in Studying Outcomes." In M. A. Lieberman, Leonard D. Borman, and Associates, *Self-Help Groups for Coping with Crisis: Origins, Members, Processes, and Impact.* San Francisco: Jossey-Bass, 1979.

Locke, H. J., and Wallace, K. M. "Short, Marital-Adjustment and Prediction Tests: Their Reliability and Validity." *Marriage and Family Living,* 1959, *21,* 251-255.

Luce, R. D., and Raiffa, H. *Games and Decisions.* New York: Wiley, 1957.

Luckey, E. B. "Marital Satisfaction and Congruent Self–Spouse Concepts." *Social Forces,* 1960, *39,* 153-157.

Lundy, R. M. "Assimilative Projection and Accuracy of Prediction in Interpersonal Relations." *Journal of Abnormal and Social Psychology,* 1956, *52,* 33-38.

MacDonald, A. P. "Identification and Measurement of Multidimensional Attitudes Toward Equality Between the Sexes." *Journal of Homosexuality,* 1974, *1,* 165-182.

Mace, D. R. "Marriage Enrichment Concepts for Research." *The Family Coordinator,* 1975a, *24,* 171-173.

Mace, D. R. "We Call It ACME." *Small Group Behavior,* 1975b, *6,* 31-44.

Mace, D. R., and Mace, V. "Marriage Enrichment—Wave of the Future?" *The Family Coordinator,* 1975, *24,* 131-135.

Mace, D. R., and Mace, V. *Marriage Enrichment in the Church.* Nashville: Broadman, 1976a.

Mace, D. R., and Mace, V. "Marriage Enrichment—A Preventive Group Approach for Couples." In D. H. Olson (Ed.), *Treating Relationships.* Lake Mills, Iowa: Graphic, 1976b.

Mace, D. R., and Mace, V. "The Selection, Training, and Certification of Facilitators for Marriage Enrichment Programs." *The Family Coordinator,* 1976c, *25,* 117-125.

Mace, D. R., and Mace, V. *How to Have a Happy Marriage.* Nashville: Abingdon, 1977.

Mace, D. R., and Mace, V. "The Marriage Enrichment Movement: Its History, Its Rationale, and Its Future Prospects." In L. Hopkins and others, *Toward Better Marriages: The Handbook of the Association of Couples for Marriage Enrichment (ACME).* Winston-Salem, N.C.: Association of Couples for Marriage Enrichment, 1978a.

Mace D. R., and Mace, V. "Measure Your Marriage Potential: A Simple Test That Tells Couples Where They Are." *The Family Coordinator,* 1978b, *27,* 63–68.

McHugh, G. *Marriage Counselor's Manual and Teacher's Handbook for Use With the Sex Knowledge Inventory, Form X Revised.* Saluda, N.C.: Family Life Publications, 1979.

McHugh, G., and McHugh, T. G. *Counselors and Educators Manual for the Sex Attitudes Survey and Profile.* Saluda, N.C.: Family Life Publications, 1976.

McHugh, T. G. *Teachers and Counselors Manual for the Sex Knowledge Inventory, Form-Y (Vocabulary and Anatomy).* Saluda, N.C.: Family Life Publications, 1977.

Madden, M. E., and Janoff-Bulman, R. "Blame, Control, and Marital Satisfaction: Wives' Attributions for Conflict in Marriage." *Journal of Marriage and the Family,* 1981, *43,* 663–674.

Mager, R. F. *Preparing Instructional Objectives.* Belmont, Calif.: Fearon, 1962.

Malamud, D. I. "Communication Training in the Second-Chance Family." In S. Miller (Ed.), *Marriages and Families: Enrichment Through Communication.* Beverly Hills, Calif.: Sage, 1975.

Manson, M. P., and Lerner, A. *The Marriage Adjustment Sentence Completion Manual.* Beverly Hills, Calif.: Western Psychological Services, 1962.

"Marriage Communication Labs." Indianapolis, Ind.: Division of Homeland Ministries, Christian Church, 1975. (Mimeographed.)

Maslow, A. *Toward a Psychology of Being.* (2nd ed.) New York: D. Van Nostrand, 1968.

Maxwell, J. W. "A Rational-Emotive Approach to Strengthening Marriage." In N. Stinnett, B. Chesser, and J. DeFrain (Eds.), *Building Family Strengths: Blueprints for Action.* Lincoln: University of Nebraska Press, 1979.

Meador, B. D., and Rogers, C. R. "Client-Centered Therapy." In R. Corsini (Ed.), *Current Psychotherapies.* Itasca, Ill.: Peacock, 1973.

Mehrabian, A., and Reed, H. "Some Determinants of Communication Accuracy." *Psychological Bulletin,* 1968, *70,* 365–381.

Middleman, R. R. "The Skill Component of Professional Social Work Education: Semantics, Pragmatics and Instructional Heuristics." Invitational paper presented at the annual program meeting of the Council on Social Work Education, Phoenix, Arizona, 1977.

Middleman, R. R., and Goldberg, G. *Social Service Delivery: A Structural Approach to Social Work Practice.* New York: Columbia University Press, 1974.

Milholland, T. A., and Avery, A. W. "Effects of Marriage Encounter on Self-Disclosure, Trust, and Marital Satisfaction." *Journal of Marital and Family Therapy,* 1982, *8,* 87–89.

Miller, J. G. *Living Systems.* New York: McGraw-Hill, 1978.

Miller, N. E., and Dollard, J. *Social Learning and Imitation.* New Haven, Conn.: Yale University Press, 1941.

Miller, S. (Ed.). *Marriages and Families: Enrichment Through Communication.* Beverly Hills, Calif.: Sage, 1975.

Miller, S., Corrales, R., and Wackman, D. B. "Recent Progress in Understanding and Facilitating Marital Communication." *The Family Coordinator,* 1975, *24,* 143–152.

Miller, S., Nunnally, E. W., and Wackman, D. B. *Alive and Aware.* Minneapolis: Interpersonal Communication Programs, 1975.

Miller, S., Nunnally, E. W., and Wackman, D. B. "Minnesota Couples Communication Program [MCCP]: Premarital and Marital Groups." In D. H. Olson (Ed.), *Treating Relationships.* Lake Mills, Iowa: Graphic, 1976.

Miller, W. R., and Lief, H. I. "The Sex Knowledge and Attitude Test (SKAT)." *Journal of Sex and Marital Therapy,* 1979, *5,* 282–287.

Mishler, E. G., and Waxler, N. E. *Interaction in Families.* New York: Wiley, 1968.

Moos, R. H., Insel, P. M., and Humphrey, P. *Combined Preliminary Manual: Family, Work and Group Environment Scales.* Palo Alto: Consulting Psychologists Press, 1974.

Murphy, D. C., and Mendelson, L. A. "Communication and Adjustment in Marriage: Investigating the Relationship." *Family Process,* 1973, *12,* 317-325.

Murrell, S. *Community Psychology and Social Systems: A Conceptual Framework and Intervention Guide.* New York: Behavioral Publications, 1973.

Murstein, B. I. "Sex Drive, Person Perception, and Marital Choice." *Archives of Sexual Behavior,* 1974, *3,* 331-348.

Murstein, B. I., and Beck, G. D. "Person Perception, Marriage Adjustment, and Social Desirability." *Journal of Consulting and Clinical Psychology,* 1972, *32,* 396-403.

National Marriage Encounter. *Marriage Enrichment Resource Manual.* St. Paul, Minn.: National Marriage Encounter, 1978.

Navran, L. "Communication and Adjustment in Marriage." *Family Process,* 1967, *6,* 173-184.

Nelson, R. C., and Friest, W. P. "Marriage Enrichment Through Choice Awareness." *Journal of Marital and Family Therapy,* 1980, *6,* 399-407.

Newmark, C. S., and Woody, G., and Ziff, D. "Understanding and Similarity in Relation to Marital Satisfaction." *Journal of Clinical Psychology,* 1977, *33,* 83-86.

Novak, A. L., and van der Veen, F. "Family Concepts and Emotional Disturbance in the Families of Disturbed Adolescents with Normal Siblings." *Family Process,* 1970, *9,* 157-171.

Nowinski, J. K., and LoPiccolo, J. "Assessing Sexual Behavior in Couples." *Journal of Sex and Marital Therapy,* 1979, *5,* 225-243.

Nunnally, E. W. "Effects of Communication Training Upon Interaction Awareness and Empathic Accuracy of Engaged Couples: A Field Experiment." Unpublished doctoral dissertation, Department of Sociology, University of Minnesota, 1971.

Nunnally, E. W., Miller, S., and Wackman, D. B. "The Minnesota Couples Communication Program." In H. A. Otto (Ed.), *Marriage and Family Enrichment: New Perspectives and Programs.* Nashville: Abingdon, 1976.

Nunnally, J. C., and Wilson, W. H. "Method and Theory for Developing Measures in Evaluation Research." In E. L. Struening and M. Guttentag (Eds.), *Handbook of Evaluation Research.* Vol. 1. Beverly Hills, Calif.: Sage, 1975.

Olson, D. H. "Measurement of Family Power by Self-Report and Behavioral Methods." *Journal of Marriage and the Family*, 1969, *31*, 545-550.

Olson, D. H. "Marital and Family Therapy: Integrative Review and Critique." *Journal of Marriage and the Family*, 1970, *32*, 501-538.

Olson, D. H. "Review and Critique of Behavior Modification Research with Couples and Families: or Are Frequency Counts All That Really Count?" Revision paper presented at the annual meeting of the Association for the Advancement of Behavior Therapy, New York, Oct. 1972.

Olson, D. H. "Bridging Research, Theory, and Application: The Triple Threat in Science." In D. H. Olson (Ed.), *Treating Relationships*. Lake Mills, Iowa: Graphic, 1976a.

Olson, D. H. "Inventories of Premarital, Marital, Parent-Child, and Parent-Adolescent Conflict." Unpublished manuscript, University of Minnesota, 1976b.

Olson, D. H., and others. *Family Inventories*. Minneapolis: University of Minnesota, 1982.

Olson, D. H., and Ryder, R. G. "Inventory of Marital Conflicts (IMC): An Experimental Interaction Procedure." *Journal of Marriage and the Family*, 1970, *32*, 443-448.

Olson, D. H., and Ryder, R. G. *Inventory of Marital Conflict: Procedure Manual*. Minneapolis: University of Minnesota, 1977.

Olson, D. H., and Sprenkle, D. H. "Emerging Trends in Treating Relationships." *Journal of Marriage and Family Counseling*, 1976, *2*, 317-329.

Olson, D. H., Sprenkle, D. H., and Russell, C. S. "Circumplex Model of Marital and Family Systems I: Cohesion and Adaptability Dimensions, Family Types, and Clinical Applications." *Family Process*, 1979, *18*, 3-28.

Olson, D. H., and Straus, M. A. "A Diagnostic Tool for Marital and Family Therapy: The Sim Fam Technique." *The Family Coordinator*, 1972, *21*, 251-258.

Osgood, C. E., Suci, G. J., and Tannenbaum, P. H. *The Measurement of Meaning*. Urbana: University of Illinois Press, 1957.

Otto, H. A. *More Joy in Your Marriage*. New York: Hawthorn Books, 1969.

Otto, H. A. "Marriage and Family Enrichment Programs in North America—Report and Analysis." *The Family Coordinator,* 1975, *24,* 137-142.

Otto, H. A. (Ed.) *Marriage and Family Enrichment: New Perspectives and Programs.* Nashville: Abingdon, 1976.

Otto, H. A. "Developing Human Family Potential." In N. Stinnett, B. Chesser, and J. DeFrain (Eds.), *Building Family Strengths: Blueprints for Action.* Lincoln: University of Nebraska Press, 1979.

Otto, H. A., and Otto, R. "The More Joy in Your Marriage Program." In H. A. Otto (Ed.), *Marriage and Family Enrichment: New Perspectives and Programs.* Nashville: Abingdon, 1976.

Patterson, G. R. *Families: Applications of Social Learning to Family Life.* Champaign, Ill.: Research Press, 1971.

Patterson, G. R. "Changes in Status of Family Members as Controlling Stimuli: A Basis for Describing Treatment Process." In L. Hamerlynck, L. Handy, and E. Mash (Eds.), *Behavior Change: Methodology, Concepts, and Practice.* Champaign, Ill.: Research Press, 1973.

Patterson, G. R., and Cobb, J. A. "A Dyadic Analysis of 'Aggressive' Behaviors: An Additional Step Toward a Theory of Aggression." In J. P. Hill (Ed.), *Minnesota Symposia on Child Psychology.* Vol. 5. Minneapolis: University of Minnesota Press, 1971.

Patterson, G. R., and Hops, H. "Coercion, a Game for Two: Intervention Techniques for Marital Conflict." In R. E. Ulrich and P. T. Mountjoy (Eds.), *The Experimental Analysis of Social Behavior.* New York: Appleton-Century-Crofts, 1972.

Patterson, G. R., Hops, H., and Weiss, R. L. "Interpersonal Skills Training for Couples in Early Stages of Conflict." *Journal of Marriage and the Family,* 1975, *37,* 295-302.

Patterson, G. R., and Reid, J. B. "Reciprocity and Coercion: Two Facets of Social Systems." In C. Neuringer and J. Michael (Eds.), *Behavior Modification in Clinical Psychology.* New York: Appleton-Century-Crofts, 1970.

Patterson, G. R., Weiss, R. L., and Hops, H. "Training in Marital Skills: Some Problems and Concepts." In H. Lutenberg (Ed.),

Handbook of Behavior Modification. New York: Appleton-Century-Crofts, 1976.

Pfeiffer, J. W., and Heslin, R. *Instrumentation in Human Relations Training.* Iowa City: University Associates, 1973.

Pfeiffer, J. W., and Jones, J. E. (Eds.) *The 1974 Annual Handbook for Group Facilitators.* La Jolla, Calif.: University Associates, 1974.

Pfeiffer, J. W., and Jones, J. E. *A Handbook of Structured Experiences for Human Relations Training.* Vol. 5. San Diego, Calif.: University Associates, 1975.

Pierce, R. M. "Training in Interpersonal Communication Skills With the Partners of Deteriorated Marriages." *The Family Coordinator,* 1973, *22,* 223-226.

Piercy, F. P., and Schultz, K. "Values Clarification Strategies for Couples' Enrichment." *The Family Coordinator,* 1978, *25,* 175-178.

Pinsof, W. M. "Family Therapy Process Research." In A. S. Gurman and D. P. Kniskern (Eds.), *Handbook of Family Therapy.* New York: Brunner/Mazel, 1981.

Pless, I. B., and Satterwhite, B. "A Measure of Family Functioning and Its Application." *Social Science and Medicine,* 1973, *7,* 613-621.

Powell, G. S., and Wampler, K. S. "Marriage Enrichment Participants: Levels of Marital Satisfaction." *Family Relations,* 1982, *31,* 389-393.

Program Development Center of Northern California. *A Programmed Course for the Writing of Performance Objectives.* Bloomington, Ind.: Commission on Educational Planning, 1972.

Prunty, K. G. "The Care-Lab: A Family Enrichment Program." In H. A. Otto (Ed.), *Marriage and Family Enrichment: New Perspectives and Programs.* Nashville: Abingdon, 1976.

Quick, E., and Jacobs, T. "Marital Disturbance in Relation to Role Theory and Relationship Theory." *Journal of Abnormal Psychology,* 1973, *82,* 309-316.

Rachman, S. "Clinical Applications of Observational Learning, Imitation and Modeling." *Behavior Therapy,* 1972, *3,* 379-397.

Rappaport, A. F. "Effects of an Intensive Conjugal Relationship Modification Program." Unpublished doctoral dissertation, Pennsylvania State University, 1971.

Rappaport, A. F. "Conjugal Relationship Enhancement Program." In D. H. Olson (Ed.), *Treating Relationships*. Lake Mills, Iowa: Graphic, 1976.

Rappaport, A. F., and Harrell, J. "Behavioral-Exchange Model for Marital Counseling." *The Family Coordinator*, 1972, *21*, 203-212.

Rathus, S. A. "A 30-item Schedule of Assessing Assertive Behavior." *Behavior Therapy*, 1973, *4*, 398-406.

Raush, H. L., Grief, A. C., and Nugent, J. "Communication in Couples and Families." In W. R. Burr, and others (Eds.), *Contemporary Theories About the Family: Research-Based Theories*. Vol. I. New York: Free Press, 1979.

Raush, H. L., and others. *Communication, Conflict, and Marriage: Explorations in the Theory and Study of Intimate Relationships*. San Francisco: Jossey-Bass, 1974.

Ravich, R. A. "The Use of an Interpersonal Game-Test in Conjoint Marital Psychotherapy." *American Journal of Psychotherapy*, 1969, *23*, 217-229.

Regula, R. R. "The Marriage Encounter: What Makes It Work?" *The Family Coordinator*, 1975, *24*, 153-159.

Rhyne, D. "Bases of Marital Satisfaction Among Men and Women." *Journal of Marriage and the Family*, 1981, *43*, 941-955.

Riskin, J. M., and Faunce, E. E. "An Evaluative Review of Family Interaction Research." *Family Process*, 1972, *11*, 365-455.

Ritter, B. "The Use of Contact Desensitization, Demonstration Plus Participation and Demonstration Alone, in the Treatment of Acrophobia." *Behavior Research and Therapy*, 1969, *7*, 157-164.

Roach, A. J., Frazier, L. P., and Bowden, S. R. "The Marital Satisfaction Scale: Intervention Research." *Journal of Marriage and the Family*, 1981, *43*, 537-546.

Rogers, C. *On Becoming a Person*. Boston: Houghton Mifflin, 1961.

Rollins, B. C., and Feldman, H. "Marital Satisfaction Over the Family Life Cycle." *Journal of Marriage and the Family,* 1970, *32,* 20-28.

Rorschach, H., and Oberholtzer, E. "The Application of the Interpretation of Forms to Psychoanalysis." *Journal of Nervous and Mental Diseases,* 1924, *60,* 225-248.

Rose, S. *Group Therapy: A Behavioral Approach.* Englewood Cliffs, N.J.: Prentice-Hall, 1977.

Rosen, R. C., and Schnapp, B. J. "The Use of a Specific Behavioral Technique (thought stopping) in the Context of Conjoint Couples Therapy: A Case Report." *Behavior Therapy,* 1974, *5,* 261-264.

Rosenthal, P., and Novey, T. "Measurement of Stroking Behavior in Couples." *Transactional Analysis Journal,* 1976, *6,* 205-208.

Rosman, B. "Outcome and Other Criteria in the Evaluation of Family Therapy." Paper presented at the American Orthopsychiatric Association Meeting, New York, Oct. 1977.

Rowland, K. F., and Haynes, S. N. "A Sexual Enhancement Program for Elderly Couples." *Journal of Sex and Marital Therapy,* 1978, *4,* 91-113.

Royce, W. S., and Weiss, R. L. "Behavioral Cues in the Judgment of Marital Satisfaction: A Linear Regression Analysis." *Journal of Consulting and Clinical Psychology,* 1975, *43,* 816-824.

Ruben, A. G. "Creating a Mature Marriage: The CAMM Program." Miami, Fla.: The CAMM Program, 1980.

Ruben, B. D., and Budd, R. W. *Human Communication Handbook.* Rochelle Park, N.J.: Hayden Book Company, 1975.

Ruesch, J., Block, J., and Bennett, L. "The Assessment of Communication: I. A Method for the Analysis of Social Interaction." *Journal of Psychology,* 1953, *35,* 59-80.

Santa-Barbara, J., and Epstein, N. B. "Conflict Behavior in Clinical Families: Preasymptotic Interactions and Stable Outcomes." *Behavioral Science,* 1974, *19,* 100-110.

Satir, V. *Peoplemaking.* Palo Alto, Calif.: Science and Behavior Books, 1972.

Satir, V. "Family Life Education—A Perspective on the Educator." In S. Miller (Ed.), *Marriages and Families: Enrichment Through Communication.* Beverly Hills, Calif.: Sage, 1975.

Sauber, S. R. "Primary Prevention and the Marital Enrichment Group." *Journal of Family Counseling,* 1974, *2,* 39-44.

Schauble, P. G., and Hill, C. G. "A Laboratory Approach to Treatment in Marriage Counseling: Training in Communication Skills." *The Family Coordinator,* 1976, *25,* 277-284.

Schiavi, R. C., and others. "The Assessment of Sexual Function and Marital Interaction." *Journal of Sex and Marital Therapy,* 1979, *5,* 169-224.

Schlein, S. P. "Training Dating Couples in Empathic and Open Communication: An Experimental Evaluation of a Potential Preventative Mental Health Program." Unpublished doctoral dissertation, Division of Industrial and Family Studies, Pennsylvania State University, 1972.

Schmitt, A., and Schmitt, D. "Marriage Renewal Retreats." In H. A. Otto (Ed.), *Marriage and Family Enrichment: New Perspectives and Programs.* Nashville: Abingdon, 1976.

Schutz, W. C. *The FIRO Scales: Manual.* Palo Alto, Calif.: Consulting Psychologists Press, 1967.

Sharan (Singer), S. "Family Interaction with Schizophrenics and Their Siblings." *Journal of Abnormal Psychology,* 1966, *71,* 345-353.

Sherwood, J., and Scherer, J. "A Model for Couples: How Two Can Grow Together." In S. Miller (Ed.), *Marriages and Families: Enrichment Through Communication.* Beverly Hills, Calif.: Sage, 1975.

Shostrom, E. L. *Manual for the Personal Orientation Inventory (POI): An Inventory for the Measurement of Self-Actualization.* San Diego, Calif.: Educational and Industrial Testing Service, 1966.

Singer, M. T. "The Consensus Rorschach and Family Transaction." *Journal of Projective Techniques,* 1968, *32,* 348-351.

Singer, M. T., and Wynne, L. C. "Principles for Scoring Communication Defects and Deviances in Parents of Schizophrenics: Rorschach and TAT Scoring Manuals." *Psychiatry,* 1966, *29,* 260-288.

Smith, L., and Smith, A. "Developing a National Marriage Communication Lab Training Program." In H. A. Otto (Ed.), *Marriage and Family Enrichment: New Perspectives and Programs.* Nashville: Abingdon, 1976.

Smith, M. A. *A Practical Guide to Value Clarification.* San Diego, Calif.: University Associates, 1977.

Smith, R. M., Shoffner, S. M., and Scott, J. P. "Marriage and Family Enrichment: A New Professional Area." *The Family Coordinator,* 1979, *28,* 87-93.

Spanier, G. B. "Measuring Dyadic Adjustment: New Scales for Assessing the Quality of Marriage and Similar Dyads." *Journal of Marriage and the Family,* 1976, *38,* 15-28.

Spanier, G. B. "The Measurement of Marital Quality." *Journal of Sex and Marital Therapy,* 1979, *5,* 288-300.

Spanier, G. B., and Lewis, R. A. "Marital Quality: A Review of the Seventies." *Journal of Marriage and the Family,* 1980, *42,* 825-839.

Speer, D. C. "Family Systems: Morphostasis and Morphogenesis, or Is Homeostasis Enough?" *Family Process,* 1970, *9,* 259-278.

Stedman, J. M. "Marriage Encounter: An Insider's Consideration of Recent Critiques." *Family Relations,* 1982, *31,* 123-129.

Stein, E. V. "MARDILAB: An Experiment in Marriage Enrichment." *The Family Coordinator,* 1975, *24,* 167-170.

Stinnett, N., Chesser, B., and DeFrain, J. (Eds.). *Building Family Strengths: Blueprints for Action.* Lincoln: University of Nebraska Press, 1979.

Straus, M. A., and Tallman, I. "SIMFAM: A Technique for Observational Measurement and Experimental Study of Families." In J. Aldous and others (Eds.), *Family Problem Solving.* Hinsdale, Ill.: Dryden, 1971.

Strodtbeck, F. L. "Husband-Wife Interaction Over Revealed Differences." *American Sociological Review,* 1951, *16,* 468-473.

Stroup, A. L. "Marital Adjustment of the Mother and the Personality of the Child." *Marriage and Family Living,* 1956, *18,* 109-113.

Stryker, S. "Role-Taking Accuracy and Adjustment." *Sociometry,* 1957, *20,* 286-296.

Stuart, R. B. "Operant-Interpersonal Treatment for Marital Discord." *Journal of Consulting and Clinical Psychology,* 1969, *33,* 675–682.

Stuart, R. B. "Token Reinforcement in Marital Treatment." In P. H. Glasser and L. N. Glasser (Eds.), *Families in Crisis.* New York: Harper & Row, 1970.

Stuart, R. B. *Marital Pre-Counseling Inventory: Counselors Guide.* (Rev. Ed.) Champaign, Ill.: Research Press, 1974.

Stuckert, R. P. "Role Perception and Marital Satisfaction." *Journal of Marriage and the Family,* 1963, *25,* 415–419.

Tharp, R. G. "Psychological Patterning in Marriage." *Psychological Bulletin,* 1963, *60,* 97–117.

Thelen, M. H., and Rennie, D. "The Effect of Vicarious Reinforcement on Imitation: A Review of the Literature." In B. A. Maher (Ed.), *Progress in Experimental Personality Research.* New York: Academic Press, 1972.

Thibaut, J. W., and Coules, J. "The Role of Communication in the Reduction of Interpersonal Hostility." *Journal of Abnormal and Social Psychology,* 1952, *47,* 770–777.

Thomas, E. J. *Marital Communication and Decision Making.* New York: The Free Press, 1977.

Thomas, E. J., Carter, R. D., and Gambrill, E. D. "Some Possibilities of Behavioral Modification with Marital Problems Using 'SAM' (Signal System for the Assessment and Modification of Behavior)." In R. D. Rubin and others (Eds.), *Advances in Behavior Therapy.* New York: Academic Press, 1971.

Thomas, E. J., Walter, C. L., and O'Flaherty, K. "A Verbal Problem Checklist for Use in Assessing Family Verbal Behavior." *Behavior Therapy,* 1974, *5,* 235–246.

Thomas, E. J., and others. "A Signal System for the Assessment and Modification of Behavior (SAM)." *Behavior Therapy,* 1970, *1,* 252–259.

Tiggle, R. B., and others. "Correlational and Discrepancy Indices of Understanding and their Relation to Marital Satisfaction." *Journal of Marriage and the Family,* 1982, *44,* 209–215.

Travis, R. P., and Travis, P. Y. "The Pairing Enrichment Program: Actualizing the Marriage." *The Family Coordinator,* 1975, *24,* 161–165.

Travis, R. P., and Travis, P. Y. "A Note on Changes in the Caring Relationship Following a Marriage Enrichment Program and Some Preliminary Findings." *Journal of Marriage and Family Counseling,* 1976a, *2,* 81-83.

Travis, R. P., and Travis, P. Y. "Self-Actualization in Marital Enrichment." *Journal of Marriage and Family Counseling,* 1976b, *2,* 73-80.

Turner, A. J. "Couples and Group Treatment of Marital Discourse. An Experiment." Unpublished manuscript, Huntsville Community Mental Health Center, Alabama, 1972.

Vander Haar, D., and Vander Haar, T. "The Marriage Enrichment Program—Phase 1." In H. A. Otto (Ed.), *Marriage and Family Enrichment: New Perspectives and Programs.* Nashville: Abingdon, 1976,

Van Eck, B., and Van Eck, B. "The Phase II Marriage Enrichment Lab." In H. A. Otto (Ed.), *Marriage and Family Enrichment: New Perspectives and Programs.* Nashville: Abingdon, 1976.

Vincent, J. P., Weiss, R. L., and Birchler, G. R. "A Behavioral Analysis of Problem Solving in Distressed Married and Stranger Dyads." *Behavior Therapy,* 1975, *6,* 474-487.

Vinter, R. D. (Ed.). *Readings in Group Work Practice.* Ann Arbor, Mich.: Campus Publishers, 1967.

Wampler, K. S. "The Effectiveness of the Minnesota Couple Communication Program: A Review of Research." *Journal of Marital and Family Therapy,* 1982, *8,* 345-355.

Wampler, K. S., and Powell, G. S. "The Barrett-Lennard Relationship Inventory as a Measure of Marital Satisfaction." *Family Relations,* 1982, *31,* 139-145.

Wampler, K. S., and Sprenkle, D. H. "The Minnesota Couple Communication Program: A Follow-Up Study." *Journal of Marriage and the Family,* 1980, *42,* 577-584.

Watzlawick, P., Weakland, J. H., and Fisch, R. *Change: Principles of Problem Formation and Problem Resolution.* New York: Norton, 1974.

Waxler, N., and Mishler, E. G. "Scoring and Reliability Problems in Interaction Process Analysis: A Methodological Note." *Sociometry,* 1966, *29,* 28-40.

Webb, E. J., and others. *Unobtrusive Measures: Nonreactive Research in the Social Sciences*. Chicago: Rand McNally, 1966.

Weiss, C. H. *Evaluation Research*. Englewood Cliffs, N.J.: Prentice-Hall, 1972.

Weiss, R. L., Hops, H., and Patterson, G. R. "A Framework for Conceptualizing Marital Conflict, a Technology for Altering It, Some Data for Evaluating It." In L. A. Hamerlynck, L. C. Handy, and E. J. Mash (Eds.), *Behavior Changes: Methodology Concepts and Practice*. Champaign, Ill.: Research Press, 1973.

Wieman, R. J. "Conjugal Relationship Modification and Reciprocal Reinforcement: A Comparison of Treatments for Marital Discord." Unpublished doctoral dissertation, Department of Psychology, Pennsylvania State University, 1973.

Wieman, R. J., Shoulders, D. L., and Farr, J. H. "Reciprocal Reinforcement in Marital Therapy." *Journal of Behavior Therapy and Experimental Psychiatry*, 1974, *5*, 291-295.

Wildman, R. "Structured Versus Unstructured Marital Intervention." Unpublished doctoral dissertation, Georgia State University, 1976.

Wills, T. A., Weiss, R. L., and Patterson, G. R. "A Behavioral Analysis of the Determinants of Marital Satisfaction." *Journal of Consulting and Clinical Psychology*, 1974, *42*, 802-811.

Witkin, S. L., and Rose, S. D. "Group Training in Communication Skills for Couples: A Preliminary Report." *International Journal of Family Counseling*, 1978, *6*, 45-56.

Wynne, L. C. "Consensus Rorschachs and Related Procedures for Studying Interpersonal Patterns." *Journal of Projective Techniques*, 1968, *32*, 352-356.

Yates, A. J. *Behavior Therapy*. New York: Wiley, 1970.

Zarle, T. H., and Boyd, R. C. "An Evaluation of Modeling and Experimental Procedures for Self-Disclosure Training." *Journal of Counseling Psychology*, 1977, *24*, 118-124.

Zinker, J. C., and Leon, J. P. "The Gestalt Perspective: A Marriage Enrichment Program." In H. A. Otto (Ed.), *Marriage and Family Enrichment: New Perspectives and Programs*. Nashville: Abingdon, 1976.

Name Index

A

Allison, M. Q., 321
Amidon, E. J., 296
Avery, A. W., 41-42, 290, 297, 325
Azrin, N. H., 32, 299, 307

B

Bach, G. R., 46, 256, 307
Bach, T. R., 307
Badgley, R. F., 284, 291, 310
Baker, B. O., 307
Baker, F., 307
Bales, R. F., 206, 296, 307-308
Ball, J., 3, 308
Bandura, A., 70, 308
Barnlund, D. C., 98, 319
Barton, K., 282, 283, 290, 308
Bass, B. M., 288, 308
Bateson, G., 308
Beck, G. D., 201, 284, 326
Behrens, M. L., 285, 289, 291, 308
Bell, H. M., 282, 288, 308
Benne, K., 308

Bennett, L., 283, 285, 287, 288, 331
Benson, L., 308
Berenson, B. G., 7, 27, 311
Berger, M., 308
Bernard, J., 122, 199, 202, 203, 308
Bertalanffy, L., 308
Bertcher, H. J., 56, 309
Bienvenu, M. J., 285, 290, 291, 299, 305, 309
Birchler, G. R., 10, 309, 335
Blanchard, K. H., 91, 94, 95, 317
Blaylock, B., 310
Blazier, D. C., 283, 289, 290, 309
Block, J., 283, 285, 287, 288, 331
Blount, H. C., 302
Bodin, A. M., 285, 287, 309
Boies, K. G., 70, 309
Bond, G. R., 194, 323
Bons, P. M., 91, 314
Boomer, D. S., 285, 286, 316
Bormann, E. G., 80, 94, 309
Bosco, A., 38, 309
Bowden, S. R., 206, 301, 330
Bowen, M., 8, 310
Boyd, E., 23, 310

Boyd, L. A., 310
Boyd, R. C., 196, 283, 285, 290, 336
Bradford, L. P., 91, 98, 310
Breedlove, J., 322
Broderick, C., 46, 310
Brown, L. B., 286, 287, 289, 291, 310
Buckley, W., 199, 310
Budd, R. W., 280, 331
Buerkle, J. V., 284, 291, 310
Burgess, E. W., 282, 288, 290, 310
Buros, O. K., 283, 284, 310
Burr, W. R., 8, 310
Byrne, D., 310

C

Calden, G., 46, 310
Campbell, D. T., 211, 215, 216, 310-311
Capers, B., 43, 311
Capers, H., 43, 311
Carkhuff, R. R., 7, 27, 285, 290, 311
Carnes, P. J., 23, 311
Carter, R. D., 203, 286, 311, 334
Cartwright, D., 86, 91, 311
Cattell, R. B., 282, 283, 290, 308, 313
Certo, S. C., 279, 311
Chemers, M. M., 91, 314
Cherry, C., 311
Chesser, B., 311, 333
Christensen, L., 311
Clarke, C., 40, 311
Clinebell, C. H., 46, 312
Clinebell, H. J., 35, 36, 40, 46, 279, 312
Cobb, J. A., 328
Cookerly, J. R., 283, 284, 288, 312
Cooper, G. L., 312
Corrales, R., 21, 325
Corsini, R. J., 283, 285, 287, 288, 312
Coules, J., 334
Croake, J. W., 312
Cromwell, R. E., 205, 208-209, 282, 312
Curtis, J. H., 312

D

Davis, A., xiii
Davis, E. C., 64, 196, 312
Dean, D. G., 312
Deci, E. L., 70, 313
DeFrain, J., 333
Degiovanni, I. S., 45, 314
Delhees, K. H., 282, 283, 290, 313
Demarest, D., 37-38, 313
DeYoung, A. J., 41, 313
Dibatista, B., 201, 313
Dielman, T. E., 308
Dixon, D. N., 32, 34, 300, 313
Doherty, W. J., 40-41, 42, 313
Dollard, J., 70, 325
Dreyer, A. S., 285, 291, 313
Dreyer, C. A., 285, 291, 313
Drum, D. J., 3, 8, 279, 313
Dyer, E. D., 51, 313
Dymond, R., 313

E

Earle, R. B., Jr., 293
Edmonds, V. H., 201, 284, 313
Edwards, A. L., 288, 313
Egan, G., 7, 285, 287, 314
Elbert, S., 283, 287, 288, 289, 295, 314
Elliott, S., 23, 314
Ely, A. L., 28, 192, 295, 304, 314
Epstein, N., 45, 65, 68, 187, 188-189, 197, 203, 286, 314, 318, 331

F

Fagen, R. E., 316
Fahlberg, N., 318
Farr, J. H., 30, 336
Faules, D., 314
Faunce, E. E., 330
Feffer, M., 314
Feldman, H., 8, 52, 331
Ferreira, A. J., 282, 314
Fiedler, F. E., 91, 314
Fiore, A., 304
Fisch, R., 19, 335
Fisher, R., 32, 34, 192, 314-315

Flanders, N. A., 296, 315
Follingstad, D. R., 300, 317
Forer, B. R., 283, 284, 288, 315
Foster, A. L., 286, 291, 315
Fournier, D. G., 205, 208-209, 282, 312
Frank, E., 315
Frazier, L. P., 206, 301, 330
Frederiksen, L. W., 70, 193, 315
Fretz, B. R., 315
Friedman, A. S., 286, 288, 315
Friedman, C. J., 286, 288, 315
Friest, W. P., 45, 326

G

Gambrill, E. D., 203, 334
Gant, R. L., 30, 315
Garland, D. R., 12, 21, 29, 132, 185, 193, 195, 245n, 279, 315
Genovese, R. J., 37, 40, 315
Goldberg, G., 243, 245n, 325
Golding, S. L., 283, 286, 291, 320-321
Goldstein, A. P., 29-30, 315
Goodrich, D. W., 285, 286, 316
Goosman, E. T., 283, 289, 290, 309
Gordon, T., 38, 117, 122, 251, 316
Gottman, J., 285, 316
Gough, H. G., 283, 288, 316
Green, H., 316
Grief, A. C., 330
Guerney, B. G., Jr., 9, 27-28, 33, 192, 219, 220-221, 222, 285, 286, 287, 288, 290, 291, 295, 297, 304, 306, 314, 316, 317
Gurman, A. S., 12, 24, 28, 33, 184, 191-192, 195, 202, 204, 316

H

Haiman, F. S., 98, 319
Haley, J., 19, 316
Hall, A. D., 316
Hambleton, R. K., 91, 317
Hardcastle, D. R., 283, 285, 316
Hardin, G., 316
Hare, A. P., 98, 317
Harrell, J., 30, 33, 192, 317, 330
Harris, T. A., 21, 317

Hartford, M., 98, 317
Hawkins, J. L., 201, 317
Haynes, S. N., 196, 282, 284, 285, 287, 289, 290, 300, 317, 331
Hayward, D., 317
Heilbrun, A. B., Jr., 283, 288, 316
Hekmat, H., 317
Heller, K., 315
Henry, S., 98, 317
Herbst, P. G., 286, 287, 289, 291, 317
Hersey, P., 91, 94, 95, 317
Heslin, R., 299, 329
Hicks, M., 200, 317
Hill, C. C., 23, 332
Hill, R., 19, 318
Hill, W., 283, 285, 318
Hinkle, J. E., 40, 318
Hobart, C. W., 318
Hobbs, D. E., Jr., 51, 318
Hof, L., 1, 44, 45, 54, 55, 65, 68, 187, 188-189, 197, 210, 231, 279, 318
Hoffman, D. K., 287, 320
Hoffman, L., 20, 318
Hopkins, L., 13, 14, 35, 36, 37, 38, 64, 140, 318
Hopkins, P., 38, 318
Hops, H., 31, 32, 193, 203, 300, 328-329, 336
Humphrey, P., 285, 288, 291, 325
Hunt, R. A., 318
Huntington, R. M., 285, 287, 318
Hurvitz, N., 301

I

Insel, P. M., 285, 288, 291, 325
Inselberg, R. M., 290, 318-319
Ivey, A. E., 7, 245n, 319

J

Jackson, D. D., 319
Jackson, E., 203, 314
Jacobs, T., 18, 329
Janis, I. L., 70, 319
Janoff-Bulman, R., 324
Jayaratne, S., 211, 319
Jayne-Lazarus, C., 45, 314

Joanning, H., 24-25, 319
Jones, J. E., 241, 280, 285, 290, 291, 329
Jones, R., 32, 299, 307
Jones, S. E., 98, 319
Jourard, S. M., 290, 319
Julian, A., 196, 320

K

Kahn, M., 285, 319
Kahn, R. L., 319
Karen, R. L., 283, 284, 288, 319
Karlsson, G., 319
Katz, D., 319
Katz, M., 284, 319
Kaufmann, R. F., 46, 319
Kelly, G. A., 70, 320
Kelmann, P. R., 320
Kenkel, W. F., 287, 320
Kersten, L. K., 320
Kieren, D., 285, 291, 320
Kilmann, P. R., 196, 320
Kirkpatrick, C., 282, 289, 290, 320
Kligfield, B., 38, 320
Kniskern, D. P., 12, 24, 28, 33, 184, 191-192, 195, 202, 204, 316
Knott, J. E., 3, 8, 279, 313
Knox, D., 30, 46, 284, 288, 289, 290, 320
Knudson, R. M., 283, 286, 291, 320-321
Koch, L., 42, 321
Koch, T., 42, 321
Komisar, D. D., 283, 321
Krupar, K. R., 279, 321
Kupfer, D., 315

L

L'Abate, L., 2, 3, 4, 6, 9-10, 45-46, 53, 54, 55, 74, 152, 196, 279, 285, 287, 321
LaForge, R., 283, 288, 321
Laing, R. D., 321-322
Lake, D. G., 293
Larsen, G. R., 193, 322
Laube, H., 23, 311
Lazarus, A. A., 30, 70, 322
Leavitt, H. J., 322

LeBow, M. D., 30, 322
Lee, A. R., 322
LeMasters, E. E., 51, 322
Leon, J. P., 43, 236, 336
Lerner, A., 283, 284, 288, 324
Leslie, G. R., 51, 322
Lester, J., xiii
Lester, M. E., 42, 313
Levinger, G., 284, 291, 322
Levy, R. L., 211, 319
Lewis, J. M., 20, 21, 322
Lewis, R. A., 333
Liberman, R., 30, 193, 322
Lieberman, M. A., 194, 323
Lief, H. I., 290, 325
Locke, H. J., 282, 289, 304, 323
LoPiccolo, J., 305, 306, 326
Lucas, W. L., 312
Luce, R. D., 323
Luckey, E. B., 323
Lundy, R. M., 323
Lyon, R. S., 312

M

McCabe, P., 40-41, 313
MacDonald, A. P., 289, 323
McDonald, C., 302
McDonald, P. J., 302
Mace, D. R., 3, 8, 35, 36, 37, 39, 40, 74, 165, 170-171, 323-324
Mace, V., 3, 8, 35, 36, 37, 39, 40, 74, 165, 170-171, 323-324
McHugh, G., 290, 324
McHugh, T. G., 290, 324
Madden, M. E., 324
Mager, R. F., 68, 324
Malamud, D. I., 324
Mann, L., 70, 319
Manson, M. P., 283, 284, 288, 324
Maple, F., 56, 309
Marler, P., xiii
Maslow, A., 35, 43, 324
Mathews, V. D., 300
Maxwell, J. W., 44, 324
Meador, B. D., 25-26, 324
Mease, W., 308
Mehrabian, A., 324-325
Mendelson, L. A., 299, 325-326
Middleman, R. R., 7, 69, 243, 245n, 325

Mihanovich, C. S., 300
Miles, M. B., 293
Milholland, T. A., 41-42, 290, 297, 325
Miller, J. G., 20, 325
Miller, N. E., 70, 325
Miller, S., 21, 24, 117, 130, 192, 325, 326
Miller, W. R., 1, 44, 45, 54, 55, 65, 68, 187, 188-189, 197, 210, 231, 279, 290, 318, 325
Minuchin, S., 295, 314
Mishler, E. G., 19, 325, 335
Moore, M., 40, 318
Moos, R. H., 285, 288, 291, 325
Moreault, D., 196, 320
Mueller, R. A. H., 322
Murphy, D. C., 299, 325-326
Murrell, S., 18, 326
Murstein, B. I., 201, 284, 288, 326

N

Naster, B. J., 32, 299, 307
Navran, L., 304, 326
Nelson, R. C., 45, 326
Newmark, C. S., 326
Novak, A. L., 282, 284, 289, 326
Novey, T., 286, 331
Nowinski, J. K., 306, 326
Nugent, J., 330
Nunnally, E. W., 21, 24, 25, 117, 130, 192, 325, 326
Nunnally, J. C., 326

O

Oberholtzer, E., 286, 287, 289, 331
O'Callaghan, J. B., 321
O'Flaherty, K., 334
Olson, D. H., 18, 56, 185, 203, 206, 282, 284, 286, 287, 288, 289, 291, 293, 294, 297, 298, 303, 304, 327
Olson, D. H. L., 205, 208-209, 282, 312
Osgood, C. E., 283, 284, 327
Otto, H. A., 2, 4, 35, 36, 37, 39-40, 46, 122, 280, 327-328
Otto, R., 328

P

Patrick, J. A., 320
Patterson, G. R., 30, 31, 32, 193, 203, 300, 328-329, 336
Pfeiffer, J. W., 241, 280, 285, 290, 291, 299, 329
Phillipson, H., 322
Pierce, R. M., 27, 28, 192, 329
Piercy, F. P., 280, 329
Pinsof, W. M., 209-210, 282, 329
Platt, M., 200, 317
Pless, I. B., 284, 285, 289, 329
Porterfield, A. L., 285, 316
Powell, G. S., 59, 283, 286, 290, 291, 329, 335
Prunty, K. G., 329

Q

Quick, E., 18, 329

R

Rachman, S., 70, 329
Raiffa, H., 323
Rappaport, A. F., 28-29, 30, 193, 330
Rathus, S. A., 283, 330
Raush, H. L., 330
Ravich, R. A., 283, 286, 287, 330
Ray, D. L., 201, 317
Reed, H., 324-325
Regula, R. R., 42, 330
Reid, J. B., 30, 328
Rennie, D., 70, 334
Rhyne, D., 51, 52, 200, 201, 330
Riskin, J. M., 330
Ritter, B., 70, 330
Roach, A. J., 206, 301, 310, 330
Robinson, E. A., 320
Rogers, C. R., 25, 26-27, 122, 324, 330
Rogers, R., xiii
Rollins, B. C., 8, 52, 331
Rorschach, H., 286, 287, 289, 331
Rose, S. D., 33, 34, 193, 331, 336
Rosen, R. C., 331
Rosenthal, P., 286, 331
Rosman, B., 191, 314, 331

Rowland, K. F., 196, 331
Royce, W. S., 331
Ruben, A. G., 46, 331
Ruben, B. D., 280, 331
Ruesch, J., 283, 285, 287, 288, 331
Rupp, G., 55, 321
Russell, C. S., 294, 327
Ryder, R. G., 40-41, 203, 297, 298, 313, 327

S

Santa-Barbara, J., 286, 331
Sarbin, T. R., 307
Satir, V., 74, 331-332
Satterwhite, B., 284, 285, 289, 329
Sauber, S. R., 40, 332
Saunders, B., 23, 314
Schaefer, M. T., 303, 304
Schauble, P. G., 23, 332
Scherer, J., 332
Schiavi, R. C., 332
Schlein, S. P., 192, 297, 332
Schmitt, A., 43-44, 332
Schmitt, D., 43-44, 332
Schnapp, B. J., 331
Schultz, K., 280, 329
Schutz, W. C., 44-45, 298, 332
Sciara, A. D., 32, 34, 300, 313
Scott, J. P., 35, 333
Sechrest, L. B., 315
Sexton, J., 37-38, 313
Sexton, M., 37-38, 313
Sharan (Singer), S., 287, 291, 332
Sherwood, J., 332
Shoffner, S. M., 35, 333
Shostrom, E. L., 43, 283, 287, 288, 292, 332
Shoulders, D. L., 30, 336
Singer, M. T., 285, 286, 287, 288, 289, 332
Smith, A., 332-333
Smith, L., 332-333
Smith, M. A., 280, 333
Smith, R. M., 35, 333
Sommers, A. A., 283, 286, 291, 320-321
Spanier, G. B., 56, 211, 293, 333
Speer, D. C., 333

Sprenkle, D. H., 18, 24, 294, 327, 335
Stanley, J. C., 211, 215, 216, 310-311
Stedman, J. M., 42, 333
Steger, J. C., 305, 306
Stein, E. V., 40, 333
Stinnett, N., 333
Stinson, T., 91, 317
Stover, L., 295, 304
Straus, M. A., 286, 287, 289, 291, 327, 333
Strodtbeck, F. L., 286, 287, 289, 333
Stroup, A. L., 282, 289, 290, 333
Stryker, S., 333
Stuart, R. B., 30, 31, 32, 193, 284, 285, 287, 289, 290, 334
Stuckert, R. P., 334
Suchotliff, L., 314
Suci, G. J., 283, 284, 327
Suezek, R. F., 283, 288, 321
Sullivan, J. C., 300, 317
Sweeney, A. B., 282, 283, 290, 313
Swensen, C. H., 304

T

Tallman, I., 285, 286, 287, 289, 291, 320, 333
Tannenbaum, P. H., 283, 284, 327
Tharp, R. G., 334
Thelen, M. H., 70, 334
Thibaut, J. W., 334
Thomas, E. J., 203, 286, 311, 334
Tiggle, R. B., 283, 289, 334
Travis, P. Y., 43, 283, 287, 288, 293, 334-335
Travis, R. P., 43, 283, 287, 288, 293, 334-335
Turner, A. J., 195, 335

V

Vander Haar, D., 335
Vander Haar, T., 335
van der Veen, F., 282, 284, 289, 326
Van Eck, B. and B., 335
Vincent, J. P., 309, 335

Vinter, R. D., 59, 60, 98, 335

W

Wackman, D. B., 21, 24, 117, 130, 192, 325, 326
Wadeson, H., 292
Wallace, K. M., 282, 289, 323
Wallace, L., 311
Walter, C. L.,334
Wampler, K. S., 24, 25, 59, 283, 286, 290, 291, 329, 335
Watzlawick, P., 19, 335
Waxler, N. E., 19, 325, 335
Weakland, J. H., 19, 319, 335
Webb, E. J., 336
Weisburg, C., 201, 317
Weiss, C. H., 186, 187, 211, 215, 336
Weiss, R. L., 31, 32, 193, 203, 283, 289, 300, 309, 328-329, 331, 335, 336

Wieman, R. J., 30, 32, 34, 193, 246n, 336
Wildman, R., 10, 336
Wills, T. A., 203, 336
Wilson, W. H., 326
Winter, W. O., 282, 314
Withers, G., 201, 313
Witkin, S. L., 33, 34, 336
Woody, G., 326
Wyden, P., 46, 256, 307
Wynne, L. C., 285, 286, 287, 288, 289, 332, 336

Y

Yates, A. J., 70, 336

Z

Zander, A., 86, 91, 311
Zarle, T. H., 196, 283, 285, 290, 336
Ziff, D., 326
Zinker, J. C., 43, 236, 336

Subject Index

A

Ability, and group maturity, 91, 92-93

Acceptance of Other Scale, 285, 291

Active listening: in communication skills group, 128-129, 134, 135, 136; in marriage enrichment retreat, 143

Active Listening exercise: analysis of, 243-246; in communication skills group, 120-121; goals and objectives related to, 233; handouts for, 245-246; in marriage enrichment retreat, 143

Activities, structured: advantages of, 231; goals and objectives related to, 233-279; listing of, 231-280; sources of, 279-280

Adjective Checklist, 283, 288

Adjustment: concept of, 199; evaluation tools for, 282, 288; levels of, and programs, 53-59

Adjustment Inventory, 282, 288

Affective learning: activities for, 238, 239, 242, 247, 248, 250, 253, 256, 257, 260, 263, 264, 266, 269, 270, 271, 272, 274, 277, 278; in communication skills program, 111, 121, 125, 127; concept of, 67; in marriage enrichment retreat, 139-140, 143; steps in, 71; workshop for, 45

Agreement, evaluation tool for, 282

American Association of Marriage and Family Therapists, 13

Anonymous Statements: analysis of, 237-239; goals and objectives related to, 233

Art Techniques, 285, 292

Assertion, evaluation tools for, 282-283

Assertion training, theory of, 45

Assessing Our Sexual Relationship exercise: analysis of, 274-276; in communications skills group, 135; goals and objectives related

345

to, 233, 234, 235; handout for, 276; in marriage enrichment retreat, 149

Association of Couples for Marriage Enrichment, 274, 307; criteria of, 13; founding and objectives of, 35; and maintenance of skills, 75

Attending exercise: analysis of, 241-243; in communication skills group, 114, 117; goals and objectives related to, 233, 235

Attitudes or knowledge about spouse, evaluation tools for, 283

Attitudes toward relationship, evaluation tools for, 283-284

Awareness wheel, in General Systems theory, 21

B

Baptist Marriage Enrichment System, 308; and church-related theory, 38-39, 43

Baptists: and marriage enrichment movement, 5n, 35; programs of, 38-39

Behavior Exchange Program, in behavioral theory, 33

Behavioral learning: activities for, 242, 243, 247, 252, 269, 278; in communication skills program, 110, 120, 125, 127, 132; concept of, 67; in marriage enrichment retreat, 140, 143; and motivation, 70-71; steps in, 69-71

Behavioral theory: analysis of, 29-34; background of, 29-32; evaluation research on, 33-34; programs in, 32-33

Brainstorming About Sex exercise: adaptations of, 223, 235; analysis of, 277-278; in communication skills group, 134; goals and objectives related to, 233

C

Caring: evaluation tools for, 284; unpossessing, in Rogerian theory, 26

Caring Relationship Inventory, 43, 284, 288, 290, 291, 292-293

Case study, use of, 211

Catholics, and marriage enrichment movement, 5n, 35. See also Marriage Encounter

Choice Awareness, theory of, 45

Christian Church, and marriage enrichment movement, 5n, 35

Church of God, and marriage enrichment movement, 35

Church-related programs: analysis of, 34-42; background on, 4-5, 34-36; development of, 218; evaluation research on, 40-42; examples of, 36-40, 138-150; and group format, 37-38; marriage enrichment retreat as, 139-150; and weekend retreats, 37, 38-39, 41, 43, 139-150

Client-centered therapy. See Rogerian theory

Closeness, evaluation tools for, 284

Coercion, in behavioral theory, 30-31

Cognitive learning: activities for, 236, 237, 238, 240, 242, 247, 248, 250, 252, 253, 256, 257, 260, 263, 264, 266, 269, 271, 272, 274; in communication skills group, 111, 134; concept of, 67; steps in, 68-69; workshop for, 45

Cohesion: activities for, 233; in communication skills group, 125, 134; evaluation tools for, 284; and group maturity, 91, 93-94; and loss of members, 180-181

Color Matching Test, 285, 286

Commitment, activities for building, 235

Communication: activities for, 233, 241-251; in behavioral theory, 30, 33; in church-related theory, 38; evaluation tools for, 285-286; in General Systems theory, 21-23, 24-25; in Rogerian theory, 27, 28

Communication Research Associates, 279, 312

Communication skills group: active listening in, 120-121, 128-129, 134, 135, 136; affective learning in, 111, 121, 125, 127; Assessing Our Sexual Relationship in, 135; Attending exercise in, 114, 117; beginning session of, 112-114; behavioral learning in, 110, 120, 125, 127, 132; Brainstorming About Sex in, 134; cognitive learning in, 111, 134; cohesiveness in, 125, 134; conflict management and decision making session of, 128-134; conflictual stage of development by, 129-130, 132-134; Couple Time exercise in, 137; Daily Rating of Spouse's Communication in, 127, 134, 137; Decision Making exercise in, 136; expectations in, 114; feedback in, 126-127, 128; Fill in the Blank exercise for, 127; generalization and maintenance from, 112; Getting Acquainted exercise for, 113; goal-planning activity for, 138; homework in, 127-128, 134, 137; I-messages in, 130-131; Inside and Outside Circles exercise in, 134; interdependent phase of development by, 134; leadership of, 112; learning activities in, 112-138; learning objectives in, 110-111; marital conflict in, 132-134; meetings of, 112; membership in, 111-112; Naming exercise for, 113-114; paraphrasing of feeling in, 122-125; Priorities exercise in, 137; program for, 110-138; reinforcement in, 121; roles and values session of, 136-137; sexuality session in, 134-136; Sharing My Feelings with You exercise in, 137; skill learning session in, 114-128; and suspending judgment in conflict, 122-125; terminating session of,

137-138; theoretical approach of, 111; Understanding One Another exercise in, 125-126; Win/ Win Conflict Negotiation activity in, 132

Communication Skills Workshop: in behavioral theory, 33; research on, 34

Compatibility, evaluation tools for, 284

Conflict, indirect, 101-102

Conflict management: activities for, 234, 251-263; evaluation tools for, 286-287; in marriage enrichment retreat, 144-145

Conflict phase of group development: analysis of, 100-103; in communication skills group, 129-130, 132-134; in marriage enrichment retreat, 146-147

Conflictual couple: and group discussion, 161-164; identifying and coping with, 158-164; and positive aspects, 159-161

Confrontation: and dragee, 172-173; evaluation tools for, 282-283; guidelines for, 165; and member aggressiveness, 165

Congruence, in Rogerian theory, 25-26

Conjugal Relationship Enhancement: research on, 28-29, 34; in Rogerian theory, 27-28

Consensus Rorschach, 285

Conventionalism, evaluation tool for, 284

Couple Time exercise: analysis of, 264-265; in communication skills group, 137; goals and objectives related to, 234

Couples. See Conflictual couple; Fearful couple; Relationship

Creative Marriage Enrichment Program, theory of, 44-45

D

Daily Rating of Spouse's Communication: in communication skills

group, 127, 134, 137; as handout, 246
Day at Home, 286, 287, 289, 291
Decision making: activities for,
234; evaluation tools for, 284,
287
Decision Making exercise: analysis
of, 253-254; in communication
skills group, 136; goals and objectives related to, 234; handout for, 255
Dependent phase of group development: analysis of, 99-100; in
marriage enrichment retreat, 141
Dragee: ambivalence of, 171-173;
and confrontation, 172-173; and
discomfort with group experience, 174; group as, 174-175;
identifying and coping with,
170-175; issues for, 171
Dyadic Adjustment Scale, 56, 211,
282, 293

E

Edwards Personal Preference Schedule, 288
Effectiveness: concept of, 198-199;
criteria of, 199-202; factors in,
188; levels of, 202-204
Empathy: evaluation tools for, 291;
in Rogerian theory, 26
Encounter Group Checklist, 285,
287
ENRICH (Enriching and Nurturing
Relationship Issues, Communication, and Happiness), 56, 283,
285, 286, 288, 289, 290, 293-294
Evaluation: advantages of, 185-186;
analysis of, 183-216; background on, 183-186; barriers to,
183-184; before and after design
of, 193, 211-212, 214; on behavioral theory, 33-34; on church-
related programs, 40-42; coding
system in, 209-210; defined, 186;
and effectiveness criteria, 226;
of effects, types of, 188-189; of
efficiency, 191-192; experimental design in, 192-193, 211-216;

focus of, 187-198; on General
Systems theory, 24-25; of group,
206-207; of group process variables, 197-198; instruments for,
207-210, 281-306; of levels of
effectiveness, 202-204; of mediating and treatment goals, 191;
method development for, 226-
228; methods of, requirements
for, 227; model of, 204-207,
225-226; need for, 184-185, 224;
and objectives of intervention,
198-204; observational methods
of, 205-206; and population
variables, 197; practitioner designs in, 211-212; of program effectiveness, 199-202; and program goals, 186-187; randomly
assigned control groups for, 192,
213-214; on Rogerian theory,
28-29; of self-help groups, 194;
self-report methods of, 204-205;
of specific interventions, 194-
195; status and prospects of,
223-228; of structural variables,
195-197; and theoretical approaches, 190-194
Expectations: in communication
skill group, 114; and member aggressiveness, 164-165. See also
Norms

F

FACES II (Family Adaptability and
Cohesion Evaluation Scales), 56,
282, 283, 284, 286, 289, 294
Facilitative Self Disclosure Scale,
285, 290
Families, disturbed, communication
in, 19-20
Family Agreement Measure, 285,
286, 287
Family Attitude Measure, 282, 283,
290
Family Concept Q Sort, 282, 284,
289
Family Dinner Time, 285, 291
Family Environment Scale, 285,
288, 291

Family Functioning Index, 284, 285, 289
Family Interaction Apperception Test, 283, 287, 288, 289
Family Interest Scale, 282, 289, 290
Family Life Questionnaire, 289, 295
Family Strengths, 282, 284, 288
Family Task, 285, 287, 291, 295-296
Fearful couple, identifying and coping with, 175-177
Feedback: in communication skills group, 126-127, 128; negative and positive, in General Systems theory, 18-19
Feelings: expression of, activities for, 234; paraphrasing of, in communication skills group, 122-125
Ferreira-Winter Questionnaire, 282
Fighting for Optimal Distance: analysis of, 256-257; goals and objectives related to, 234, 235
Fill in the Blank: analysis of, 266-268; in communication skills group, 127; goals and objectives related to, 234, 235; handout for, 268
Flanders' Interaction Analysis Categories, 287, 296
Flexibility (relationship), evaluation tools for, 284-285

G

General Systems theory: analysis of, 17-25; background of, 17-20; and communication theory, 111; and developmental changes, 18-19; evaluation research on, 24-25; programs in, 21-23; and Rogerian theory, 29
Generalizing: activities for, 235; from communication skills group, 112; from marriage enrichment retreat, 142; from programs, 74-75
Genuineness, in Rogerian theory, 25-26
Gestalt theory, and marriage enrichment programs, 43

Getting Acquainted: analysis of, 235-237; in communication skills group, 113; goals and objectives related to, 233
Goals, activities for defining, 233
Groups: analysis of problems common to, 151-182; conflict phase of, 100-103; conflictual couple in, 158-164; dependence phase of, 99-100; development activities for, 233; development of, 97-108; discomfort of, with problems, 153; dragee resistance in, 170-175; evaluation of participation in, 285; fearful couple in, 175-177; formation activities for, 235-241; identifying and coping with problems in, 158-179; interaction in, evaluation tools for, 287; interdependence phase of, 103-105; leadership strategies for, 152-158; loss of members in, 179-181; maturity of, 91-97; member aggressiveness in, 164-170; pregroup phases of, 98-99; psychological and task maturity of, 91-92; termination phase of, 105-108; value differences in, 177-179

H

Handling Problems Change Scale, 288
Happiness, evaluation tools for, 289-290
Henry Ittleson Center Family Interaction Scales, 285, 289, 291
Hill Interaction Matrix, 283, 285
Home Responsibilities exercise: analysis of, 263-264; goals and objectives related to, 234; in marriage enrichment retreat, 147-148
Homework: in communication skills group, 127-128, 134, 137; evaluation of, 196
Hope, activities for building, 235
How You Tell Me You Love Me: analysis of, 248-249; goals and objectives related to, 233-234

Human services, and marriage enrichment, 2-4

I

I-messages: in church-related groups,
38; in communication skills
group, 130-131
Inside and Outside Circles: analysis
of, 271-272; in communication
skills group, 134; goals and objectives related to, 233, 235
Interaction, evaluation tools for,
285-287
Interaction Process Analysis, 206,
287, 296-297
Interdependent phase of group development: analysis of, 103-105;
in communication skills group,
134; in marriage enrichment retreat, 149
Intermarital taboo, and church-related theory, 36, 140
Interpersonal Behavior Project
Method, 283, 286, 291
Interpersonal Checklist, 283, 288
Interpersonal Communication Inventory, 285, 290, 291
Interpersonal needs, theory of, 44-
45
Interpersonal Relationship Scale,
285, 287, 291, 297
Intimacy: activities on, 235, 271-
279; evaluation tools for, 287
Inventory of Marital Conflict (IMC),
205, 286, 287, 297-298

J

Jews, and marriage enrichment
movement, 35, 38

K

Kenkel Decision Making Test, 287

L

Leaders: and consultation, 15-16;
and counseling contracts, 158;

and crisis intervention, 15-16;
functions of, 86-87; in group
conflict phase, 102-103; in interaction with group, 222; modeling function of, 15, 16, 114-117,
182; and norm development, 82-
84; paraprofessional, criteria for,
13-14; professional, criteria for,
14-16; professional, role of, 10-
12; qualifications of, 12-16; responsibilities of, related to group
problems, 166-167, 170; role
play by, 117-120, 123-125, 128-
129, 130-131; skills of, 220;
strategies of, for group problems,
152-158; teaching function of,
14; in termination phase, 106;
training of, 74; training workshops for, 14; two, 73-74; values
of, 177-179
Leadership: of communication skills
group, 112; designated, 86; evo-
lution of, 87-88; functional, 86-
88; and group development,
107-108; and group maturity,
91-97; for marriage enrichment
retreat, 142; model of, 94-97;
for programs, 72-74, 86-97; roles
in, evaluation tools for, 289;
styles in, 88-91; task and socioemotional functions in, 86-87
Learning. See Affective learning;
Behavioral learning; Cognitive
learning
Learning systems theory, activity
for, 233
Listening. See Active listening
Listing Our Strengths exercise:
analysis of, 239-240; goals and
objectives related to, 233
Locke Marital Adjustment Scale,
282, 289
Loss, feelings of, and loss of members, 181
Love Attitude Inventory, 284, 288
Love Letters: analysis of, 278-279;
goals and objectives related to,
234, 235
Loving, evaluation tools for,
284

M

Maintenance. *See* Generalizing
Marital Attitudes Evaluation Empathy Ratio (MATE), 283, 287, 288, 291, 298-299
Marital Communication Inventory, 282, 285, 299
Marital Communication Scale, 285
Marital Conventionalism Scale, 284
Marital Happiness Scale, 289, 299-300
Marital Interaction Coding System, 285, 286, 287, 300
Marital Precounseling Inventory, 284, 285, 287, 289, 290
Marital Problem Checklist, 288, 289, 300-301
Marital Problem Story Completion Test, 283
Marital Projection Series, 285, 287
Marital relationship. *See* Relationship
Marital Roles Inventory, 282, 288, 289, 301
Marital Satisfaction Scale, 206, 207, 282, 283, 289, 301-302
Marriage Adjustment Form, 282, 288, 290
Marriage Adjustment Sentence Completion Survey, 283, 284, 288
Marriage Analysis, 283, 289, 290
Marriage Climate Analysis, 302-303
Marriage Communication Labs, 324; and church-related theory, 38, 40, 46
Marriage counseling, marriage enrichment distinct from, 5-10
Marriage Encounter: authoritarian leadership of, 89-90; and church-related theory, 37, 40, 59, 78; evaluation of, 40-42, 191; leadership team for, 72
Marriage enrichment: advantages of, 7-9; approach selection for, 46-47, 66-67; background on, 1-5; behavioral theory of, 29-34; church-related theory of, 4-5, 34-42; concept of, 1-2; contraindicated, 54; development,

goals, and leadership of, 1-16; development of, 217-218, 228; and developmental needs, 8; educational approach of, 220-222; evaluation of, 183-216; functions of, 152; General Systems theory of, 17-25; and Gestalt theory, 43; goals of, 4, 17, 36; group context of, 8-9, 228-229; group development and leadership in, 76-108; and growth enhancement, 220-221; human service professions background of, 2-4; and interpersonal skills, 7; limitations of, 9-10; marriage counseling distinct from, 5-10; other theoretical approaches to, 42-46; problems in groups for, 151-182; program design for, 48-75; purpose of, 217-218; and Rankian theory, 44; rational-emotive approach to, 44; Rogerian theory of, 25-29; status and prospects of, 217-229; theoretical foundations of, 17-47; therapy combined with, 9-10, 222; and transactional analysis, 43; and troubled marriages, 6-7, 53-54
Marriage Enrichment Program for Couples, theory of, 45-46
Marriage enrichment retreat: active listening in, 143; affective learning in, 139-140, 143; Assessing Our Sexual Relationship in, 149; behavioral learning in, 140, 143; conflictual phase of development by, 146-147; crisis intervention in, 153-157; dependence phase of development by, 141; example of, 138-150; generalization and maintenance from, 142; group discussion in, 146; group goals for, 141; Home Responsibilities exercise in, 147-148; interdependent phase of development by, 149; leadership for, 142; learning activities of, 142-150; marital conflict resolution in, 144-145; membership for,

140-141; objectives of, 139-140; reinforcement in, 149-150; Sharing My Feelings with You exercise in, 144; and support group, 143, 150; theoretical approach of, 140; Win/Win Conflict Negotiation activity in, 144

Marriage Evaluation, 284, 285, 288, 302

Marriage Expectation Inventory, 284, 286, 289, 290, 302-303

Marriage Inventory, 288, 289, 290

Marriage Personality Inventory, 283, 284

Marriage Sentence Completion Test, 283, 284, 288

Member aggressiveness: by advising others, 169-170; and confrontations, 165; and expectations, 164-165; and group norms, 165-166; identifying and coping with, 164-170; responsibilities related to, 166-168, 170; self-disclosure as, 168-169

Methodists: and marriage enrichment movement, 5n, 35; programs of, 37, 38, 46

Minnesota Couples Communication Program (MCCP): evaluation of, 24-25, 191; in General Systems theory, 21

Minnesota Multiphasic Personality Inventory (MMPI), 203

Modeling: in group programs, 58-59; by leaders, 15, 16, 114-117, 182

Moravians, and marriage enrichment movement, 35

Mormons, and marriage enrichment movement, 35

N

Naming exercise: analysis of, 237; in communication skills group, 113-114; goals and objectives related to, 233

National Marriage Encounter, 279, 326; and church-related theory, 37, 38

Needs (relationship), evaluation tools for, 287

Negotiation: in behavioral theory, 30, 33; in General Systems theory, 21-23

Nonequivalent control group, use of, 215-216

Nonverbal Communication: analysis of, 249-251; goals and objectives related to, 233, 234, 235

Norms: activities for defining, 233; building of, 78-84, 104; common, 80-81; defined, 80; group-generated, 82; and member aggressiveness, 165-166

O

Orientation Inventory, 288

P

Pair Inventory (Personality Assessment of Intimacy in Relationships), 287, 290, 303-304

Pairing Enrichment Program, theory of, 43

Paraphrasing, in communication skills group, 122-125

Personal growth, evaluation tools for, 288

Personal Orientation Inventory, 43, 283, 287, 288

Positive regard, in Rogerian theory, 26

Posttest-only control group, use of, 214-215

Power distribution, activities on, 234

Presbyterians, and marriage enrichment movement, 35

Pretest-posttest design, use of, 193, 211-212, 214

Primary Communication Inventory, 286, 304

Priorities: analysis of, 270-271; in communication skills group, 137; goals and objectives related to, 234, 235

Prisoner's Dilemma Game, 286

Problem-Solving Areas: analysis of, 257-259; goals and objectives related to, 234; handout for, 259

Problems (relationship), evaluation tools for, 288-289

Program Development Center of Northern California, 68, 71, 329

Programs in marriage enrichment: beginning, 77-86; in behavioral theory, 32-33; and changes in setting, 85-86; for communication skills, 110-138; design and implementation of, 48-75; development of, 66-72; development process for, 49; effectiveness of, 65; evaluation of, 183-216; examples of, 109-150; expectations in, 80, 81; in General Systems theory, 21-23; generalizing and maintaining content of, 74-75; goals for, evaluation of, 186-187; and group development, 97-108; homogeneity and heterogeneity in, 49-50; implementation of, 76-108; and intervention goals, 48; leadership for, 72-74, 86-97; learning objectives in, 67-72; and marital adjustment levels, 53-59; and marital life cycle stages, 50-53; marriage enrichment retreat as, 138-150; membership determination for, 49-64; modeling in, 58-59; norm building in, 78-84, 104; recruitment for, 60-62; referrals to, 61-62; relationship building in, 78-84; in Rogerian theory, 27-28; rules in, 63; screening for, 54-58, 62-64; self-introductions in, 79; setting for, 84-86; size of group for, 59-60; structure in, 54, 64-66

Q

Q Sort Technique, 283, 285, 287, 288

Quakers: and laissez-faire leadership, 90; and marriage enrichment movement, 5n, 35; programs of, 37, 39

R

Rankian theory, and marriage enrichment, 44

Rathus Assertiveness Scale, 283

Rational-emotive approach, 44

Ravich Interpersonal Game Test, 283, 286, 287

Rebirth Theory of Psychology, 44

Reciprocal behavioral change, in behavioral theory, 32-33, 34

Reciprocity, in behavioral theory, 30-31

Reinforcement: in behavioral theory, 30-32, 34; in communication skills group, 121; in marriage enrichment retreat, 149-150

Relationship: adjustment levels in, 53-59; attitudes toward, 283-284; building, 78-84; in communication skills group, 132-134; concept of, 18; conflict resolution for, 144-145, 234, 251-263, 286-287; flexibility in, 284-285; healthy, characteristics of, 20; and life cycle states, 50-53; maintaining, 83-84; needs in, 287; problems in, 288-289; satisfaction in, 289-290; structure of, 291; troubled, and marriage enrichment, 6-7, 53-54

Relationship Change Scale, 286, 287, 290, 291

Relationship Inventory, 283, 286, 290, 291

Research. See Evaluation

Resistance. See Dragee; Fearful couple

Retreat. See Marriage enrichment retreat

Revealed Difference Technique, 286, 287, 289

Rogerian theory: analysis of, 25-29; background of, 25-27; and communication skills, 111; evaluation research on, 28-29; programs in, 27-28

Roles: activities on, 234; evaluation tools for, 289

Rorschach test, 203, 286, 287, 289

S

Satisfaction: concept of, and evaluation, 199-202; evaluation tools for, 289-290
Satisfaction Change Scale, 290
Scale of Marriage Problems, 284, 286, 289, 304-305
Screening: interviews for, 62-63; for marital adjustment level, 54-58; no opportunity for, 57-58; and pregroup phases, 99
Self-Actualization Theory, 43
Self awareness, evaluation tools for, 290
Self-disclosure: evaluation of, 196; evaluation tools for, 290; as member aggressiveness, 168-169
Self Disclosure Questionnaire, 290
Self-esteem, in General Systems theory, 21
Self-Feeling Awareness Scale, 286, 290
Self-help groups: evaluation of, 194; theory of, 46
Semantic Differential Test, 283, 284
Sentence Completion Blank, 290
Sex Attitude Survey and Profile, 290
Sex Knowledge and Attitude Test, 290
Sex Knowledge Inventory, 290
Sex Role Survey, 289
Sexual Communication Inventory, 286, 290, 305
Sexual Compatibility Test, 286, 291
Sexual Interaction Inventory, 282, 283, 290, 291, 305-306
Sexuality: activities on, 235, 271-279; evaluation tools for, 290-291
Shared meaning process, in General Systems theory, 21
Sharing My Feelings with You: analysis of, 272-273; in communication skills group, 137; goals

and objectives related to, 234, 235; handout for, 273; in marriage enrichment retreat, 144
Show and Tell: analysis of, 240-241; goals and objectives related to, 233, 234
Signal System for the Assessment and Modification of Behavior, 286
Simulated Family Activity Measurement, 286, 287, 289, 291
Skill learning. See Behavioral learning
Skills: in behavioral theory, 33; in Rogerian theory, 28
Southern Baptist Convention, Sunday School Board of, 38
Special Times: analysis of, 269-270; goals and objectives related to, 233, 234, 235
Spousal Adaptibility Test, 285, 291
Spouse: attitudes or knowledge about, 283; roles of, 20
Static-group comparison, use of, 212
Stress, evaluation tools for, 288-289
Stroking Scale, 286
Suspending judgment, in communication skills group, 122-125
Systems Marriage Enrichment Program, in General Systems theory, 23

T

Termination phase of group development: analysis of, 105-108; in communication skills group, 137-138
Thematic Apperception Test, 286, 288, 289
Therapy, marriage enrichment combined with, 9-10, 222
Time, use of, activity on, 234
Transactional analysis, and marriage enrichment, 43
Trust, evaluation tool for, 291

U

Understanding, evaluation tools for, 291

Understanding One Another exercise: analysis of, 247-248; in communication skills group, 125-126; goals and objectives related to, 233, 234

Unpossessing caring and confirmation, in Rogerian theory, 26

V

Values: activities on, 234, 263-271; clarification of, 178-179; differences of, in groups, 177-179

Verbal Interaction Task, 286, 290, 306

Verbal Problem Checklist, 286

W

Wechsler Adult Intelligence Scale, 286, 287, 291

Weekend retreats: advantages of, 64, 196; in church-related programs, 37, 38-39, 41, 43; example of, 138-150

Weekly sessions: advantages of, 64, 196; example of, 110-138

Why We Fight: analysis of, 260-262; goals and objectives related to, 234; handout for, 261-262

Willingness to Change Scale, 283, 289

Win/Win Conflict Negotiation: analysis of, 251-253; in communication skills group, 132; goals and objectives related to, 234; handout for, 253; in marriage enrichment retreat, 144

Workshop in Couples Communication and Negotiation Skills, in General Systems theory, 21-23

Worldwide Encounter, and church-related theory, 38

Y

Yale Marital Interaction Battery, 284, 291